China's New Confucianism

Politics and Everyday Life in a Changing Society

With a new preface by the author

Daniel A. Bell

Princeton University Press • Princeton and Oxford

Published by Princeton University Press, 41 William Street, Princeton,
New Jersey 08540

In the United Kingdom: Princeton University Press, 6 Oxford Street,
Woodstock, Oxfordshire OX20 1TW

press.princeton.edu

Fourth printing, and first paperback printing, with a new preface, 2010
Paperback ISBN: 978-0-691-14585-3

THE LIBRARY OF CONGRESS HAS CATALOGED THE CLOTH EDITION
OF THIS BOOK AS FOLLOWS

Bell, Daniel (Daniel A.), 1964–
China's new confucianism : politics and everyday life in a changing society /
Daniel A. Bell.
p. cm.
Includes index.
ISBN 978-0-691-13690-5 (hardcover : alk. paper)
1. China—Politics and government—2002– 2. China—Social conditions—2000–
3. Confucianism—China. I. Title.
JQ1510.B45 2008
306.20951—dc22   2008000733

British Library Cataloging-in-Publication Data is available

This book has been composed in Electra LT Std

Printed on acid-free paper. ∞

Printed in the United States of America

7   9   10   8   6

For my mother and Anthony

Contents

Preface to the Paperback Edition   ix

Acknowledgments   xxiii

Introduction   xxvii

PART ONE   **Politics**   1

1. From Communism to Confucianism:
Changing Discourses on China's Political Future   3

2. War, Peace, and China's Soft Power   19

3. Hierarchical Rituals for Egalitarian Societies   38

PART TWO   **Society**   57

4. Sex, Singing, and Civility:
The Costs and Benefits of the Karaoke Trade   59

5. How Should Employers Treat
Domestic Workers?   75

6. The Politics of Sports:
From the 2006 World Cup to the 2008 Olympics   91

PART THREE   **Education**   105

7. A Critique of Critical Thinking   107

8. Teaching Political Theory in Beijing   128

9. On Being Confucian:
Why Confucians Needn't Be Old, Serious,
and Conservative   148

CONTENTS

APPENDICES

1. Depoliticizing the *Analects*   163

2. Jiang Qing's *Political Confucianism*   175

Index   231

Preface to the Paperback Edition: Toward a Progressive and Humane Confucian Ethics?

Since the publication of the hardcover of *China's New Confucianism* in 2008, the revival of Confucianism in China has only intensified. But what exactly explains this phenomenon and what makes it so controversial? And what are the challenges of promoting Confucianism in China and the West?

Why the Revival of Confucianism?

Communism has lost its capacity to inspire the Chinese. But what is replacing it? And what should replace it? Clearly there is a need for a new moral foundation for political rule in China, and the Chinese government has moved closer to an official embrace of Confucianism. The 2008 Summer Olympics highlighted Confucian themes, quoting the *Analects of Confucius* at the opening ceremony and in booklets handed out to visiting journalists, and downplayed any references to China's experiment with Communism. Cadres at the newly built Communist Party School in Shanghai proudly tell visitors that the main building is modeled on a Confucian scholar's desk, with the tower representing the power of the word. Abroad, the government has been promoting Confucianism via branches of the Confucius Institute, a Chinese language and culture center similar to France's Alliance Française and Germany's Goethe Institute.

Of course there is resistance as well. Elderly cadres, still influenced by Maoist antipathy to tradition, often condemn any efforts to promote ideologies outside a rigid Marxist framework. But the younger cadres in their forties and fifties tend to support such efforts, and time is on their side. It's easy to forget that the 76-million-strong Chinese Communist

Party is a large and diverse organization. The party itself is becoming more meritocratic—it now selects high-performing students and encourages them to join—and the increased emphasis on the selection of educated cadres is likely to translate into more sympathy for Confucian values.

But the revival of Confucianism is not just government-sponsored. There has also been a resurgence in interest among academics in China. Rigorous experiments by psychologists show that there are striking cognitive differences between Chinese and Americans, with Chinese more likely to use contextual and dialectical approaches to solving problems. Economists take the family as the relevant unit of economic analysis and try to measure the economic effect of such Confucian values as filial piety. Feminist theorists draw parallels between care ethics and the Confucian emphasis on empathy, particularity, and the family as a school of moral education. Theorists of medical ethics discuss the importance of family-based decision-making in medical settings. Those working in the field of business ethics research the influence of Confucian values on business practices in China. Surveys by political scientists show that attachment to Confucian values has increased during the same period that China has modernized. Sociologists study the thousands of experiments in education and social living in China that are inspired by Confucian values.

The renewed academic interest is also driven by normative concerns: an increasing number of critical intellectuals are turning to Confucianism for ways of dealing with China's current social and political predicament. Without entirely rejecting Westernization, they believe that stable and legitimate political arrangements need to be founded, at least partly, on political ideals from their own traditions. Theorists of international relations look to early Confucian thinkers for foreign-policy insights. Legal theorists search for less-adversarial modes of conflict resolution grounded in traditional practices. Philosophers draw upon the ideas of great Confucian thinkers of the past for thinking about social and political reform in China. And Confucian educators work on long-term moral transformation by teaching the Confucian classics to young children.

Of course, such political and academic developments are supported by economic factors. China is a rising economic power, and with economic might comes cultural pride. The Weberian view that Confucianism is not conducive to economic development has come to be widely questioned in view of the economic success of East Asian countries with a Confucian heritage. Unlike with Islam, Hinduism, and Buddhism, there has never been an organized Confucian resistance to economic modernization, and such values as respect for education and concern for future generations may have contributed to economic growth. And now, poised to become a global power, it's China's turn to affirm its cultural heritage.

But modernity also has a downside: it often leads to a kind of atomism and psychological anxiety. The competition for social status and material resources becomes fiercer and fiercer, with declining social responsibility and other-regarding outlooks. Communitarian ways of life and civility break down. Even those who make it to the top ask "what now?" Making money, people realize, doesn't necessarily lead to well-being. It is only a means to the good life, but what exactly is the good life—is it just about fighting for one's interests? Most people—in China, at least—do not want to be viewed as individualistic. The idea of simply focusing on individual well-being seems too self-centered. To really feel good about ourselves, we also need to be good to others. Here's where Confucianism comes in: the tradition is based on the assumption that the good life lies in social relationships. To be fully human involves an ethic of social responsibility and political commitment. In China, Confucian ethics is the obvious resource to help fill the moral vacuum that so often accompanies modernization.

In short, this mixture of political, academic, economic, and psychological trends helps to explain the revival of Confucianism in China. These trends are likely to continue, and I would surmise that the revivalism is likely to intensify in the future. But Confucianism is a rich and diverse tradition, and it's worth asking which interpretation of Confucianism ought to be revived.

If the concern is to develop a feasible and desirable political theory for the Chinese context, then it depends on what Chinese people actually think now: any interpretation must be consistent with basic aspirations, though it should also push to improve those aspirations. For example, the interpretation should draw and build on widely shared values like concern for the disadvantaged. The interpretation would also depend on what Chinese intellectuals regard as pressing needs, such as the need for a new source of ideological legitimacy for the state. Interpretations of Confucianism will also depend upon claims that can be supported by empirical evidence. For example, it would be important to test the idea that caring for elderly parents helps to develop a sense of empathy that is extended to others.

The revival of Confucianism in mainland China is too recent to strongly affirm the superiority of any one interpretation. My own sympathies lie with critical intellectuals like Jiang Qing, who put forward proposals for political change inspired by Confucian values that often differ substantially from the status quo. Such views are discussed in the book, and I've been an active participant in public debates about political Confucianism. I freely confess, however, that it has been an uphill struggle to persuade intellectuals in Western countries that Confucianism can offer a progressive and humane path to social and political reform in China.   .

Neither Democratic Nor Authoritarian

Why does the revival of Confucianism often worry Westerners? One reason may be a form of self-love. For most of the twentieth century, Chinese liberals and Marxists engaged in a totalizing critique of their own heritage and looked to the West for inspiration. It may have been flattering for Westerners—look, they want to be just like us!—but there is less sympathy now that Chinese are taking pride in their own heritage and turning to their own traditions for thinking about social and political reform. But more understanding and a bit of open-mindedness can take care of that problem.

Another reason might be that the revival of Confucianism is associated with the revival of Islamic "fundamentalism" and its anti-Western tendencies. Perhaps the revival of closed-minded and intolerant Christian "fundamentalism" in the United States also comes to mind. But the revival of Confucianism in China is not so fundamentally opposed to liberal social ways (other than extreme individualist lifestyles, where the good life is sought mainly outside of social relationships). What it does propose is an alternative to Western political ways, and that may be the main worry. But I think this worry stems from an honest mistake: the assumption that less support for Western-style democracy means increased support for authoritarianism. In China, packaging the debate in terms of "democracy" versus "authoritarianism" crowds out possibilities that appeal to Confucian political reformers.

Confucian reformers generally favor more freedom of speech in China. What they question is democracy in the sense of Western-style competitive elections as the mechanism for choosing the country's most powerful rulers. One clear problem with "one person, one vote" is that equality ends at the boundaries of the political community: those outside the community are neglected. The national focus of the democratically elected political leaders is part of the system, so to speak: they are meant to serve the community of voters, not foreigners living outside the political community. Even democracies that work well tend to focus on the interests of citizens and neglect the interests of foreigners. But political leaders, especially leaders of big countries like China, make decisions that affect the rest of the world (consider global warming), and they need to consider the interests of the rest of the world when they make decisions.

Hence, reformist Confucians put forward political models that are meant to work better than Western-style democracy in terms of securing the interests of all those affected by the policies of the government. The ideal is not necessarily a world where everybody treats each other as an equal—Confucians realize that care diminishes in intensity as it extends from intimates to strangers—but one where the interests of nonvoters would be taken more seriously than in most nation-centered democracies. And the key value for realizing global political ideals is meritocracy, meaning equality of opportunity in education and government, with positions of leadership being distributed to the most virtuous and qualified members of the community. The idea here is that everybody has the potential to become morally exemplary, but in real life the capacity to make competent and morally justifiable political judgments varies between people and an important task of the political system is to identify those with above-average capacity. One idea might be to give extra votes to elderly people: Confucians assume that wisdom normally increases with age as people's life experience deepens; when adult children care for elderly parents, for example, they cultivate such virtues as empathy and humility. Moreover, the elderly are usually less subject to the sexual passions that often get in the way of sound judgment. So if the elderly continue to strive for self-improvement and maintain social networks, perhaps they should be given extra shares of political power.

Another proposal is for a meritocratic house of government, with deputies selected by such mechanisms as free and fair competitive examinations, that would have the task of securing the interests of nonvoters typically neglected by democratically selected political decision-makers such as foreigners, future generations, ancestors, and minority groups (note the difference with legal institutions like the U.S. Supreme Court, which theoretically do not have the power to legislate and do not have a mandate to protect the interests of noncitizens outside the national territory). A meritocratic house of government would balance and complement a democratic house, and, however imperfect, the idea is to better approximate the ideal of government that secures the interests of all those affected by its policies. The value of political meritocracy is deeply embedded in East Asian political discourse, and political proposals to realize it are not typically seen as eccentric or dangerous.

One obvious objection to examinations is that they cannot test for the kinds of virtues that concerned Confucius—flexibility, humility, compassion, and public-spiritedness—and that, ideally, would also characterize political decision-makers in the modern world. It is true that examinations won't test perfectly for those virtues, but the question is whether deputies chosen by such examinations are more likely to be virtuous than those chosen by democratic elections.

There are reasons to believe so. Drawing on extensive empirical research, Bryan Caplan's book *The Myth of the Rational Voter: Why Democracies Choose Bad Policies* (Princeton University Press, 2008) shows that voters are often irrational, and he suggests tests of voter competence as a remedy. Such proposals have a zero chance of being considered seriously in the United States, where the constitutional system is fixed in its basic outlines and anti-intellectualism runs deep in the political culture. In China, however, the political future is more wide open, and tests of competence in the form of examinations can be considered as proposals for political reform. The examinations would test for basic economic literacy (and knowledge of international relations), but they would also cover knowledge of the Confucian classics, testing for memorization as well as interpretation. There is an assumption that learning the classics does indeed improve the virtue of the learner. But that's not the end of the story. The leading Confucian political thinker, Jiang Qing, argues that the examinations could set a framework and moral vocabulary for subsequent political actions, and successful candidates would also need to be evaluated in terms of how they perform in practice.

In any case, there is no reason to be dogmatic about different ways of realizing meritocracy before proposals are actually implemented. China is a huge and diverse country, and it is a good laboratory to try out different experiments in political reform. Since Deng Xiaoping opened the doors to economic reform over thirty years ago, various economic experiments have been carried out at different levels of government, with the central government taking what works and implementing the reforms in the whole country. Experiments in village-level democracy have been underway for a couple of decades, and more recently there has been talk of intraparty democracy as well as democratic experiments in cities like Shenzhen and Guiyang. Why not also try out some institutional experiments in meritocracy and see what works? Once we have a better idea of what works at lower levels of government, it might not be so risky to try something at the national level.

The debate over whether Confucianism should be institutionalized as a state religion has generated even more controversy in China. Some Confucians do not take a strong view regarding religion. Following the example of early Confucian thinkers, including Confucius himself, they leave open metaphysical commitments, focusing their efforts on the problems of earthly life. Hence, it's not inconceivable to be a Confucian in social and political life and, say, a Buddhist or Christian in one's spiritual life. Early Confucianism was not meant to provide a final answer to existential questions about human suffering and life after death, and it leaves open the idea that religions may do a better job in that respect.

But other Confucian reformers like Jiang Qing do take Confucianism seriously as a religion with a metaphysical foundation, and draw the implication that there should be official state sponsorship of Confucianism as a kind of religion. The idea is that Confucianism needs to be taught in schools and promoted in villages and communities with some sort of financial support from the state. Partly, the idea is to train future rulers in Confucian ethics so that they will rule with moral sensitivity. As Jiang Qing puts it, we need to be careful about the state (mis)using Confucianism, but Confucianism can also use the state: if future rulers are trained in the Confucian classics, they will likely rule with more moral sensitivity. But he emphasizes that other religions would be tolerated, and compares his ideal to the Danish or UK systems, in which there is state support for an official religion but other religions and sects (whether foreign or not) are permitted and able to flourish. And he explicitly makes room for the political representation of other Chinese religions like Buddhism and Daoism in his proposed House of Historical Continuity.

Still, the idea of state support for Confucianism does seem to go well beyond the North European model, especially in terms of state backing for Confucianism in education and community life. Jiang Qing has also proposed the reintroduction of state-supported Confucian burial rituals following natural disasters such as the Sichuan earthquake (though he allows for the possibility that members of minority groups could follow their own burial rituals). Another way in which "official Confucianism" would influence policy is that civil servants would be able to take paid leave for a limited period of mourning in the event of the death of a parent, similar to the two-month period of mourning leave granted to civil servants in South Korea. To a certain extent, Confucian values already influence state policy (for example, elderly parents are entitled to a share of property if an adult child dies intestate in mainland China, Hong Kong, and Taiwan, notwithstanding different political and legal systems), and making Confucianism official would make such policies matters of public debate and perhaps lead to improvements. If such proposals for "official Confucianism" are implemented in ways that show tolerance and respect for other religious practices, they are worth taking seriously. The history of "official Confucianism" in Imperial China does offer reason to be wary of state misuses of Confucianism, but it also offers some inspiring moments. In the late sixteenth century, as Yu Ying-shih notes, Matteo Ricci was amazed to discover that the Chinese religious atmosphere was highly tolerant, with Confucianism, Buddhism, and Taoism all seen as capturing a vision of the same Dao ("Way").

Popularizing Confucianism

I make no claim to being a neutral observer of Confucianism. Over the past couple of years, I've been writing on Chinese society and politics for the popular media, focusing mainly on Confucian values and practices that I consider to be morally defensible and politically promising in the Chinese context (for my op-eds and essays, see my website, which may be accessed through http://press.princeton.edu/titles/9173 .html). In China, I've been fortunate to work with an excellent and efficient translator, Professor Wu Wanwei of Wuhan University, who translates and distributes my articles. We work closely together and adopt the following strategy: first, we try the print media, such as the *Global Times*, the international news arm of the official *People's Daily*. Not surprisingly, I've been asked to delete sensitive material, and I've often acceded to the demands. Here's the principle I try to follow: if it's just a matter of changing the wording to make the criticism more indirect, no problem; if it's a matter of deleting one or two minor arguments that do not affect the overall point of the article, then I negotiate and compromise, usually accepting some changes; if it's a matter of changing the main argument or criticism, then I withdraw the article.

Then we submit the articles to Chinese-language Web sites. Without fail, we've managed to find at least one Chinese-language Web site that takes our material without changes. I find it strange that the same material that is deemed too sensitive for newspapers can appear on Web sites for public debate. On the one hand, it shows that the Internet has played an important role in expanding the range of political debate in China. On the other hand, it shows that the print media still has some sort of sacred value in China. It could be that the printed page implies some sort of official government approval and thus is more likely to be influential.

In the West, to (over)simplify, the problem is the opposite: it's much easier to publish an op-ed harshly critical of the Chinese government than one that strives for balance or proposes unfamiliar political alternatives. And the chance of a major Western newspaper publishing an op-ed that commends the Chinese government for work well done is even slimmer. Still, I've had quite good luck over the past couple of years. I've been asked to contribute articles and op-eds on the revival of Confucianism, and that usually goes according to plan. Other times, I'll try different op-ed pieces with occasional success and frequent rejections. One rarely knows why Western newspapers turn down op-eds (unless the writer has a special relationship with the editor), but I suspect it's often because my contributions are viewed as too "pro-China." Unlike their Chinese counterparts, the editors of Western newspapers will rarely cite political reasons to reject a piece (with one exception, in my case: the Asian edition of the *Wall Street Journal* refused to publish an op-ed because they oppose the legalization of sex work as a matter of policy).

I confess I did not have much luck writing for conservative publications, though I did try on several occasions. My hunch is that they seem averse to less-than-hostile political commentary about China. I did have more luck writing for centrist publications (or left of center, depending on one's perspective) like the *New York Times* and *Newsweek*. But most of my writings were published on the Web sites of openly leftist publications. Even then, however, I've had troubles. A leading British leftist newspaper turned down an op-ed that was critical of imperial attitudes toward China. The Chinese translation was subsequently accepted by the *Global Times*, and I can say I was glad for the options opened by the Chinese press. Another time, I had complained to the editor of a Western newspaper that their headlines made me seem like an apologist for the Chinese government, and asked to be consulted about headlines in the future (Chinese newspapers seem more open to consulting authors in this respect). Shortly thereafter, the editor chose another misleading headline and sub-headline, and in a moment of pique I complained in a comment attached to my own article. The editor deleted my comment (though comment is supposed to be free), threatened me with a defamation lawsuit, and said he would cut off my relationship with his paper if I ever did it again. I swallowed my pride and tried to smooth over the relationship, but still feel uneasy about it.

I do not mean to imply that there is equivalence between the Western and the Chinese press, that it's just a matter of different constraints with the same result. In the case of China, the constraints are clearly political and more uniformly applied (academic publications tend to be more open than the popular media: the rule seems to be, the greater the social influence, the greater the constraints). It is almost impossible to openly criticize rulers by name or to suggest concrete institutional alternatives to the status quo at the national level. Nor is it possible to openly say what almost everyone knows to be true: that Marxist-Leninism is basically dead as a ruling philosophy. In the West, there are more media outlets of different political orientations and the constraints are not so straightforwardly set according to the parameters of the ruling party. Obviously I hope the Chinese press loosens up and becomes more like the Western press in that respect (or like the press in Hong Kong, which is basically free and vibrant). So do many public-spirited Chinese journalists: they are often frustrated that they can't report what they investigate, and they feed the information to Western journalists without taking any credit. But—and here's where I will lose the sympathy of most Western journalists—I still think there is room for a distinctive Confucian-inspired approach to the media. When the television news during the 2008 Paralympics opened with a shot of President Hu Jintao singing along with disabled children, I didn't view that as a problem. Quite the contrary—I was watching it with an elderly Chinese relative, who was clearly moved by what she saw. Such news segments have the effect of increasing sympathy for the disabled. Yes, it may also increase sympathy for Hu Jintao, but perhaps we should sympathize with the politicians who are actually doing something good.

What kind of model do I have in mind? The free-market media model is far from ideal because it often translates into the domination of corporate interests and titillating news that diverts attention away from real social problems (a journalist friend from abroad told me that her stories on the Paralympics were often shot down by her editor on the ground that they wouldn't sell papers). The UK model, where regulatory agencies urge balance, might offer more informed and diverse perspectives. But a culturally sensitive approach to media regulation in China, arguably, would also draw upon the Confucian tradition of moral education. Yes, there can and should be more independent and critical media that tells the truth about social problems and blames the government when it's at fault. But that doesn't rule out government support for media outlets that have the mandate to strive not for the party's interests but for widely endorsed social values like concern for the poor. Such media might involve the portrayal of moral exemplars, appeal to people's better nature, and help to generate sympathy for the disadvantaged. This model need not—and should not—be authoritarian because it would also allow for private media to operate without constraints (other than depictions of extreme violence and pornography). More concretely, it might mean an independent regulatory agency that funds public media according to its success at promoting the goals of diversity, high-quality programming, and moral education. The latter value would make the Chinese model unique—and may strike Westerners who prioritize the value of individual autonomy as moralizing and potentially unfair—but there are areas of justifiable difference that need to be tolerated, if not respected.

Beyond China?

What about the possibility that Confucianism can actually enrich political values and practices in Western countries? Different political theories should allow for the possibility of mutual enrichment. In its best moments, Confucianism has shown openness to other traditions like Legalism, Buddhism, and Daoism, to the point that it's often hard to separate the theories in practice. In its encounter with Western political theories, however, Confucianism has been the student rather than the teacher, and it's worth asking under what conditions Confucianism might be seen as compelling by Western liberals. One condition is that Western societies undergo prolonged crises of confidence. It is a sad truth, perhaps, that people are more inclined to learn from others when their own ways prove to be problematic. Chinese intellectuals looked to the West when traditional ways of social and political life broke down, and it may take a similar crisis of confidence in the West before large numbers of Western intellectuals turn to Confucianism for hope and inspiration (at a conference on the "China model" that took place shortly after the global financial crisis, an influential Western journalist joked, "Give us time, we've only had a few months of humiliation").

But the key obstacle to universalizing Confucianism, perhaps, is the gap between theory and practice. If it's just talk, nobody will listen. At the moment, there is a long way to go. The Chinese media tends to serve the party rather than the disadvantaged. The state resorts to thuggish tactics against some social critics. Social welfare reformers look more to Europe than to Japan and South Korea. There has hardly been any reform of political institutions inspired by lower-level reforms. The elderly do not get even one vote for choosing top decision-makers, never mind extra votes. A meritocratically selected political institution designed to represent the interests of future generations and foreigners exists only in the dreams of Confucian reformers. There are obvious constraints on religious freedom in China, and the state gives more funds to the promotion of Marxism than to the study of the Confucian classics and the revival of Confucian rituals. In short, progressive and humane Confucian values need to be translated into practice. Once the Chinese government acts morally, in accordance with Confucian ideals, then it can articulate and promote its soft power to the rest of world.

Beijing
January 2010

Acknowledgments

In spring 2006, I wrote an essay on my teaching experience in Beijing that was published in the periodical *Dissent*. The essay seemed to generate much interest—more, in fact, than anything I had previously written—and I was encouraged to write other China-related essays in a similar vein. Three other essays were published in *Dissent* (fall 2006, spring 2007, winter 2008). So my first thanks is to *Dissent*, which published earlier versions of chapters 1, 5, 6, and 8. I would also like to thank the *Guardian* for offering a forum—the comment is free blog—where I can test some of my ideas. I am also grateful to Zhao Tingyang, who commissioned an earlier version of chapter 2 that was published in *Diogenes*, March 2008; the organizers of a conference on ritual held at Hong Kong Baptist University, where I presented a more academic version of chapter 3; to Richard Bellamy, who commissioned an earlier version of chapter 9 that was published in *Government and Opposition* 43, no. 1 (2008); to the organizers of a conference on the thought of Jiang Qing held in Zhuhai, June 2007, where I presented an earlier version of appendix 2 (a Chinese version, translated by Xie Huiyuan, will be published by Shanghai VI Horai Publishers); and to Wang Hui, who commissioned an earlier version of appendix 1 that was published in the Chinese-language periodical *Du Shu*, August 2007 (translated by Wu Wanwei). All these essays have been substantially revised for this book.

I have a feeling that my writing improves with age. But the main reason for improvement has nothing to do with my abilities. As I get older, I make more friends, and this expanding network of friends means that I can get more critical—and kind—feedback on my work. I've sent each chapter in this book to several friends, and the book has been revised several times in reaction to their comments. In fact, I've made so many changes that I've lost track of which idea has been improved in response to which comment by which friend. So I've decided to leave out any attributions of thanks in the text itself. The liberal individualist might say that I've plagiarized other people's ideas. The Confucian might say that I should not use my name qua individual author and that the book should be regarded as part of a tradition. Well, I'm not sure what to say. Perhaps I should say that it's safe to assume the good ideas in the book are communal creations, but that I'm solely responsible for the bad ones.

Let me thank the following friends (in alphabetical order) for helpful conversations and comments on earlier versions of particular chapters: Roger Ames, Peter Baehr, Sébastien Billioud, Joe Carens, Chan Sin Yee, Chen Lai, Ci Jiwei, Cui Zhiyuan, Corinna Delkeskamp-Hayes, John Delury, Avner de-Shalit, Christopher Detweiler, John Dryzek, Paul Dumouchel, James Fallows, Fawaz Gerges, Dan Gutmann, He Baogang, John Holden, Ian Holliday, Hong Xiuping, Jiang Qing, Parag Khanna, David Kelly, Li Qiang, Li Wanquan, Liang Zhiping, Lu Keli, Andrei Markovits, Antony Ou, Peng Guoxiang, Thomas Pogge, Qian Jiang, Sidney Rittenberg, Henry Rosemont, Jr., Masayuki Sato, Gopal Sreenivasan, Caroline Tong, Wei Zhengxiang, Wu Wanwei, and Zhao Juan. Let me also thank Richard Baum and members of the Internet group Chinapol, for useful exchanges of ideas and resources. I owe special thanks to the following friends who wrote detailed written comments on large chunks of the book: Steve Angle, Bai Tongdong, Joseph Chan, Fan Ruiping, Steve Geisz, Randy Peerenboom, and Paik Wooyeal. Let me also thank Jia Peijuan, Jiang Haibo, Kong Xinfeng, and Wu Yun for research assistance. I would also like to express my gratitude to Wan Junren and my colleagues at Tsinghua for providing a supportive and stimulating environment for teaching and research.

I owe most to the following people: P. J. Ivanhoe, my friend from afar, who read through two versions of the manuscript and wrote detailed comments each time; my editor Ian Malcolm, for his kindness and helpful suggestions; Michael Walzer, coeditor of *Dissent*, for his comments, friendship, and inspiring theorizing; the memory of my grandmother Thérèse and uncles Jean-Claude and Maurice, who will forever form part of my identity; my relatives in Canada, China, France, Japan, and the United States for emotional support; my wife Bing and son Julien, for unrestrained yet loving criticism; and my mother and Anthony, to whom this book is dedicated.

A Note on Chinese Sources

The translations from Chinese language material, unless otherwise indicated, are my own. I have used pinyin romanization, except where it wouldn't make any sense to the non-Chinese reader and the correct character might not be obvious to the Chinese reader, in which case I have used simplified Chinese characters (though I do think the traditional complex form is more aesthetically pleasing and I hope more use will be made of that form in the future). For the classical Chinese, I have made use of the original sources along with the following translations: for *The Analects* of Confucius, the philosophical translation by Roger T. Ames and Henry Rosemont, Jr.; for Mencius, the translation by D. C. Lau; and for Xunzi, the translation by John Knoblock. However, these translations have been modified to suit my own style and vocabulary.

Introduction

What's the big story about the rise of modern China? Is it the continuing human rights abuses? The expansion of personal freedoms? The development of local democracy? The resilience of the authoritarian state? Or perhaps the economic miracle, with hundreds of millions lifted out of poverty? Or the hundreds of millions still living in poverty? The answer, of course, is all of the above. A joke about China is that one can say anything about it without getting it right. Another joke is that one can say anything about it without getting it wrong. Yet another joke is that the longer one stays in the country, the more intimate the grasp of the language, culture, and history, the less confident one feels about judgments and predictions. Still, there may be room for one more China story. My story is informed by personal experience living and working in Beijing. The main plot concerns the revival of the Confucian tradition in politics and everyday life. The moral of the story is that creative adaptation of the legacy can be helpful for dealing with the challenges of contemporary China. And I will try to tell the story in plain language accessible to all those who try to understand China.

My story begins by asking a few questions about modern China. In politics, why do Communist Party leaders invoke centuries-old Confucian values? Why do social critics also invoke those values? There are, perhaps, even more puzzling questions. Why do senior Communist Party leaders dye their hair black? And why do some local officials get promoted if they care for their elderly parents? Why do social critics use Mencius to criticize imperialism? We might also ask why hierarchical rituals contribute to material equality? In social life, there are more puzzles. Why is paid sex often preceded by singing duets? Why does the crime rate spike just before the Chinese New Year? Why do Chinese cheer for Goliaths in international sporting events? Why do domestic helpers want to be treated like family members? It's also worth asking some questions about my own students. Why do they send me critical emails rather than raise objections in class? Why do they sing together? And why do they want me to sing with them?

I do not mean to imply that there are simple answers to these questions. Any serious analysis needs to discuss the various economic, political, and psychological forces that help to explain such phenomena. My vantage point living in Beijing, reading Chinese-language debates, and talking to Chinese from various walks of life, offers some insight into those forces. To invoke a classical metaphor, however, one also needs to understand the "roots" of modern society. China specialists in the West often focus their energies on study of the "branches" (such as democracy, civil society, property rights) that seem to owe their origin to Western "roots." As a result, they often misconstrue or miss altogether the contemporary branches that arise from China's own roots and show little capacity for predicting what new branches might sprout from its powerful and venerable traditions. On the other hand, specialists in Chinese thought often spend their time on historical interpretations of texts. They sometimes gesture at implications for modern society, but rarely spell them out in any detail. In my view, any sound understanding of China needs to explore both the roots and the branches. I will try to uncover and explore distinctive and deep aspects of Chinese culture and point to contemporary manifestations. I will also try to sort out the good from the bad, and to suggest—in all humility!—how traditional values and practices can be adapted and made defensible in contemporary Chinese society and perhaps beyond. My aim is not to promote any particular political agenda, but to enrich the discourse of possibilities.

Well, maybe I should take that back. I do have an agenda and I should come clean about my normative commitments. I worry that much thinking and policymaking in Western countries is based on crude stereotypes about China, such as the view that there is totalitarian control of intellectual discourse. The reality is much more complex. My hope is that greater awareness of philosophical traditions and current discourses in China will reduce the risk of conflicts based on misunderstandings. In the worst-case scenario, such misunderstandings can poison international relations and lead to war. There are crazy people in both the United States and China who seem to be planning, if not hoping, for war between the two countries. Those people should be stopped by others who appreciate and care for what's good about both countries. I will leave the positive accounts of American culture to others (personally, I love the choice of cereals in supermarkets, driving fast on open highways, and the sports scene). This book will discuss some of the positive features of Chinese culture. What I hope to show is that China shouldn't be condemned just because it doesn't look like us. We should allow for justifiable moral diversity. That's the key to international peace. But perhaps I shouldn't overstate the political importance of this kind of book. Maybe it's just a matter of contributing a few insights that will help visitors to China enjoy their experience.

This will sound more arrogant, but let me go ahead. I also have an agenda for China. I realize it's reckless for a foreigner to try to tell the Chinese what they should be doing. But I can't stop myself. I care about my new home. I also like Confucian values, and I hope they can be revived in contemporary China. But which Confucian values should be revived? Well, it depends. Confucianism is a long tradition with different strands and different combinations of values with different traditions. Today, there are at least three strands. One is the strand popularized by Yu Dan, whose book on the *Analects of Confucius* has sold more copies than any book since Mao's *Little Red Book* (actually, most of Mao's books were distributed for free). Her account of the *Analects* seems relatively apolitical. She aims to help people deal with the pressures of modern society. We shouldn't worry too much about external goods like status and money. What matters is our inner attitude. So long as our hearts are in the right place, things will be OK. Of course, such views are not really apolitical. They deflect attention from the economic and political conditions that actually cause people's misery. Anyone concerned with those conditions needs to invoke more political interpretations of Confucianism.

But here we run into more trouble. Even since the Han dynasty (more than two thousand years ago), the most prominent political interpretations have been manipulated by Chinese governments for their own purposes. Here Confucianism has been combined with Legalism, China's other main political tradition, to justify such practices as blind obedience to the ruler, the use of harsh punishments, and the subordination of women. But there is another interpretation of Confucianism—let's call it "left Confucianism"—that stresses such values as the obligation of intellectuals to criticize bad governments and the obligation of the state to provide for the material well-being of the people. Such values owe their origin mainly to the "original Confucianism" of Confucius, Mencius, and Xunzi, before Confucianism became established as state orthodoxy. In imperial times, the critical tradition was carried forward by such scholars as Huang Zongxi and Gu Yanwu. And today, new leftists such as Gan Yang are calling for the creation of a "Confucian socialist republic." Confucian scholars such as Jiang Qing openly acknowledge that their interpretation of the Confucian tradition most closely parallels socialist ideals: not the "actually existing socialism" in China today, but the socialist ideals defended by Karl Marx and others. This Confucian tradition aims to influence contemporary politics, but it also remains separate from state power and orthodoxy, always ready to point to the gap between the ideals and the social reality. That's the tradition I find inspiring.

Let me address the worry that I'm using the Confucian label simply to promote progressive or socialist ideas that owe their origin to Western roots. I do not deny that such "Western" values as democracy, solidarity, human rights, and the rule of law need to be adopted in China. But they also need to be *adapted* in China. They need to be enriched, and sometimes constrained, by Confucian values. For example, Western progressives and left Confucians can agree that the government's first obligation is to provide for the disadvantaged in society. To a certain extent, they can also agree about what it means to be disadvantaged: it means being deprived of the material goods that underpin any decent conception of the good life. Beyond that, however, there will be important differences. In the Western mind, those deprived of the opportunity to choose their political leaders are also disadvantaged. In the Confucian mind, it is not necessarily the case. A more serious harm is being deprived of family members and friends that make up the good life. Hence, when Mencius says the government should give first consideration to "old men without wives, old women without husbands, old people without children, and young children without fathers," he doesn't just mean that those people are materially poor. Nor does he mean that they are disadvantaged because they lack democratic rights. For Mencius, they are disadvantaged (partly, if not mainly) because they are deprived of key human relations.

The choice of topics reflects my experience as a Western-trained scholar living and working in China as well as my own personal interests and commitments. My book has three parts. The first part discusses recent political debates and developments. The second part deals with social issues such as sex, sports, and the treatment of domestic workers. The last part discusses education and my own experience as a teacher and self-styled Confucian educator. In each part, I will point to some of the modern branches and "Confucian" roots that help to explain seemingly puzzling phenomena in contemporary China. I will also be drawing upon my "left Confucian" commitments to evaluate some of those phenomena and propose alternatives if need be. In terms of style, I've deliberately avoided heavy-going academic jargon and done my best to minimize footnotes and qualifications. It wasn't always easy—in my usual academic mode, the challenge is to avoid adding footnotes to footnotes—but the reader can judge if I succeeded.[1]

Part One
POLITICS

1. From Communism to Confucianism:
Changing Discourses on China's Political Future

In the United States, the political future is constrained, for better or worse, by constitutional arrangements that have been in place for more than two centuries. Barring dramatic developments that few would welcome, such as nuclear war or major terrorist attacks, it is highly unlikely that the political system will change much over the next few decades. In China, by contrast, the political future is wide open. According to the formulation of the Chinese Communist Party (CCP), the current system is the "primary stage of socialism," meaning that it's a transitional phase to a higher and superior form of socialism.[1] The economic foundation, along with the legal and political superstructure, will change in the future. For independent intellectuals, the only remotely plausible justification for the current system of economic liberalization combined with tight political control is that it is a temporary necessity given the need to provide social order during the disruptive period of economic development (and many would reject this claim). Nobody argues that the current political system should remain in place once the economy is developed.

The question is, what comes after economic development? In China, the debates on this question are somewhat constrained due to political controls as well as the widely felt need to deal with China's more immediate economic and social problems. There also seems to be an aversion to "utopian thinking," which is an understandable reaction to Mao's disastrous attempts to sweep away the past during the Great Leap Forward and the Cultural Revolution. Still, few doubt that there's a need for a different—and more inspiring—political model in the future.

In private discussions, there is room for speculation, and I will report on some possibilities.

The End of (Marxist) Ideology

Officially, the philosophy of Karl Marx underpins the legitimacy of the ruling CCP, and thus Marxism is the place to start for thinking about China's political future. It's true that the CCP no longer emphasizes class struggle, hatred of the rich, and opposition to private property. In fact, capitalists can now join the CCP, and the legal system is being reformed (slowly) so that it more closely approximates that of capitalist countries. But such developments may reflect a better understanding of Marxist theory than in Mao's day. The CCP need not abandon the commitment to communism as the long-term goal so long as it recognizes that poor countries must go through capitalism on the way.

The capitalist mode of production treats workers as mere tools in the productive process and puts technology to use for the purpose of enriching a small minority of capitalists. But it does have an important virtue: it has the consequence of developing the productive forces more than any previous economic system. The reason is that capitalists compete with each other to make a profit; hence they have an incentive to develop new, ever more efficient means to produce goods, creating a large material surplus without which socialism would not be feasible. If communism is implemented without developed productive forces (advanced technology and the knowledge to make use of it) that underpin material abundance, then it won't work for long. Without an "absolutely essential material premise," as Marx put it in *The German Ideology*, "want is merely made general, and with want the struggle for necessities would begin again, and the old filthy business would necessarily be restored." That's why Marx justified British imperialism in India: yes, it would be exploitative and miserable for Indian workers, but the foundations would be laid for socialist rule. The CCP's defense of brutal capitalism in China—as Deng Xiaoping famously put it, "To get rich is glorious"—has its roots in a similar logic.

In the Marxist framework, the moral point of the whole ugly process is to free the large mass of humankind from the need to engage in drudge labor. Technology will be highly developed, and at a certain point—the moment of revolution—private property will be abolished, and machines made to do work for the betterment of humanity instead of the interests of one small class. Technology will do the dirty work needed to meet people's physical needs, and people will finally be free to go fishing, read books, design and create works of beauty, and so on. Unpleasant labor will be limited to the maintenance of machinery and other tasks required to keep the system going, but this "realm of necessity" would not take up most of the working day.

But when is China supposed to implement communism? And how will the transition come about? One response is that it's not useful to think about such questions because the transition to communism will happen anyway. Marx himself was a technological optimist (see his discussion of the Factory Acts in *Capital*, vol. 1): technological developments will lead to the communist revolution no matter what theorists say about it.[2] But his faith rested on now discredited economic theories such as the falling rate of profit under capitalism and the labor theory of value. And from a normative perspective, it is important to think about policies that can speed up the process and minimize the suffering of workers along the way. Perhaps that's why Marx himself felt the need to address workers and rally them to his cause.

By invoking the rhetoric of "scientific development," the Chinese government seems officially committed to the technologically optimistic interpretation of Marx. Yet it has recently taken on board concerns about the need to minimize the suffering of workers and farmers during the process of scientific development. In October 2006, for the first time in twenty-five years, a plenary session of the CCP's Central Committee devoted itself specifically to the study of social issues. Chinese policymakers signaled a shift from no-holds-barred growth to a more sustainable model that would boost social and economic equality and enable low-income and underprivileged groups to have more access to employment opportunities, basic education, primary health care, and social security. And the government has been more active in promoting workers' rights. It successfully forced Wal-Mart to accept the state-controlled union in its Chinese outlets, and it has passed a law that aims to crack down on sweatshops and gives labor unions power to negotiate worker contracts, safety protection, and workplace ground rules for the first time since market forces were introduced in the 1980s.

Notwithstanding official rhetoric, it is unclear how much these developments stem from commitment to communism. Wu Zhongmin of the Central Party School supports the official recognition of social justice with the view that social resources should be distributed according to contribution, where members of society "are enabled to obtain according to deserts." Chinese readers would recognize the reference to Marx's account of "lower communism," but in practice the government's call for social justice seems to mean nothing more than the recognition of the need for the welfare measures that some capitalist countries have adopted to mitigate the worst excesses of capitalism (many Chinese officials of late have visited Scandinavian states to learn about their social welfare system, and such welfare states have been praised in the official media).[3] And philosophically, the commitment to the disadvantaged can be grounded in social democratic theories that emphasize social and economic rights,[4] Confucian ideas that the government should give first consideration to those deprived of resources and key social relations, or even Christian values that prioritize the needs of the poor and the humble. There is nothing distinctly Marxist about the CCP's call for more social welfare.

Leading intellectuals of the "new left" such as Wang Hui have long been calling for social justice, meaning that China's first priority should be to address the huge gap between rich and poor and to secure the interests of the disadvantaged. But their views, as one might expect, tend to be more critical of the status quo. They argue that social justice cannot be achieved without substantial political reforms, such as more autonomy for organizations of farmers and workers, democratic processes that allow for the articulation of interests, and a free press that would expose official corruption. Cui Zhiyuan of Tsinghua University is perhaps the most radical of the new leftists: he has argued for both economic and political democracy. In a fascinating essay titled "Liberal Socialism and the Future of China: A Petty Bourgeoisie Manifesto," he warns that progressive forces in China should not imitate social democratic practices pursued in Western Europe. Instead, Cui argues for labor-capital partnerships and social dividends paid to all citizens according to age and family status.[5] Only such innovations could realize the goal of empowering the large majority of Chinese workers and farmers.

But the new leftists do not ask the question of what happens after economic development, when the large majority of Chinese no longer have to spend their days toiling in fields and factories. The discourse, both official and unofficial, seems to be confined to debates about how best to provide benefits for workers and farmers given current levels of technological development, and nobody seems to be thinking about how to move toward an abundant society that frees workers from unwanted labor and when this ideal is supposed to be realized.

So why isn't communism being discussed? For scholars, there may be political constraints. Because Marxism is supposed to provide legitimacy for the government, it is the most tightly controlled political discourse in China. At Tsinghua—the university that has trained much of China's political elite, including President Hu Jintao—my Marxist colleagues do interesting and valuable work in Marxist theory (similar to Western scholars of Marxism), but they rarely apply Marx's ideals to China's current and future political reality. I was told that it's too politically sensitive to be explicit about such matters.

The tendency to avoid utopian theorizing also helps to explain the lack of theorizing about "higher communism." I visited the Translation Bureau of the Central Committee of the Chinese Communist Party—the official Marxist institute with the task of translating Marx's works into Chinese—in the hope of finding out more about Marxist theorizing about communism. The institute is flush with funds from the government, and perhaps they are relatively free to think about the appropriate conditions and mechanisms for the implementation of communism in China. But I came up empty. I was handed beautifully packaged translations of the *Communist Manifesto,* and the people I met spoke about the need to deal with the problem of economic inequality in contemporary China, but they seemed puzzled by my questions about freeing workers from drudge labor in China's communist future. Let's deal with the present problems first, they said, before worrying about the long term.

There may also be the worry that talking about communism now reduces the likelihood of achieving it. An American businessman who is well connected with China's political elite told me that Marxist theorists in the government still plan to implement higher communism in the future, but they don't want to make it explicit because communism might require expropriation of the capitalist class. If capitalists are made aware of this possibility, they might think their property rights are not stable and hence they might not be willing to invest in ways that are necessary to develop the productive forces now. The fact that foreign corporations (with some notable exceptions, like Nike) lobbied vigorously against the fairly mild Chinese proposal to upgrade workers' rights and warned that they would build fewer factories in China suggests that such fears are not entirely unfounded. Such forward-looking leaders may also worry that contemporary Chinese workers may not be willing to sacrifice in the interests of future generations. If workers are made aware of the plan to implement communism in the future, they might not be willing to undergo the sacrifices that are required to get there.

I would surmise, however, that the main reason Chinese officials and scholars do not talk about communism is that hardly anybody really believes that Marxism should provide guidelines for thinking about China's political future. The ideology has been so discredited by its misuses that it has lost almost all legitimacy in society. In reality, even the "communist" government won't be confined by Marxist theory if it conflicts with the imperative to remain in power and to provide stability and order in society. For practical purposes, it's the end of ideology in China. Not the end of all ideology, but the end of Marxist ideology.[6] To the extent there's a need for a moral foundation for political rule in China, it almost certainly won't come from Karl Marx.

The Revival of Confucianism

In China, the moral vacuum is being filled by Christian sects, Falun Gong, and extreme forms of nationalism.[7] But the government considers that such alternatives threaten the hard-won peace and stability that underpins the country's development, so it has encouraged the revival of China's most venerable political tradition: Confucianism. Like most ideologies, however, Confucianism can be a double-edged sword.

"Confucius said, 'Harmony is something to be cherished,'" President Hu Jintao noted in February 2005. A few months later, he instructed China's party cadres to build a "harmonious society." Echoing Confucian themes, Hu said China should promote such values as honesty and unity, as well as forge a closer relationship between the people and the government. In March 2007, the prime minister, Wen Jiabao—regarded as relatively liberal—made even more explicit references to tradition: "From Confucius to Sun Yat-sen, the traditional culture of the Chinese nation has numerous precious elements, many positive aspects regarding the nature of the people and democracy. For example, it stresses love and humanity, community, harmony among different viewpoints, and sharing the world in common (*tian xia wei gong*)." Political practices also reflect such values: Communist Party officials in Henan province are assessed on the basis of Confucian values such as filial piety and family responsibility. Abroad, the government has been promoting Confucianism via branches of the Confucius Institute, a Chinese language and culture center similar to France's Alliance Française and Germany's Goethe Institute (so far, however, the emphasis has been on language teaching rather than the promotion of culture). The first Confucius Institute was set up in 2004, and 140 campuses have since opened in thirty-six countries (as of mid-2007).

For the government, the promotion of Confucian values has several advantages. Domestically, the affirmation of harmony is meant to reflect the ruling party's concern for all classes. Threatened by rural discontent—according to official figures, there were 87,000 illegal disturbances in 2005, and 385,000 rural people participated in "mass incidents" from January to September 2006—the government realizes that it needs to do more for those bearing the brunt of China's development (there is a joke in China, that development benefits everyone except farmers, workers, and women). China's widening income gap is approaching Latin American levels and threatens to divide the country into separate classes. The call for harmony, in other words, is an implicit recognition that things are not so harmonious; but unlike Maoist days, the conflicts must be resolved peacefully, not through violent class conflict. Internationally, the call for peace and harmony is meant to disarm fears about China's rise. The government is saying that growing economic

power won't translate into military adventurism and that peaceful resolution of conflicts is the way to go.

How does Confucianism resonate in society at large? Given that the
CCP spent its first three decades in power trying to extirpate every root
and branch of Confucianism that it regarded as a feudal and reaction-
ary worldview hindering progress, it would seem to be a losing battle. It
could be argued, however, that the parts of Marxism that really took
hold in the population—the importance of material well-being and an
aversion to otherworldly outlooks—did so because they resonated with
deeper Confucian roots. And those parts of the CCP's program that
failed to take hold—such as the attempt to replace family ties with ties
to the state during the Cultural Revolution—did so because they con-
flicted with central Confucian values and habits.

The Marxist label can be misleading. Li Zehou and Jin Guantao
have argued that Chinese-style Marxism was actually a continuation of
traditional ways. Mao's belief that political change comes about via
people's moral transformation owes more to Confucianism than to historical materialism. The Maoist practice of "self-criticism" echoes the
Confucian idea that demands should be directed at oneself before being directed at others. The idea that rulers should be morally upright
has Confucian roots,[8] as does the practice of invoking model workers
who are supposed to set an example for others. Even the seemingly
trivial fact that senior Communist Party leaders dye their hair black can
be traced to the Mencian idea that "white haired people" should be
cared for rather than engaged in heavy work (IA.7): still today it might
seem strange for "white haired people" to have too many responsibilities.[9] Again, nothing in the Marxist tradition about hair color. So the
break with tradition may not have been as "totalizing" as advertised.

Less controversial, perhaps, is the claim that Confucian values still
inform ways of life, especially regarding family ethics. Filial piety, for
example, is still widely endorsed and practiced: few object to the law
that adult children have an obligation to care for their elderly parents.
Filial piety is learned at a young age—my son, in primary school, was
graded according to how well he showed filial piety to parents—and it
appears in various social settings, such as the Chinese equivalent of
soap operas, which often revolve around relationships with elderly parents. The best-selling works of the martial arts novelist Jin Yong uphold

Confucian values such as filial piety (Nicolas Zufferey, "Du Confucius au romancier Jin Yong," in *La Pensée en Chine aujourd'hui*, ed. Anne Cheng).[10] In practice, it means that adult children feel obliged to care for and spend time with their elderly parents: it is not uncommon to see extended families at restaurants.[11] Even criminals seem to take heed of the value of filial piety: the crime rate spikes just before the Chinese New Year, when filial sons and daughters are supposed to bring gifts to their parents.

The family-centered Confucian ethics informs the ways buildings are designed. In Beijing, the buildings occupied mainly by foreigners tend to have large lobbies, but the apartments themselves are not always so impressive. In contrast, the public spaces of buildings for Chinese of the same class are often cramped, dark, and less than welcoming, with the apartments—the centers of family life—surprisingly spacious and well decorated. Such cultural differences also affect the way people interact in social settings outside the home. In bars and clubs, for example, Westerners tend to prefer public drinking along an open bar, whereas Chinese often prefer the "family-like" atmosphere of private rooms where they can drink and talk with intimate friends.

Many intellectuals have turned to Confucianism to make sense of such social practices and to think of ways of dealing with China's current social and political predicament. The most famous is Yu Dan, who has written a self-help book on the *Analects of Confucius* that has sold over ten million copies (including six million pirated copies). She is a national star who often appears on television to lecture about the benefits of Confucian values for everyday life. Yu Dan also visits Chinese prisons and lectures prisoners about Confucian values.[12] My graduate students and colleagues express a certain amount of skepticism regarding the academic value of Yu Dan's work—she deliberately avoids controversial themes and resorts to ahistorical simplifications to make her points. Sociologically speaking, however, it's interesting that so many people seem to derive comfort from Confucian values (see appendix 1).

Over the last decade or so, the teaching of the Confucian classics has moved back into the mainstream of society. Courses on Confucianism are among the most popular on university campuses (conversely, courses on Marxism struggle to get students, unless they are made compulsory; and universities have substantially cut compulsory

Marxist courses). The teaching curriculum for secondary schools now includes teaching of the classics, and thousands of experimental schools have been set up that focus largely on the classics. According to the Beijing University philosophy professor Chen Lai, more than ten million children are now studying the Confucian classics, including many ad hoc initiatives outside the formal educational system.[13] Schools for the study of the classics have also been set up by entrepreneurs. Several high-profile companies in China instill training in "culture" that is grounded in Confucian values. China's most widely used executive-coaching system uses a blend of Confucian values and Western corporate methods (as founder Eva Wong puts it, "Confucianism is in our blood"). Of course, such efforts are meant to increase workers' loyalty and promote economic productivity, but these companies also emphasize corporate responsibility and philanthropy (for example, the head of China's largest dairy company, Niu Gensheng, has pledged to donate all his shares to a charitable foundation that aims to "promote the harmonious community in China").

On the academic front, there has been an explosion of conferences and books on Confucianism in China, to the point that even the most dedicated Confucian could not keep up.[14] But unofficial interpretations of Confucianism often diverge from the governmental line. Perhaps the most influential academic work on Confucianism is Jiang Qing's *Political Confucianism* (not yet translated into English). Jiang defends the basic values of Confucianism and argues that they are appropriate for China now and in the future. The book is an implicit challenge to the political status quo—by ignoring it, he not so subtly strips it of value—thus helping to explain why it took five years to get permission for the book to be published.

Jiang could not develop the institutional implications in that book, but the Web allows for more free speech. In an article widely distributed on the Web, he argues that the Marxist curriculum in government party schools should be replaced by Confucian material.[15] Jiang and other Confucian intellectuals have been getting the attention of the government, including meetings with top government officials. It is not entirely fanciful to surmise that the Chinese Communist Party will be relabeled the Chinese Confucian Party in the next couple of decades.

But relabeling won't suffice if the government really plans to adopt Confucianism. The government also needs to change the way it does things. Perhaps the biggest challenge to the government is the Confucian emphasis on meritocracy. The Confucian view is that political leaders should be the most talented and public-spirited members of the community, and the process of choosing such leaders should be meritocratic, meaning that there should be equal opportunity for the best to rise to the top. Historically, Confucian meritocracy was implemented by means of examinations, and there have been proposals to revive and update Confucian examinations for contemporary China. There are obvious implications for political reform: Performance on an exam, rather than party loyalty, would determine who occupies what government post.[16]

A Challenge to Western-Style Liberal Democracy?

Does Confucianism also pose a challenge to Western-style liberal democracy? There are reasons to think that they are compatible, if not mutually reinforcing. Many theorists argue that they are compatible (see, e.g., Sor-Hoon Tan's book *Confucian Democracy*). In political practice, they have often proved to be compatible: Wang Juntao, a leading Chinese dissident who was jailed for five years over the 1989 Tiananmen prodemocracy protests, argues that many of the key figures in the various democracy movements in contemporary Chinese history drew inspiration from Confucian values (see his contribution in *Confucianism for the Modern World*, ed. Daniel A. Bell and Hahm Chaibong).[17] Such influential early-twentieth-century figures as Sun Yat-sen, Kang Youwei, and Liang Qichao received a Confucian education, and they argued that democratic institutions such as parliamentary systems, elections, and equal rights are natural extensions of Confucianism. Jiang Qing, the contemporary Confucian intellectual, contrasts his Confucian theory with Western-style liberal democracy and argues that Confucianism is more appropriate for China. But his institutional proposals take on board certain liberal assumptions like the freedom of religion: he argues for the establishment of Confucianism as a state religion and compares the system to state religions in the United Kingdom and Sweden with other religions not being prohibited.

Even official sources point to the possibility of reconciling Confucianism with liberal democracy. On October 12, 2006, the newspaper *Nanfang Zhoumou* (Southern Weekly)—perhaps the leading intellectual newspaper in China—published an editorial on the meaning of the term "harmonious society." It invokes the quote in the *Analects of Confucius* that exemplary persons seek "harmony, not conformity." Then it breaks down the characters in the term "harmony," with the explanation that the first literally refers to "grain into the mouth," meaning people and social security, and the second refers to "everything can be spoken," meaning democracy and the freedom of speech. The editorial goes on to say that the welfare state requires democracy and the rule of law as an underlying framework.

The Confucian emphasis on meritocracy—rule by the most talented and public-spirited members of the community—might seem to conflict with democracy, but there have been institutional proposals to combine the two desiderata. In a manuscript titled *A Faith in Life and the Kingly Way of Politics* (unpublished in mainland China), Jiang Qing puts forward an interesting proposal for a tricameral legislature that includes representation for people's representatives, Confucian elites chosen by competitive examinations that test for knowledge of the Confucian classics, and elites entrusted with the task of cultural continuity (see appendix 2). The last proposal—the elites would include descendants of Confucius's family—stands about as much chance of being realized as proposals for reinstituting more seats for hereditary aristocrats in the British House of Lords. But the possibility of a bicameral legislature, with one political institution composed of democratic leaders chosen by free and fair competitive elections, and another of meritocratic leaders chosen by free and fair competitive examinations, is more consistent with commitments to Confucian meritocracy and modern-day democracy.

But which institution should have priority? Here things become more complicated. At the local level, all sides in the debate recognize that leaders should be democratically elected. The Chinese government introduced direct village elections in 1988 to maintain social order and combat corruption of leaders, and they have since occurred in some 700,000 villages across China, reaching 75 percent of the nation's 1.3 billion people. Of course, such elections are not free of problems. There have been worries about the quality of decision-making and the extent to which local elections really curb the power of local cadres and wealthy elites. In response, the government has backed experiments with deliberative democracy at the local level designed to address such problems (see *The Search for Deliberative Democracy in China*, ed. Ethan Leib and He Baogang). Such experiments hold the promise of aiding the democratic education process and securing more fair outcomes from that process. Once democracy becomes institutionalized at the local level, it can then be further extended to township, city, and provincial levels.

But empowering democratically elected leaders at the national level is far more controversial. It is one thing to debate and vote on the price of water and electricity and the relocation for farmers—one expects that local citizens with the detailed knowledge required for making choices that intimately affect their daily lives are best placed to make such judgments. It is another to ask voters to make informed judgments about empirically complex issues like settling interprovincial disputes or assessing the trade-off between economic growth and safeguarding the environment for future generations, the sorts of issues that may be only distantly related to their lives. And what about asking "the people" to make life-and-death decisions such as whether or not to go to war or how best to curb virulent contagious infections? With respect to decision-making at the national level, one hopes not just for fair representation and local solidarity, but also for deliberators with the ability to process large amounts of information as well as sensitivity to the interests of different kinds of people, including foreigners and future generations that are affected by national policies.

It is not just the government that balks at the prospects of turning over the levers of the Chinese state to eight hundred million rural residents with primary-school education. Few academics teaching in mainland Chinese universities—including those who call themselves "liberals"—favor countrywide democracy within the next decade or so (and discussions are completely free in the context of alcohol-fueled dinners with friends). The influential intellectual Yu Keping titled his recent book *Democracy Is a Good Thing*, but the lead essay argues that "our construction of political democracy must be closely integrated with the history, culture, tradition and existing conditions in our nation" (5). In practice, it means that elections should be extended all the way up to the choice of representatives for the National People's Congress, but only from candidates screened by the party. Even those critical of the lack of commitment to democracy among contemporary Chinese intellectuals may betray certain assumptions that are difficult to reconcile with rule by elected politicians. Cai Dingjian of the Chinese University of Law and Politics has written an essay (in Chinese) titled "In Defense of Democracy! A Response to Contemporary Antidemocratic Theory." The essay is an important academic and political contribution to the debate on democratization in China. Cai argues forcefully against some of the most frequent objections to democratic rule in China—that it benefits only majorities, that it undermines stability and economic development, and that it contributes to corruption. To support the view that the "quality" of the people[18] does not undermine the prospects of democracy, however, he draws on Singapore's founding father Lee Kuan Yew's point that Singapore's Chinese immigrants (largely from poor and uneducated backgrounds) have succeeded in establishing a good society based on the rule of law. What Singaporean Chinese can do, mainland Chinese can do, whether it's the rule of law or democracy. But Singapore's "rule of law" relies on legal punishments that control detailed aspects of everyday life: as the joke goes, Singapore is a "fine" city. And Singapore wasn't anything close to a democracy at China's level's of wealth and education (the same is true of Taiwan and South Korea). Today, there are elections, but Singapore-style democracy means overwhelming dominance of the ruling People's Action Party along with harsh punishments for opposition politicians that range from public humiliation to bankruptcy and exile. Even more worrisome, Lee himself is perhaps the most notorious defender of rule by meritocratically selected political elites,[19] a view he supports with dubious eugenic theories. Lee's view is that education won't suffice; there will always be a minority of people endowed with superior innate intelligence (such as his own son, the current prime minister of Singapore, and other family members that control key levers of the economy), and they should be society's leaders. And the rulers themselves get to decide on who counts as "the best and brightest." This is not, to put it mildly, the kind of model supporters of democracy should endorse.[20]

So for the foreseeable future, it is highly unlikely that democratic rule at the national level will emerge in China. The proposal most likely to garner support from government officials and intellectual elites who are best positioned to think about and implement political reform[21] is for a strong, meritocratically chosen legislature that has constitutional priority over the democratically elected house. The proposal might gain additional support if it incorporates the following features:

> The deputies in the meritocratic house are chosen (by examinations) for seven- or eight-year terms and there are strict penalties for corruption.

> The examinations test for the Confucian classics, basic economics, world history, and a foreign language, and they are set by an independent board of academics randomly chosen from China's universities that is sequestered from the rest of society during the examination process.[22]

> There is substantial deliberation before decisions are taken in the meritocratic house, and most debates are televised and transmitted to the public on the Web.

> The national democratic legislature's main function is to transmit the people's (relatively uninformed) preferences to the meritocratic house. At the provincial, township, city, and village levels, the top decision-makers are chosen by means of competitive elections, and decisions are taken in deliberative forums.

> Freedom of the press is basically secure, and there are many opportunities to raise objections and present grievances to deputies at the national level.

Farfetched? It's no less so than scenarios that envision a transition to Western-style liberal democracy (because both scenarios assume an end to one-party rule), and it answers the main worry about the transition to democracy: that it translates into rule by uneducated people.[23] As more Chinese gain access to education, and democratic values and practices become more entrenched, the democratic legislature can be empowered relative to the meritocratic house. Strong democrats may prefer to abolish the meritocratic house in due course—or at least reduce it to an advisory and symbolic function if it helps to strengthen the democratic system[24]—but there may be a case for more permanent empowerment of the meritocratic house when democratic processes threaten to get out of hand. During a seminar at Tsinghua University in October 2006, the comparative political scientist Adam Przeworski noted that nonpartisan institutions play an important role in resolving conflicts when partisan politics cannot produce sufficient consensus for nonviolent decision-making, and that the meritocratic house could serve this function in the Chinese context. Like the Thai king, it would intervene only in exceptional cases.

There may be the worry that the strong meritocratic system becomes entrenched—fossilized, like the American constitutional system—and hard to change once it's in place. But what if it works well? The deputies debate at length. They favor policies that prioritize the needs of the disadvantaged. They consider the interests of all those affected by policies, including foreigners and future generations. For long-term planning, they favor technological change that frees workers from the need to engage drudge labor. They also try to limit the environmental impact of new technologies.[25] And what if the large majority of Chinese seem satisfied with strong meritocracy? Should we complain just because the system doesn't satisfy our ideas about democratic rule, or should we allow for the possibility that there are morally legitimate, if not superior, alternatives to Western-style liberal democracy?

2. War, Peace, and China's Soft Power

In late 2006, China Central Television broadcast a twelve-part documentary titled *The Rise of Great Powers*. The series was based on research by a distinguished team of Chinese historians who also briefed the ruling Politburo about their findings. More surprisingly, perhaps, the series was remarkably balanced, akin, perhaps, to what one might watch on the National Geographic Channel. It described the reasons nine countries rose to become great powers and to the extent there was any viewpoint, it seemed to be "pro-Western." The program clearly implied that Britain and the United States were the only enduring great powers among the nine nations surveyed. Aggression through force, as demonstrated by the examples of Germany and Japan in World War II, is to be avoided at all costs. In the modern world, competition is led by business and innovation, not military force, and cultural success is measured by contributions to humanity and science. A familiar list of liberal-democratic goods contribute to competition and cultural flowering: the rule of law (the series showed how the United States managed to protect intellectual property), an open society in which ideas can be rapidly spread to a wider circle of the people, and political systems that allow for orderly transitions of power and checks on the abuse of political power.

The series led to widespread public debate, including reactions by intellectuals who argued that aping Western ways won't be sufficient for China to project its "soft power": the values and practices that win over the hearts and minds of foreigners. To an important extent, such soft power must be built on local cultural resources. Already, Chinese culture—in the form of food, painting, medicine, martial arts, and so on—has spread and enriched other societies (centuries earlier, Chinese technology had spread and enriched other societies). But Chinese *po-litical* values have not spread so successfully. In the 1960s, the Chinese government promoted the idea of peasant-based revolution and class struggle, inspiring Maoists around the globe. But such ideas are widely discredited now, especially within China itself. The United States is identified with freedom and democracy, and one can perhaps dig deep enough in Chinese culture to find such values, but it's hard to believe that China will ever replace the United States as the guardian of such values (I do not mean to imply that the United States is doing at good job at what it's supposed to do). So which values should China promote abroad? The contemporary Chinese intellectual Kang Xiaoguang has argued that Chinese soft power should be based on Confucian culture, the most influential Chinese political tradition.[1] But which Confucian values should form the core of China's soft power? Here Kang is a bit vague, and it's worth exploring this question in more detail.

From State Sovereignty to Global Harmony

Confucianism is often blamed for justifying "authoritarian national-ism," but the real blame lies with Legalism, China's other important political tradition. Legalists such as Han Fei Zi (ca. 280—233 BCE) had special contempt for Confucian thinkers who stressed tolerance and rule by morality. Han Fei did not deny that light rule had its place in a golden age of social harmony and material abundance. But in his own day—the Warring States period—such policies would lead to dis-aster, and Confucians were naively drawing inappropriate lessons from accidental features of past societies. What's needed, Han Fei argued, is to strengthen state power by means of harsh laws and punishments, and he stressed over and over again that moral considerations should not get in the way.

Not surprisingly, such ideas tended to have special sway in times of war and chaos. The ruthless king of Qin drew on Han Fei's advice to conquer and rule all of China under the title of First Emperor of the Qin dynasty. After Japan was forcefully opened to the outside world by Western powers, the Meiji Restoration (1868–90) rulers shed Confu-cian values and stressed Legalist ideas such as "Enrich the state, strengthen the military" and "Deal out to each its sure reward and punishment." Legalist ideas also came to the fore in twentieth-century China. Following the "century of humiliation" at the hands of foreign powers (ca. mid–nineteenth to mid–twentieth centuries), China's leaders drew upon Legalist ideas to strengthen the state and build its capacity to protect itself from foreign interference and internal chaos. Mao himself justified his actions with reference to Legalist ideas and compared himself to the first Qin emperor.

This background helps to explain the Chinese focus on state sovereignty. When Chinese authorities respond to the criticisms of international human rights groups with the claim that foreigners should not interfere with China's internal affairs, Western observers tend to dismiss such responses as mere covers for silencing human rights demands. That may be partly true, but it's not the whole story. There is often genuine concern, based upon recent historical memory with colonialism and imperialism, that opening up China to interference by foreigners will open a Pandora's box, with China plunging into civil war, poverty, and chaos. And it's not just authoritarian rulers who say that. I've heard many Chinese intellectuals make similar points.

But such sentiments are receding with time. Clearly China is stronger than before, and it doesn't have to worry as much about foreign incursions. The realities and responsibilities of being a great power are gradually rendering preoccupation with state sovereignty obsolete. "To each his own" in international affairs no longer makes any sense. With China's economic integration in the global market, it has the power to influence economic actors around the globe (and vice versa). In the United States, the "Made in China" label has become a source of anxiety: parents worry about toys with lead paint, diners worry about unsanitary food, and even pet owners worry about consuming poisonous Chinese products. The influx of cheap Chinese manufactured goods is threatening producers in Mexico. Retailers in Zambia fret about competition from small Chinese shopkeepers. The environmental consequences of China's economic growth—greenhouse gas emissions, acid rain and dust storms in Japan and South Korea, particulate pollution over Los Angeles—threaten the rest of the world. China has been blamed for the slaughter in Darfur because it sells weapons to Sudan and fills the country's coffers with oil revenues. It has also been condemned for cozying up to brutal and unpopular dictators in Burma and Zimbabwe. If China affects the rest of the world, how can it ask the rest of the world not to interfere with its own internal affairs?

Faced with such concerns, China has begun to play a more responsible and cooperative role in international affairs. It has shown willingness to settle long-standing territorial disputes with its neighbors. According to Taylor Travel, China has "frequently used cooperative means to manage its territorial conflicts, revealing a pattern far more complex than many portray . . . it has offered substantial compromises in most of these settlements, usually receiving less than 50% of the contested land" (*International Security*, fall 2005, 46). Economic pressure from China contributed to the successful war on drugs in Southeast Asia's Golden Triangle (opium production has largely shifted to Afghanistan). The government has issued a plan for dealing with climate change meant partly to reassure outsiders. It played a critical role in defusing the nuclear crisis in North Korea and persuading the Sudanese government to allow a UN–African Union hybrid peacekeeping force to deploy to Darfur (Erica Downs, *China Security*, summer 2007, 60-61). It ended developmental assistance to Zimbabwe and joined the UN Security Council in condemning Burma's rulers for its violent crackdown on peaceful protesters. It has sent four thousand soldiers and police to participate in fourteen UN peacekeeping missions: more than any of the other five members of the UN Security Council (Bates Gill and Yanzhong Huang, "Sources and Limits of China's 'Soft Power,'" *Survival*, summer 2006, 22). In the largest emergency package for foreign countries that China has ever provided, it sent $83 million to the countries hit by the tsunami off Indonesia's coast. It even offers financial help to rich countries: after Hurricane Katrina hit the southern United States, the Chinese government offered $5.1 million in aid to the United States.

Of course, such efforts often fall short of what the Chinese government ought to do. But what exactly is the government supposed to do? What moral principles should inform Chinese foreign policy, the way China deals with the rest of the world? Legalism cannot provide any guidance, since it advocates amoral disregard for other countries. But Confucianism has resources to offer, and such issues are being debated by Chinese intellectuals. The point is not only to provide moral guidance for state policy, but also to provide moral resources for social critics that expose the inevitable gap between the reality and the ideal. Just as American critics of foreign policy expose the gap between the democratic ideals of their Founding Fathers and the U.S. government's actual deeds, so Chinese critics can draw upon Confucian ideals to evaluate the way their government actually deals with other countries.

Far from defending narrow nationalism, Confucianism veers toward the other extreme of utopian cosmopolitanism. One of the most celebrated passages in Confucian literature is the account of Da Tong, the age of Great Harmony, taken from the *Record of Rites* (*Liji*), a work compiled during the Han dynasty (206 BCE—220 CE) on the basis of older materials. The ideal, traditionally taken as representing Confucius's highest ideal in the social order, refers to a golden age in which the world was shared in common by all (*tian xia wei gong*):

> When the Great Way was practiced, the world was shared by all alike. The worthy and the able were promoted to office and men practiced good faith and lived in harmony. Therefore they did not regard as parents only their own parents, or as sons only their own sons. The aged were cared for till the end of their lives, the able-bodied pursued proper employment, while the young were nurtured in growing up. Provisions were made to care for widows, widowers, the orphaned and the sick. Men had their tasks while women had their hearths. They hated to see goods lying about in waste, yet they did not hoard them for themselves; they disliked the thought that their energies were not fully used, yet they used them not for private ends. Therefore all evil plotting was prevented and thieves and rebels did not arise, so that people could leave their outer gates unbolted. This was the age of Great Harmony.[2]

This ideal had special importance in early modern China. The Confucian reformer Kang Youwei, often thought to be conservative in his own day (he favored restoration of the imperial system), wrote a book on the Great Harmony that was only published in 1935, seven years after his death. He divided the world's development into three stages: an "uncivilized stage," followed by an intermediate stage (*xiaokang*, or moderate prosperity, similar to capitalist democracy),[3] and then Great Harmony, also known as *Taiping Shi* (Global Peace). Kang described an ideal society composed of people freed from particular attachments and where all goods are shared in common: "Now to have states, families, and selves is to allow each individual to maintain a sphere of selfishness. . . . Therefore, not only states should be abolished, so that there would be no more struggle between the strong and the weak; families should also be done away with, so that there would no longer be inequality of love and affection among people; and finally selfishness itself should be abolished, so that goods and services would not be used for private ends. . . . The only true way is sharing the world in common by all (*tian xia wei gong*)."[4] Many Chinese leaders at the turn of the twentieth century agreed with Kang's ideal. Sun Yat-sen, for example, accepted Kang's suggestion that the East West School be changed to the Da Tong school (the motto *tian xia wei gong* is now inscribed on Sun Yat-sen's tomb). In 1917, the youthful Mao wrote to his friend Li Jinxi that "Da Tong is our goal" (as one might expect, he dropped such ideas once he become ruler). Even Liang Qichao (1873-1927), Kang's student who leaned more to liberty than equality, wrote that "the Chinese people have never considered national government as the highest form of social organization. Their political thinking has always been in terms of all mankind, with world peace as the final goal, and family and nation as transitional stages in the perfecting of World Peace (*Tian Xia*)."[5]

Such ideals have resurfaced in contemporary debates. Zhao Tingyang, a scholar at the Chinese Academy of Social Sciences, wrote an essay defending the ideal of Tian Xia that has been widely discussed in intellectual circles. According the Zhao, China has the potential to become "a power that is responsible to the world, a power that is different from various empires in world history. To be responsible to the world, rather than merely to one's own country, is, theoretically speaking, a perspective of Chinese philosophy, and practically speaking, a brand-new possibility, that is, to take Tian Xia as a preferred unit of analysis of political/economic interests, to understand the world from the perspective of Tian Xia. [The ideal is] to analyze problems with 'the world' as the unit of thinking, going beyond the Western mode of thinking in terms of the nation-state, to take responsibility to the world as one's own responsibility, and to create a new world idea and a new world institution."[6]

But now there's a different twist. In the early twentieth century, dreams of an ideal world that transcends the state-centric international system may have owed more to China's weak position relative to Western powers. One psychologically appealing way of restoring the traditional glory of Chinese culture was to simply wish away the world of competing states. Now that China looks set to become a great power, if not the great power, the Chinese state is viewed as the carrier of cosmopolitan values that will spread throughout the rest of the world. Of course, the world may not be so receptive: in a political institution of global scope informed by the Confucian ideal of Tian Xia, other cultural and moral systems are implicitly downgraded to second-class status. This is not to deny that Zhao's proposal has some virtues. It is fine—indeed, desirable—for the Chinese state to pursue world peace. Some of Zhao's practical recommendations, such as the ideal of free immigration, are also worth pursuing.[7] But the ideal of Tian Xia must make room for cultural diversity.[8] At the very least, it seems wrong to deny the possibility that there are morally legitimate differences regarding social and political organization, that different ways of protecting and promoting cultural ideals can give rise to different political institutions (and different kinds of states). As a practical matter, it is difficult to imagine that one global ruler or political institution will ever be able to secure political legitimacy among all the different cultures and worldviews. Rather than arguing for cosmopolitan political institutions inspired by Confucian principles—with the not-so-implicit agenda that the Chinese state will take the leading role in promoting, if not instantiating, such institutions[9]—those concerned with promoting China's soft power might be better off pointing to the Confucian emphasis on modesty, tolerance, and willingness to learn that Confucians have often shown when engaging with other cultural and moral systems like Buddhism and liberalism.

But the deeper problem with the cosmopolitan ideal is the ideal itself. It relies on the utopian assumption that human beings can be freed from particularistic attachments, where feelings of commonality outweigh any "selfish" ties. Such ideas may be more appropriate for small communities, but in a country of 1.3 billion people, culturally diverse and still quite poor (per capita income of roughly US$2000) per year, it is hard to imagine that such strong feelings of commonality could develop.[10] Extended to the international realm, Kang's ideal of Da Tong and Zhao's ideal of Tian Xia seem even more implausible. "To all his own" makes no more sense in international affairs than "to each his own." Obviously there are competing national interests. Like other states, China competes for access to resources and foreign investment. Even if China becomes rich, there would still be competition for cultural glory. And sometimes it's a zero-sum game. China's new Confucius Institutes aim to promote Chinese language learning abroad, leading to worries among French politicians that their language is losing global appeal. There will always be competition for Olympic gold medals.[11] Some of these pursuits may not be legitimate, but any principle of international relations needs to leave some room for legitimate national interest.

More surprisingly, perhaps, the cosmopolitan ideal is radically inconsistent with key Confucian values.[12] The ideal owes more to imported traditions like Christianity, Buddhism, and Marxism, whatever the self-understanding of its "Confucian" advocates. Another chapter from the *Record of Rites* titled *The Great Learning* helps us to interpret the Da Tong ideal. *The Great Learning*—subsequently canonized by the Song dynasty scholar Zhu Xi (1130-1200) as one of the four Confucian classics—opens with the famous passage:

> The extension of knowledge consists in the investigation of things. When things are investigated, knowledge is extended; when knowledge is extended, the will is sincere; when the will is sincere, the mind is rectified; when the mind is rectified, the personal life is cultivated; when the personal life is cultivated, the family will be regulated; when the family is regulated, the state will be in order; and when the state is in order, there is peace throughout the world (*Tian Xia*).

Starting from the moral ordering of the individual person and the family, an important goal of Confucianism is to bring order to the state and thereby to spread peace throughout the world. The ideal goal is a harmonious political order of global peace. But nowhere does *The Great Learning* state that ties to strangers should be as strong as ties to loved ones (not to mention Kang Youwei's idea that families should be abolished). The Confucian idea is that ties should be extended from intimates to others, but with diminishing intensity. And if ties between intimates and strangers conflict, the former often have priority.[13] The web of obligations that binds family members is more intense than that binding citizens, the web of obligations that binds citizens is more intense than that binding foreigners, and so on. As Joseph Chan puts it, "The Confucian view that it is natural and right for a person to show more concern for people close to him or her than to strangers would lead one to accept at least some kind of territorial boundary that distributes more resources to citizens of a community than to outsiders" ("Territorial Boundaries and Confucianism," 81). But *The Great Learning* reminds us that it shouldn't end there. It is also natural and right to seek to extend concern to outsiders to the extent possible.[14] In practice, the Confucian ideal of Great Harmony would mean a foreign policy that promotes international peace while allowing for legitimate national self-interest that can sometimes outweigh cosmopolitan ideals. It is not necessarily wrong for the Chinese state to be particularly concerned about, say, the fate of Chinese workers in other countries,[15] even if it can get more "bang for the buck" by aiding foreign workers. But the Chinese state should also show some concern for the well-being of outsiders and devote itself to working out common solutions to global problems wherever possible. Such is the "Golden Mean" (*zhongyong zhi dao*) between the extremes of state sovereignty and utopian cosmopolitanism. A foreign policy informed by the ideal of Grand Harmony that makes room for cultural difference and legitimate national self-interest is good for China and may also enhance China's soft power abroad.[16]

There remain many complex questions regarding the nature and extent of obligations owed to outsiders. But I would like to focus on perhaps the most basic question of international relations: when, if ever, should the state engage in warfare? Surprisingly, perhaps, the Confucian tradition still informs Chinese thinking on the morally justified use of state violence. And such thinking may hold valuable insights for the modern world.

War for Peace

In the early days of the U.S.-led invasion of Iraq, the Chinese-language Internet was filled with references to ancient Confucian thinkers.[17] Ming Yongqian's contribution is typical:

> Mencius said, "A true king uses virtue and humanity, a hege-
> mon uses force under the pretext of humanity and compas-
> sion." Let us first consider the idea of the hegemon. According
> to Mencius's saying, a hegemon uses force to attack others in
> the name of benevolent justice. This kind of war is an unjust
> war. . . . In ancient times as well as today, most rulers are very
> clear regarding political realities, they won't lightly abandon
> the cover of virtue to launch such wars. . . . The best contem-
> porary example is Bush's war of invasion against Iraq! He used
> the excuses of weapons of mass destruction and terrorism in
> order to obtain oil resources and to consolidate his strategic
> position in the Middle East. This is the best example of "using
> force under the pretext of humanity and compassion." Bush is
> today's hegemonic king.[18]

The distinction between the aggressive "hegemon" and the peace-loving "true king" was first articulated by Mencius over two thousand years ago and still informs the moral language that Chinese intellectuals often use to evaluate foreign policy, especially regarding morally justified warfare (in contemporary parlance, "just war"). But what exactly did Mencius say about war and peace? And does it make sense to invoke his ideas in today's vastly different political world? Why not simply stick to the language of human rights? Let us turn to these questions.

In the ideal world of Tian Xia, an era of global peace, there would be no wars, and pacifism would be the only justifiable moral stance. If no one is fighting for territory, then, as Mencius put it, "What need is there for war?" (7B.4). But Mencius was writing at the time of the War-ring States period (c. 500–221 BCE), a time of ruthless competition for territorial advantage between small walled states, and it shouldn't be too surprising that he also provided practical, morally informed guidance for this context.[19] Mencius argued that rulers have an obligation to promote the peaceful unification of the world (1A.6, 2B.12). Ideally, the ruler should rely on noncoercive means to do so: "There is a way to gain the whole world. It is to gain the people, and having gained them one gains the whole world. There is a way to gain the people. Gain their hearts and minds, and then you gain them" (4A.10). As a consequence, he was critical of rulers who launched bloody wars of conquest simply in order to increase their territory and engage in economic plunder. Seemingly fearless, Mencius goes to see King Hui of Liang and scolds him for being "overly fond of war" (1A.3). Mencius suggests that wars of conquest cannot even lead to short-term victories, and that they are disastrous for all parties concerned, including the conqueror's loved ones:

> Mencius said, "King Hui of Liang is the antithesis of humanity and compassion. The man of humanity and compassion brings upon the things he does not love the things he loves. But the man who is not humane and compassionate brings upon the things he loves, the things he does not love." Gongsun Chou said, "What does that mean?" Mencius said, "King Hui of Liang ravished his own people for the sake of territory and went to war. When defeated, he tried again and fearing that he might not succeed he drove the son he loved to fight and his son was sacrificed. That is what I meant by 'bringing upon the things he loves, the things he does not love.'" (7B.1; see also 1.A.7)

An unjust war, in short, is a war that is launched for purposes other than peace and humanity. The problem, however, is the world is filled with ruthless men, including some who gained states (7B.13) and won't be moved by moral concerns. Faced with cruel rulers of this sort, what are the morally informed practical responses?

Mencius does not counsel nonviolent resistance against tyrants who only respond to the language of force. In domestic policy, Mencius is famous for sanctioning the killing of despotic rulers (1B.8). To prevent attacks from foreign tyrants and secure the peace at home, Mencius suggests that state boundaries can be fortified: "The setting up of border posts in antiquity was to prevent violence. Today they are set up for the purpose of engaging in violence" (7B.8, see also 6B.9). So the first kind of just war approximates the modern idea of self-defense. For example, if a small territory is ruled by a capable and virtuous ruler who seeks to promote peace and humanity, and if that territory is attacked by an unjust would-be hegemon, then the ruler of that territory can justifiably mobilize the people for military action:

> Duke Wen of Teng asked, "Teng is a small state, wedged be-
> tween Qi and Chu. Should I be subservient to Qi or should I
> be subservient to Chu?"
> "This is a question that is beyond me," answered Mencius.
> "If you insist, there is only one course of action I can suggest.
> Dig deeper moats and build higher walls and defend them
> shoulder to shoulder with the people. If they would rather die
> than desert you, then all is not lost." (1B.13)

This passage suggests that the people's support is crucial for successful warfare (see also 2B.1). It also suggests the people can only be mobilized to fight if they are willing to fight, with the implication that conscription of a reluctant populace would not be effective (or morally desirable).

The second kind of just war approximates the modern idea of humanitarian intervention—Mencius labels these wars "punitive expeditions" (征), and they are meant to bring about global peace and humane government. Certain conditions, however, must be in place. First, the "conquerors" must try to liberate people who are being oppressed by tyrants: "Now the prince of Yen cruelly mistreated his own people and Your Majesty set out on a punitive expedition. Yen's people thought you were saving them from 'flood and fire' [i.e., from tyranny]" (1B.11). Mencius suggests that wicked rulers are not likely to go down without a fight and that liberation of the people may require murdering the tyrant: "He killed the ruler and comforted the people, like the fall of timely rain, and the people greatly rejoiced" (1B.11). Second, the people must demonstrate, in concrete ways, that they welcome their conquerors (7B.4, 1B.10, 1B.11, 3B.5). However, the welcome must be long-lasting, not just immediate. The real challenge is to maintain support for the invading forces after the initial enthusiasm: "The people welcomed your army [which had just carried out a punitive expedition] with baskets of rice and bottles of drink. If you [then] kill the old, bind the young, destroy the ancestral temples, and appropriate the ancestral vessels, how can you expect the people's approval?" (1B.11). Third, punitive expeditions must be launched by rulers who are at least *potentially* virtuous. One can assume that Mencius bothered to talk to some flawed rulers only because he believed they contained the seeds of virtue within them, or at least that they had sufficient good sense to respond to practical, morally informed advice. Fourth, the leader of justified punitive expeditions must have some moral claim to have the world's support: "The Book of History says, 'In his punitive expeditions Tang began with Ge.' The whole world was in sympathy with his cause. When he marched on the east, the western tribes complained. When he marched to the south, the northern tribes complained. They said, 'Why does he not come to us first?'" (1B.11).

Needless to say, this ancient world is far removed from our own, and one has to be careful about drawing implications for contemporary societies. But Ni Lexiong argues that the Warring States period shares five common characteristics with the contemporary international state system: (1) there is no real social authority higher than the state; (2) the higher social authorities exist in form rather than substance (the Zhou Son of Heaven in the Warring States period, the United Nations today); (3) national/state interest is the highest principle that trumps other considerations in cases of conflict; (4) the dominant principle in international relations is the "law of the jungle"; and (5) universal moral principles are invoked as pretexts for realizing state interests.[20] Thus it should not be entirely surprising if at least some Confucian prescriptions on just and unjust war are held to be relevant for the contemporary world of sovereign states in an "anarchical" global system.

This is not just a theoretical point. As mentioned, Mencius's views serve as a normative reference point for contemporary Chinese social critics opposed to wars of conquest. They also underpin judgments regarding just wars. For example, Gong Gang appeals to the distinction between wars of conquest and justified punitive expeditions to differentiate between recent wars in the Persian Gulf:

One can say that the first Gulf War is a just war authorized by the United Nations, similar to "a guilty duke corrected [punished] by the Son of Heaven." . . . In this war [the 2003 invasion of Iraq], the United States says it is using force to exercise humanity and compassion, that it is acting as both a true king and a hegemon. But the second Gulf war is not the same, because without the authorization of the United Nations. . . . the United States is using force under the pretext of humanity and compassion, and it is also maintaining its geopolitical, national security, and economic interests in the name of promoting democracy in the Middle East; it is obviously acting as a global hegemon.[21]

Still, one may ask, why not use the modern language of human rights to make such judgments? Michael Walzer, the most influential Western theorist of just and unjust war, explicitly argues that human rights are at the foundation of wartime morality: "Individual rights to (life and liberty) underlie the most important judgments we make about war" (*Just and Unjust War*, 3rd ed., 54). The obvious response is that "we" does not typically include Chinese intellectuals and policymakers. In the Chinese context, the language of human rights, when it has been deployed to justify military intervention abroad, has been tainted by its misuses in the international arena.[22] Given the history of colonial subjugation by Western powers, as well as the ongoing conflicts over economic resources and geopolitical interests, the language of human rights is often seen as an ideology designed to rationalize policies of exploitation and regime change. Even where military intervention in the name of human rights may have been justified—as, arguably, in the case of NATO's war on behalf of the Kosovo Albanians—it is difficult, if not impossible, to overcome Chinese skepticism regarding the real motives underlying intervention.[23]

This provides a practical reason for invoking Mencius's theory of just and unjust war in the Chinese context. What ultimately matters is the *practice* rather than the theory of human rights. So long as people are protected from torture, genocide, starvation, and other such obvious harms, there is no need to worry about the particular political and philosophical justifications. That is, states and other collective agencies should do their best to respect our basic humanity, but whether such practices are backed by human rights morality is secondary. And if Mencius's theory leads to the same judgments regarding the justice of particular wars as theories of wartime morality founded on human rights, then why not deploy his theory in the Chinese context?

Having said that, Mencius's theory will not always lead to the same judgments as theories founded on human rights—but this may speak in favor of Mencius's theory. For Mencius, the government cannot secure the peace if its people are not well fed (1A.7). Hence, the first obligation of government is to secure the basic means of subsistence of the people. By extension, the worst thing a government can do—in contemporary parlance, the most serious violation of human rights— would be to deliberately deprive the people of the means of subsistence (by killing them, not feeding them, not dealing with a plague, etc.). A ruler who engages in such acts, for the Confucian, would noncontroversially be viewed as an oppressive tyrant, and punitive expeditions against such rulers would be justified (assuming the other conditions for punitive expeditions have also been met). In contrast, the sorts of violations of civil and political rights that might be viewed as constituting tyranny by contemporary Western defenders of human rights, such as systematic denials of the right to free speech or the heavy-handed treatment of political dissidents in the name of social order, would not be viewed as violations sufficiently serious to justify humanitarian intervention by foreign powers.

Such differences in emphasis may influence judgments of just and unjust warfare in the contemporary world. For Western defenders of human rights, Saddam Hussein was noncontroversially regarded as an oppressive tyrant because he engaged in the systematic violation of civil and political rights: liberal defenders of humanitarian intervention such as Michael Ignatieff and Thomas Friedman supported the invasion of Iraq largely on those grounds. The invasion of Iraq, in their view, could democratize that country and set a political model for the rest of the Middle East (now that Iraq has become synonymous with violence and chaos, such dreams have been set aside). For Confucians, however, so long as the Iraqi people were not being deliberately deprived of the means of subsistence, the intervention could not be justified.

In other cases, however, Confucians may be more likely to support humanitarian interventions compared to liberal defenders of humanitarian intervention. In cases of deliberately engineered famines, such as the Afghanistan government's total road blockade on Kabul in 1996, the Confucian just war theorist would argue for foreign intervention (assuming, as always, that the other conditions for foreign intervention have been met). In contrast, liberal human rights groups such as Amnesty International denounced the shooting and torture of a few victims as human rights violations and treated the manufactured starvation of thousands as background.[24] Similarly, if it is true that the North Korean government has been deliberately promoting policies that result in the starvation of millions of people, the Confucian would have emphasized the need for foreign intervention in North Korea rather than such countries as Iraq.[25]

It is worth asking how much of this matters in practice. Even if Confucian views inform the judgments of critical intellectuals in China, do these judgments really affect the political practices of the Chinese state? Confucian theorists of just war may prove to be just as ineffective as moralizing theorists of human rights in the American context (perhaps even more so, if the society lacks a free press and other public forums for communicating criticisms; Chinese Confucian critics tend to reserve their criticisms for foreign hegemons). It is obvious, for example, that war against Taiwan if it declares formal independence would not meet the Confucian criteria for justifiable punitive expeditions: so long as the Taiwanese government does not kill or starve its people, only moral power could be justifiably employed to bring Taiwan back into the Chinese orbit.[26] But it seems just as obvious that Confucian objections are not likely to cause the Chinese government to hold back in such an eventuality. So what exactly is the point of Confucian theorizing on just warfare?

A historical perspective may provide some insight. One feature of imperial China was that it did not expand in ways comparable to Western imperial powers, even when it may have had the technical ability to do so. Instead, it established the tributary system, with the "Middle Kingdom" at the center and "peripheral" states on the outside. In this system, the tributary ruler or his representative had to go to China to pay homage in ritual acknowledgment of his vassal status. In return, China guaranteed security and provided economic benefits, while using moral power to spread Confucian norms and allowing traditional ways of life to flourish. Needless to say, the practice often deviated from the ideal. Still, the Confucian-Mencian discourse did help to stabilize the tributary system and curb the excesses of bloodthirsty warriors and greedy merchants. There may be lessons for the future. As China once again establishes itself as an important global power, with the economic and military means to become a regional (or even global) hegemon, it will need to be constrained by more than realpolitik. More than any other discourse, Confucian theorizing on just and unjust war has the potential to play the role of constraining China's imperial ventures abroad, just as it did in the past. Confucian morality would cause the leaders to think twice about collaborating with governments implicated in the mass killings of civilians, as in Sudan. Put more positively, China would also have the power and the responsibility to carry out punitive expeditions in neighboring states (e.g., if Burma began to carry out a Rwanda-style massacre of its population). Confucian discourse could provide moral guidance in such cases, and the Chinese government wouldn't simply be reacting to international pressure.

Confucian theorizing can also have an impact below the highest levers of the state, particularly once the war is already under way. The torture of prisoners at Abu Ghraib in Iraq is a reminder that evil deeds in warfare are committed "unofficially," by soldiers acting without the explicit authority of the top commanders. Nonetheless, these soldiers took implicit cues from the top, which set the tone for the cavalier approach to the protection of prisoners' well-being. Here the Confucian emphasis on the moral quality of political and military leaders may be particularly relevant. In imperial China, the idea that those carrying out the war should be humane and compassionate informed the practice of appointing generals who were held to be exemplary persons with both moral character and military expertise. One important reason for emphasizing the moral quality of commanders is that they set the moral example for other ordinary soldiers, and their moral power radiates down to lower levels: as Confucius put it, "Under the wind, the grass must bend" (12.19). If the aim is to sensitize soldiers to moral considerations, the leaders should not, as in Clausewitz's idea of the general, simply be concerned with the practical skills required for victory.

There are, in short, two main reasons for invoking Mencius's theory of just war. The first reason is psychological. If there is rough agreement

on the aims of a theory of just war—that it should prohibit wars of conquest and justify certain kinds of wars of self-defense and humanitarian
intervention—then one should invoke the theory that is most psychologically compelling to the people being addressed. In the Chinese
context, the theory of Mencius is most likely to have causal power. The
comparison here is not just with theories of human rights, but with other
Chinese thinkers such as Mozi who have also put forward theories functionally similar to modern theories of just war. Mencius is typically
viewed as a "good guy" by contemporary Chinese, so there is no need to
qualify or apologize for aspects of his theory.

The second reason is philosophical, and it speaks to the normative
validity of Mencius's theory. Compared to alternative theories, Mencius's theory has several advantages, such as the focus on material
well-being and the lack of emphasis on religion or ethnicity as justifications for going to war. Mencius's theory can and should be taught in
military academies, both in China and elsewhere. And critical intellectuals should draw upon Mencius's views to evaluate the justice of
wars in the contemporary world. Of course, there is no reason to take
Mencius's theory (or any other theory) of just war as the final word on
the subject. One lacuna, for example, is the lack of detailed prescriptions for *jus in bello*. Besides arguing against the large-scale slaughter of
civilians (7B.3), Mencius did not explicitly draw the implications of his
views on just war for just conduct in war. Here Xunzi's insights regarding just conduct in war, as well as those of contemporary theorists,
could usefully supplement Mencius's theory.

Can Mencius's theory come to be seen as part of China's soft power
by the rest of the world? For that to happen, the theory has to come
alive. Confucian social critics should also direct their critical ammunition at the Chinese state (not just the United States), where such criticisms are more likely to be taken seriously. And the theory should be
seen as influencing the foreign policy of the Chinese state. Once the
Chinese state acts morally abroad, then it can articulate and promote
its theory to the rest of the world. Otherwise nobody will really listen.
Confucian moral values should also be seen as influencing domestic
policy. A state that deliberately kills peaceful protesters in full view of
the world's media, for example, won't be able to inspire the rest of the
world with its foreign policy.[27] An official apology for the bloody crack-

down on June 4, 1989 in Beijing would go a long way toward restoring China's moral credibility in the eyes of outsiders.[28]

Even then, however, there is no guarantee that China's foreign policy will come to express Confucian moral values. Much depends on the rest of the world's actions. The United States bears special responsibility. So long as it maintains global military dominance—with military bases in China's neighboring countries and claims to exclusive rights in what should be common areas, such as outer space—China is not likely to depend solely (or even mainly) on soft power in the international arena. In this context, China's rise may not be entirely peaceful. A more balanced world—with no country having the military capacity to exert its will in the face of global opinion—renders more likely the expression of Confucian moral values. It's also a matter of attitude. So long as Chinese influence is regarded as inherently malevolent and competitive unless it conforms to American values and practices, it will be hard for China to respond with anything but power politics. Yes, China's political opening will make its model more attractive to Americans, and forces that seek to demonize the country may not be as successful. But there is no reason to expect that China will—or should—have the same set of moral and political priorities when it engages with other countries. There are areas of justifiable moral difference that need to be tolerated, if not respected.

3. Hierarchical Rituals for Egalitarian Societies

One of the most puzzling features of East Asian societies is that they seem both rigidly hierarchical and strongly egalitarian. On the one hand, they have incorporated hierarchical rituals in everyday social life. In Japan and South Korea—perhaps the most hierarchical societies in East Asia—the greeting and parting rituals between persons of different social status are governed by bowing practices that vary in accordance with the social status of the person. Those with less status bow at sharper angles to their social superiors, and vice versa. In Korea, close friends seem relatively formal no matter what the setting: for example, two university colleagues will refer to each other as "Professor so-and-so" in the midst of late-night drinking sessions even with no one else around.

Yet Korea and Japan have relatively equal distributions of wealth compared to most countries in the industrialized world. How can it be that the same society emphasizes both social hierarchy and economic equality? One possibility is that East Asian societies simply prioritize different values. Western societies emphasize social rather than material equality. An average American would never dream of bowing to an aged person yet might not be perturbed by the gross inequalities of income in the United States. In contrast, East Asians typically feel much stronger about economic inequity than about hierarchies of status. Of course, the Chinese Communists tried to eliminate social hierarchies—all Chinese referred to each other as "comrade" during the Cultural Revolution—but traditional hierarchies have reasserted themselves with a vengeance over the past three decades or so.

In any case, I would like to make a different argument. It's not just that East Asians worry less about social than economic inequality. My *author*

view is that social inequality can actually *contribute* to economic equality. In that sense, social inequality is something positive, a value worth defending. I don't mean to sound overly bookish, but I came to this counterintuitive conclusion by reading the works of the ancient Confucian philosopher Xunzi (ca. 310–219 BCE). In this chapter, I will begin by explaining Xunzi's philosophy of ritual. Then I will show how hierarchical rituals contribute to economic equality in contemporary East Asian societies. I will end by drawing implications for political reforms in China and ask whether Xunzi's defense of hierarchical rituals has universal validity.

Xunzi on Ritual

Xunzi is widely regarded as one of the three "founding fathers" of Confucianism (along with Confucius and Mencius). He has been tainted because of his supposed influence on the Legalists—the arch-rivals of Confucians—but his ideas, arguably, did more to shape the actual politics of East Asian societies than anyone else. His writings are relatively clear and systematic, and he deliberately avoids utopian assumptions about human nature and society. In fact, he begins with the assumption that "human nature is bad" (23.1). If people follow their bodily natures and indulge their natural inclinations, aggressiveness and exploitation are sure to develop, resulting in cruel tyranny and poverty (19.1). In his own day—the Warring States period—Xunzi thought that natural desires had gotten out of hand: "In these times, people lack good teachers and models, so they are prejudiced, wicked, and not upright; there are no rituals or conceptions of moral duty, so there's rebellion and chaos and it's impossible to govern society" (23.3).

Fortunately, that's not the end of the story. Human beings can be "made good by conscious exertion" (23.1). They can learn to contain their natural desires and enjoy the benefits of peaceful and cooperative social existence. The key to transformation is ritual (23.3). By learning and participating in rituals, people can learn to contain their desires, there will be a better fit between people's actual desires and the goods available in society, and social peace and material well-being will result (19.1). Rituals provide bonds not based solely on kinship that allow people to partake of the benefits of cooperative social existence. But what exactly is ritual? Xunzi's account of ritual has the following features:

- Ritual is a social practice (as opposed to behavior involving only one person). Xunzi's examples of ritual include musical performances, marriage ceremonies, and village wine ceremonies (20.12). He discusses the treatment of the dead—funeral and mourning rites—in greatest detail (19.10-19.22). Note that rites may involve one living person and one dead person, as when the dead person's body is bathed and the dead person's hair is washed (19.16). Hence, the word "social" should be extended to mean interaction between the living and the dead, not just interaction between the living.

- Ritual is grounded in tradition (as opposed to newly invented social practices). In Xunzi's view, "Rituals have three roots: Heaven and Earth are the root of life; our ancestors are the root of commonality; rulers and teachers are the root of order" (19.4). The exemplary rulers of the past self-consciously implemented and promoted the rituals to limit human desires and establish social order: "The ancient rulers abhorred such chaos, so they established the regulations contained within rituals and moral principles in order to civilize human desires and to supply the means for their satisfaction. They ensured that desires should not lack the things that satisfy them and goods would not be exhausted by the desires. In this way, goods and desires sustained each other over the course of time. This is the origin of rituals" (19.1). By identifying the social origin of rituals with the great sage-kings of the past, Xunzi endowed rituals with the authority of tradition that would increase the likelihood people care for and follow the rituals.

- Ritual involves emotion and behavior. As Xunzi puts it, "Rites reach their highest perfection when both emotion and form are fully realized" (19.7). The main point of ritual is to civilize our animal natures,[1] and if people are just going through the outward routines without any emotion, they are not likely to transform their natures. The ritual needs to involve, or trigger, an emotional response, so that it will have an effect on the participants during the ritual and beyond the ritual itself. An "empty ritual" performed without any emotion is not a ritual in Xunzi's sense.

• The details of rituals can be changed depending on the context. As Xunzi puts it, "Rituals rely on valuables and goods to make offerings, use distinctions between noble and base to create forms, vary the quantity to make distinctions, and elaborate or simplify to render each its due. . . . Thus, exemplary persons could make the elaborate forms of ritual more florid or its simplified forms leaner, but they dwell in the mean of its course" (19.9). The relatively intelligent person who is aware of the main point of ritual—to civilize human desires—can adjust the details of the rituals in accordance with the situation so that the rituals are made to serve their point. To be effective, as noted previously, they must involve expressions of emotion. The rituals should be proportionate to the emotions involved, so the mourning rituals should last three years to deal with occasions when the pain of grief has reached its pinnacle (19.18). The exact period of mourning can be modified depending upon the context and the nature of the emotions involved (for example, Xunzi notes that there should be little or no mourning for criminals after they are buried; 19.10). Elsewhere, Xunzi notes that the period when the dead body lies in state should not be rushed so that it lasts less than fifty days partly because those coming from far away should have enough time to arrive (19.11). In the contemporary era, with periods of travel drastically shortened, Xunzi would probably agree that the changed empirical circumstances mean that the period when the dead body lies in state could also be shortened.

However, Xunzi suggests that it may also be important to impose somewhat arbitrary limits that are not perceived to be subject to individual choice. He notes that it is important to specify an end point so that daily life can be resumed: "That the mourning rite is finished in the twenty-fifth month means that even though the grief and pain have not ended and although thoughts of the dead and longing for him or her have not been forgotten, this ritual practice cuts off these things, for otherwise would not sending off the dead have no conclusion, and must there not be a definite interval for the return to daily life?" (19.18). The implication is that such limits are necessary but somewhat arbitrary; to allow for the resumption of everyday life, the limits must be perceived as coming from outside and restricting individual choice. So the rituals should not be changed too frequently or without good reason, or they will begin to be seen as wholly determined by individual choice.

• Rituals specify different treatment for different people (as opposed to practices that are meant to treat everybody equally). As Xunzi puts it, "The exemplary person has been civilized by these things, and he will also be fond of ritual distinctions. What is meant by 'distinctions'? I say that these refer to the gradations of rank according to nobility or baseness, differences between the treatment of old and young, and modes of identification to match these with poverty or wealth and relative (social) importance" (19.3). Rituals involve people with different power in common social practices that treat people differently. As we will see, such practices are essential for generating a sense of community and the emotional disposition for the powerful to care for the interests of the weak and the poor.

• Rituals are noncoercive (in contrast to legal punishments). Xunzi contrasts three types of societies: one governed by the Way and its authority, one governed by harsh and judicial investigations, and one governed by deranged madness (16.2). They are arranged in order of desirability, and the first type relies on ritual and music to secure social order. Although punishments are not used, the people willingly obey the ruler, and awesome authority holds sway (16.2). Xunzi is pragmatic, and he recognizes that punishments and legal coercion may be necessary in nonideal contexts, but if possible it is best to rely on noncoercive rituals that command willing assent and participation. It is when ritual principles are cast aside that people are deluded, and penal sanctions and punishments are numerous (27.13). There is, one might say, an inverse correlation between the use of rituals and the use of punishments in society.[2]

• Rituals are socially legitimate (as opposed to practices that are not endorsed by society at large, such as blood oaths between criminal gangs). Xunzi does not make this condition explicit, but the rituals he invokes are drawn from everyday social life and seem to be supported by social legitimacy. At the very least, they would not be undermined by laws that prohibit their expression and induce a sense of fear among practitioners.

Like other Confucians, Xunzi intended to persuade political rulers to adopt his ideas because such rulers had the most power to transform society in the desired way. In an ideal society, the wise and benevolent ruler would implement such rituals, and the whole society would be harmonious, peaceful, and prosperous. But what about nonideal society? Xunzi is famously sensitive to context and advocates different prescriptions for different contexts. So the question is how to persuade rulers to adopt rituals if the rulers have yet to be morally transformed. For such purposes, Xunzi had to appeal to their self-interest.[3] The problem, however, is that the powerful have the most to benefit from "uncivilized" society, where the strong can rely on brute force to exploit the weak. Those with power need to be persuaded that they benefit from a social system that seems to place constraints in their desires. Hence, much of Xunzi's discussion of ritual is designed to persuade political rulers that it is in their own interest to promote rituals in society. Ritual, he says, is the root of strength in the state (15.8) and the right sort of music can strengthen its military forces (20.5). One would expect most rulers to be receptive to this sort of advice.

But rituals do not only benefit rulers. Both Marxists and liberal democrats have denounced hierarchical rituals because they seem designed to benefit the ruling classes of feudal societies and thus are inappropriate for modern times. But this is a misreading of Xunzi's intentions. For Xunzi, hierarchical rituals also have the effect of benefiting the weak and poor, those who would fare worst in a "state of nature": "Without rituals, desires are unlimited, leading to contention, leading to disorder, and leading to poverty" (19.1). Of course, the tyrant himself won't be the worst hit by a system where he can exercise power without constraints. It is the weak and vulnerable who are worst hit by disorder and poverty: in a situation without ritual civility, Xunzi says, "the strong would harm the weak as well as rob them (23.9).[4] Putting ritual in practice means "being kind to the humble" (27.17). But why does Xunzi seem to emphasize rituals involving people with different power?

Hierarchical rituals seem more attractive if they are contrasted with practices that exclude people of different status: the rich and powerful do their own thing, as do the poor and the weak (consider the Indian caste system). The choice, typically, is not between hierarchical and egalitarian rituals, but between rituals that involve the powerful and the vulnerable and two different sets of rituals for those with power and those without.[5] Xunzi argues for the former. The village wine ceremony, for example, is praised because young and old take a drink from the wine cup, and "in this way we know that it is possible for junior and senior to drink together without anyone being left out" (20.12). Rituals such as common birth, marriage, and burial practices also have the effect of including the poor and the marginalized as part of the society's culture and common understandings.[6] Even castrated criminals, in Xunzi's view, are entitled to funerals (19.10).[7] The powerful are made to think of the powerless as part of the group, and they are more likely to do things for them (or at least, to refrain from the worst forms of rapacious behavior). It is no coincidence that Xunzi devotes a great deal of attention to the proper treatment of the dead. The dead, for obvious reasons, are the least capable of protecting their interests.[8] They are the worst off of the worst off. Hence, those with power—the living—need to be trained by means of certain rituals to treat them with respect. Xunzi carefully specifies the need to adorn the corpse because "if the corpse is not adorned, it becomes hideous, and if it is hideous, no grief will be felt" (19.12). He also specifies that the corpse must be gradually moved further away each time it is adorned because "if it is kept close at hand, one begins to scorn it; when having it close at hand makes it the object of scorn, one begins to weary of it; when one wearies of it, one forgets one's duty to it; and if one forgets one's duties, then one no longer shows proper respect" (19.12). The ritual should be gradually phased out so that it allows for a smooth transition to everyday life as well as an extension of the cultivated emotions of proper respect and mindfulness of duty to the needy in the world of the living: "With each move he takes it further away, whereby he ensures continued respect. With the passage of time he resumes the ordinary course of life, whereby he cares for the needs of the living" (19.12)

The real (moral) value of Xunzi's work, in my view, is that he shows how rituals—more than laws and more than verbal exhortation—have the effect of promoting the interests of those most likely to suffer from a "war of all against all." And the real cleverness of his philosophy is that he proposes a mechanism that can also be made to seem to be in the interest of those most likely to benefit from a "war of all against all."[9]

Rituals in Contemporary East Asian Societies

So now we can answer the puzzle with which we began: why are East Asian societies characterized by both social hierarchy and economic equality (relative to most countries at similar levels of economic development)? In most (if not all) societies, the rich and powerful members typically desire to distinguish themselves from the rest, and it is a challenge to motivate them to do otherwise. In socially egalitarian societies like the United States, the way to express superior power typically takes the form of wealth. But in societies governed by informal rituals that express differences in social status, the powerful need not rely on material wealth to show their "superiority" to the same extent.[10] And if the rituals involve the powerful and powerless in shared rituals, the rich are made to feel a sense of community with the powerless, and they are less likely to seek other means of domination such as material wealth. At the very least, they will feel guilty about displaying excessive wealth, and they are less likely to oppose government measures designed to secure material equality (such as high inheritance taxes, as in Japan).[11]

Unfortunately, perhaps, some hierarchical rituals have been replaced by the more egalitarian, "Western-style" handshaking rituals in mainland China, Hong Kong, and Singapore. Egalitarian rituals, however, will take place largely among members of the same class, and the powerful are less likely to learn the emotional disposition to care for the interests of the vulnerable.[12] The powerful are more likely to be physically separated from the rest, and there may be less of a sense of community between the powerful and the vulnerable. The interests of the weak and the vulnerable need to be secured primarily by means of coercive measures, such as redistributive taxation backed by harsh punishments for defectors, but the rich and powerful will often find ways to defect, and it will be difficult to enforce such laws, particularly in large countries (tax evasion by the rich is one of the most widespread and difficult-to-remedy social ills in contemporary China). Nonetheless, informal rituals still have an important role to play in securing a sense of community in China. For example, the rituals governing gift-giving, with gifts that vary in accordance with the social status of the recipient, are common in all East Asian societies. The greeting of guests and parting rituals are far more elaborate than those in most Western societies. It is common for parting guests to be accompanied all the way to the physical point of departure, and the host doesn't leave until the guest has physically disappeared from view.[13]

I would like to discuss three different settings for hierarchical rituals widely practiced in China and other contemporary East Asian societies that have the effect of promoting the interests of groups of people likely to fare worst in a "state of nature" where the powerful could otherwise freely indulge their natural inclinations. If such rituals exist and work in the way they're supposed to, the aspiration to promote rituals in modern-day society may seem more realistic. The rituals mentioned were not specifically discussed by Xunzi, but they illustrate his point that hierarchical rituals have the effect of civilizing—making civil—hierarchical social interaction that would otherwise expose the nasty underside of human beings and be particularly problematic for the weak and vulnerable.

Note, however, that my main point here is normative—to show that hierarchical rituals can have egalitarian consequences. The key argument has been inspired by reading Xunzi, but I reject those parts of Xunzi that do not bear on (or seem inconsistent with) the main argument. For example, Xunzi's main target seems to have been to limit the desires of political rulers by means of ritual. In contemporary society, however, it is not just political rulers that exercise power: socialists thinkers have shown that capitalist organizations exercise power over workers, anarchists have shown that bureaucrats exercise power over citizens, feminists have shown that men exercise power over women, Foucault has shown that hospitals, prisons, and other social organizations exercise power over individuals, and so on. My aim is to suggest that hierarchical rituals can limit the powerful and protect the interests of the disadvantaged in the various spheres of social life where power is exercised.

In addition, Xunzi's point that the rituals were first implemented by the exemplary rulers of the past cannot seem plausible in a modern context. Xunzi himself may have had political purposes in mind: perhaps he thought that identifying the origin of rituals with the great sage-kings of the past would make people more likely to follow the rituals he describes. Put another way, if people regard such rituals as arbitrary human creations or as practices that could be invented or changed at will by themselves or their less-than-perfect contemporary political leaders, the rituals may be subject to ongoing questioning and may be less effective. Just as the monarchy loses much of its magic if it's viewed simply as a conscious human creation by people just like us, so the same may be true of rituals. If the origin of an institution or practice is somehow shrouded in the mysterious past, it is more likely to command allegiance.

Fortunately, rituals needn't be seen to originate from the sage-kings to command allegiance in contemporary societies. What matters is that the ritual itself be held in awe, partly because of the authority of tradition. The ritual should also be seen to contribute to a common good or ideal valued by human beings past and present. The common good itself need not be fully attainable by reason; perhaps it is more likely to be revered if it is regarded as somewhat mysterious yet important for human well-being. As Stephen Angle puts it (drawing on Paul Woodruff), "It is crucial that reverence (and awe) be reserved for ideals of perfection that lie beyond our full ability to grasp, and thus have a tinge of mystery associated with them" (paper on file with author). Rituals should be animated by reverent feeling, so that emotions are created that forge a sense of commonality among otherwise different participants.[14] As a by-product of this process, the powerful become motivated to do more for the interests of the vulnerable in their society. Those who participate experience some sort of reverence for rituals and for the common ideals expressed by the rituals, and the feeling of solidarity emerges as a by-product of participating in the ritual: and the powerful members of the rituals are more likely to develop a concern for the disadvantaged. In sum: if the rituals are shrouded in the mysterious past, and the ritual practices and ideals expressed by the rituals are held in awe and revered without being completely understood, the rituals will more effectively serve the purpose of generating a sense of commonality among participants, including the powerful who begin the care more about the interests of the disadvantaged participants.

Let us now turn to the examples. They may seem like small matters, but as Xunzi says, "When the observance of small matters is neglected, the disorder that results is great. Such is ritual" (27.42).

• The teacher-student relationship. In East Asian societies with a Confucian heritage, the teacher has relatively high social status.[15] The teacher is typically held in high regard not just by the educated classes, but also by the bottom social and economic rungs of society.[16] Not surprisingly, the teacher-student relationship is relatively hierarchical (compared to Western societies), even in universities. Students rarely, if ever, address teachers on a first-name basis, and they show the kind of deference and respect that is initially off-putting for the Westerner who values social equality.[17] For example, in drinking sessions (the modern equivalent, perhaps, of Xunzi's account of village wine ceremonies) the student typically serves the professor and refrains from drinking before the professor, even if both parties have had a fair amount to drink. Such rituals are meant to show reverence for the ideal of commitment to learning (the pursuit of truth, in Western terms) and respect for those who have demonstrated lifelong commitment to that goal.

Such hierarchical arrangements, however, are also advantageous for the student. The teacher is meant not simply to provide a fair structure for learning and to transmit knowledge in the most effective way. The teacher is also supposed to care about the student's emotional well-being and moral development.[18] The relationship between professor and graduate student is many-sided, and it would be an important moral lapse if the teacher focused only on the student's job prospects and neglected the student's emotional and moral well-being.[19] The obligations of the teacher put additional (again, compared to Western societies) pressure on the teacher;[20] he or she is also meant to set a good moral example for the student and to gain the student's respect in nonacademic spheres of life.[21]

• Mealtime. In the animal world, the powerful beasts typically get first dibs at the food. Even communal animals, such as lions, make few allowances for the weak and the vulnerable in their community. When lions make a kill, the toughest animals eat first, and the others get the scraps. In times of scarcity, the young, the sick, and the aged are the first to perish.

Human beings have developed mealtime rituals that protect the interests of weaker members. In many societies, the weak rely on healthy members of the family to prepare and serve them an individual portion of food that keeps them alive. Unfortunately, the urge to be charitable takes a hard hit in times of scarcity, and in times of famine children and the elderly are often the first to die. But the powerful—in this case, healthy adults—are more likely to be predisposed to caring for the powerless if they are conditioned to suppress their appetites on an everyday basis. In East Asian societies, eating is a communal activity,[22] and rituals have evolved that allow weaker member of the family to get their fair share, so to speak. Communal dishes are placed at the center of the table, and healthy adults are often reluctant to be the first to start and the last to finish. They are supposed to constrain their own desires and let others indulge (the Chinese character *rang* 让 best expresses the idea of appropriate mealtime behavior).[23]

Typically, the elderly are supposed to go first, and children are conditioned at a young age to defer their gratification and not dive right into the communal food. The idea is to pay homage to the ideal of filial piety as well as to train children in the art of *rang*. In contemporary China, the practice may be breaking down due to the "little emperor" syndrome of single-child families, but many families still criticize children who act "selfishly" at mealtime.[24]

• The boss-worker relationship. In Japan, the heads of companies often engage in joint rituals with ordinary workers, such as singing company songs, eating at communal canteens, and going on group vacations. Not surprisingly, they often develop feelings for workers and are more likely to stick with workers in hard economic times (thus helping to explain the fact that the practice of lifetime employment is widespread in Japan compared to other industrialized societies). Again, the common rituals involving powerful and vulnerable groups help to protect the interests of the latter.

In China, some high-profile companies are adopting "Japanese-style" rituals in the workplace.[25] But the worst-off workers are the migrant workers. Economic development has been characterized by massive internal migration, composed largely of impoverished farmers and family members migrating to urban areas in search of better work opportunities and higher earnings. China's "floating population" consists of about 120 million migrants, and they are subject to the legal discrimination of the *hukou* (household registration system) regime that deprives them of equal access to health care, education, work, and residence. Moreover, they are routinely subject to the scorn of urbanites and suspected of criminal activity.

Many scholars seek to improve the legal status of migrant workers, but they neglect the way that common rituals involving the manager or boss and worker can improve the social standing, if not material conditions, of migrant workers. In Beijing, it is not uncommon to observe migrant workers in the restaurant trade being "subject" to group lectures, forced to undergo morning exercises, and sing group songs and chant company slogans. These rituals are typically carried out on the sidewalk in front of the restaurant, in full view of the public. They are meant to express commitment to the good of the company, and more broadly, to the ideal of progress for the country (the lectures sometimes include patriotic content).

What seems like militaristic and rigidly hierarchical set of rituals may also have some benefits for the workers. The manager-boss is involved in common rituals—exercising, singing, and sometimes joking with the workers—and he or she often develops care for their interests. The manager-boss may implement these rituals with the intent of generating feelings of loyalty on the part of the worker, but they may also cause the manager-boss to develop real feelings for the workers.[26] Such rituals can also lead to after-hours joint meals, singing sessions, and even group vacations.

In short, different rituals serve to protect the interests of different vulnerable groups: the ritual of shared dishes serves to protect the interests of the elderly, the ritual of deference for teachers serves to protect the interests of students, the ritual of morning exercises and group singing serves to protect the interests of migrant workers. Of course, this account of rituals is a bit too neat. On the one hand, it is overly optimistic. Some rituals do not always work as they should. For example, the exercises involving migrant workers can contribute to alienation if they are carried out in deadly serious ways without any hint of kindness or humor. Some rituals, even if they work as they should, lead to unintended bad social consequences. For example, the family-centered mealtime practices might lead to excessive familism, with the consequence that people are insufficiently concerned with the legitimate interests of nonfamily members.

On the other hand, my account insufficiently highlights the positive functions of rituals. Particular rituals can benefit more than one vulnerable group. For example, it is common for migrant workers to send money to disadvantaged relatives and friends in the countryside. Also, particular rituals can instill habits that can have beneficial habits in other spheres of life. For example, the norms of humility and deference at mealtime may produce the sorts of emotional disposition that leads children to be more sensitive to the interests of the elderly once they become productive adults.

There is, then, a need to consider ways that maximize the good consequences of rituals—meaning that they serve to protect the interests of the weak and the vulnerable to the greatest possible extent—and to minimize the bad ones. The next section sketches some possibilities.

Reviving Hierarchical Rituals in Contemporary China

Ritual principles, as Xunzi notes, are the guiding ropes that pull the government (27.24). So the most obvious starting place for reform would be the establishment of a government agency with the specific mission to promote rituals that help the vulnerable members of the community.[27] Its task would be to ensure that rituals generate the sorts of emotions that involve care for the interests of the weak and vulnerable, both within the ritual itself and extended to other spheres of life. My hypothesis is that rituals involving interaction between powerful and vulnerable members of society are most likely to produce such emotions. Following Xunzi, it is important not to insist on equal treatment, because unequal treatment can also (and may be more likely to) generate concern for the vulnerable. I would also like to suggest that the more such rituals govern everyday social interaction, the more likely the emotions generated—the sense of community between rich and poor, the sense of caring for the interests of the worst off—will extend to other spheres of life. If such claims are correct—and they would need further empirical validation—then the agency would have the task of promoting such rituals to the greatest possible extent.

One important task for the agency would be to create the social conditions for different groups to interact with each other. In the socially egalitarian United States, the different economic classes live largely separate lives in separate neighborhoods, and the rich do not commonly interact with the poor, with the consequence that they do not develop the motivation to care for their interests and to address the problem of economic inequality. In socially inegalitarian Japan, by contrast, there is no sharp geographical separation between rich and poor, residences and businesses; different classes interact with each other in common (socially hierarchical) rituals on an everyday basis, with the consequence that the rich are made to care for the interests of the poor. In China, the growing gap between rich and poor is widely considered to be one of the country's most pressing problems, and the agency could look to the Japanese experience in urban planning as one way to address the problem. For example, it could provide tax breaks for mixed-income housing projects that provide public spaces for intermingling between rich and poor.

The agency would also have the power to remove legal regulations that force certain rituals to operate on the boundaries of social acceptability: the idea is that getting the government out of the way is more likely to lead to social acceptance. If migrant workers operate on the boundaries of legality, for example, the fear factor may prevent the emergence of a sense of community between workers and bosses, not to mention extension of affective ties to other spheres of life. But the Confucian approach to promoting rituals would not rely first and foremost on the strong arm of punishment to promote rituals. One of the most famous passages in *The Analects of Confucius* is the following: "Lead the people by means of regulations and keep them orderly with punishments, and they will avoid punishments but will be without a sense of shame. Lead them with moral power and keep them orderly by means of rituals and they will develop a sense of shame as well as correct themselves" (2.3). In the context of our discussion, it means that fear of legal punishment is not likely to produce the sorts of emotions that generate a sense of community. If people engage in rituals because they feel forced to, the rituals are likely to become empty displays of form and devoid of the emotions that show genuine concern for the weak. People should perform rituals because they want to, not because they have to.

So it's best to think of noncoercive means to promote rituals that have the effect of helping the worst off. For example, the agency could provide subsidies for television programming that shows positive examples of how the rituals should be carried out, such as eating practices that let the weakest members of the family eat first and company activities involving bosses and migrant workers. The agency might provide rewards for model performers of rituals, such as prizes for car drivers who let disabled people cross the street. More ambitiously, perhaps, its task would also be to devise mechanisms for extending the emotions generated by such rituals to other spheres of life, similar to Xunzi's account of mourning practices that cultivate the emotions of respect and mindfulness of duty for everyday life.

In sum, there is an important role for public policy, particularly of the indirect, noncoercive variety. Still, it must be recognized that the power of ritual depends upon the kind of moral transformation that makes the powerful care for the interests of the vulnerable, and the less-than-inspiring history of governmental attempts to transform motivation (even of the indirect kind) is reason for caution. So the case for ritual should come largely from schools (e.g., teachers who emphasize rituals and set a good model for students), families (e.g., parents who encourage their children to let the elderly eat first), civil society (e.g., intellectuals who explain the benefits of ritual), and other groups in society that rely first and foremost on persuasion rather than coercion.

Beyond East Asia?

I would like to end with the thought that the defense of ritual has universal validity, as Xunzi himself no doubt believed. In fact, it has validity even if my interpretation of Xunzi is mistaken as an account of what he really believed or what he was really trying to argue. Qua intellectual historian, I hope my interpretation is correct, but what matters from a contemporary normative perspective is whether the ideas about the positive function of ritual that I've derived by reading Xunzi are applicable and do what they're supposed to do in contemporary societies. If so, they are worth promoting.

There is some evidence for the universal validity of the value of ritual transformation. For example, the rituals of sporting competitions can transform (civilize) the instinct for aggression into socially desirable motivations. As Confucius put it, "Exemplary persons are not competitive, but they must still compete in archery. Greeting and making way for each other, the archers ascend the hall, and returning they drink a salute. Even during competition, they are exemplary persons" (3.7). The task is not to try to eradicate the desire to compete (a futile, if not counterproductive effort), but rather to civilize it by various rituals, such as the rituals of sumo wrestlers or the ritual of shaking hands after tennis games, that produce a sense of social solidarity and concern for the disadvantaged.

Team competitions are perhaps even better suited for this task. By participating in a team, the players learn the value of social solidarity. At the nonelite level, the teams can include weaker players, thus promoting the virtue of concern for the weak and teaching about the need to make social institutions inclusive of the weak.[28] At the elite level, the participants and the spectators can learn about the value of good sportsmanship. And the spectators learn to respect and cheer for the underdog, perhaps contributing to more generalized concern for the weak.

Still, the defense of ritual is less likely to be taken seriously in contexts that do not have a Confucian heritage. For one thing, it is difficult to translate the key terms—li 礼 and rang 让—in ways that sound appealing to, say, English speakers. I have translated li as "ritual," but the term often has negative connotations in English; one seems to be defending mechanical and uncreative practices from outdated eras. Other common translations such as "rites" and "ritual propriety" are hardly improvements. The typical translations of rang—defer, concede, yield, give in—also seem like outdated notions from aristocratic and hierarchical times.[29]

More worrisome, perhaps, the project of promoting rituals may seem foreign in cultures that tend to invoke legalistic, rights-based solutions to the problem of how to care for the interests of the worse off. The whole social contract tradition in Western political theory, from Hobbes to Rawls, appeals to coercive laws as the main mechanism for securing the interests of those most likely suffer in a state of nature. And the rights-based welfare states in contemporary Western societies rely mainly on legal mechanisms to secure the interests of the weak and vulnerable.

Not surprisingly, Western-based human rights groups in China fault the country first and foremost for its lack of adherence to the rule of law, on the assumption that Western-style laws would help to secure the interests of the worst off. I do not mean to deny that the country would be better off with more serious commitment to the rule of law (particularly if the alternative is corrupt political processes that typically benefit the rich and powerful). But excessive focus on legal mechanisms may cause reformers to lose sight of the power of rituals, not to mention the possibility that such legalistic solutions will further undermine the sense of community that makes the powerful care for the interests of the vulnerable. To put it more positively, since rituals are already deeply embedded in the philosophical outlooks and everyday social practices in East Asian societies, it is not far-fetched to believe that social reformers can and should be more attentive to the positive function of rituals in China and elsewhere.

PART TWO
SOCIETY

4. Sex, Singing, and Civility: The Costs and Benefits of the Karaoke Trade

In 1992, my wife—then working for a Singaporean think tank—accompanied a group of visiting mainland Chinese officials on a tour of state-sanctioned brothels in Singapore. They visited high-class brothels meant for the well-to-do as well as cheaper brothels for migrant workers. Accompanied by police officials, they interviewed managers and spoke with sex workers who explained that they get regular health checks and pay taxes to the state. The Chinese officials were somewhat surprised that Singapore—supposedly an arch-conservative nanny state—openly allows prostitution, and they recognized the pragmatic benefits of legalizing the trade.[1] But they added that mainstream public morality would not tolerate similar arrangements in China.

The Economic Benefits of Sex

Since that time, the sex trade has grown at an exponential rate, and China has become one of the world's leading centers for prostitution. Just about every county in China has sex workers. According to the Public Security Bureau, there are between three and four million sex workers in China (Singapore's *Lianhe Zaobao* estimates up to twenty million). Most hotels openly tolerate (and benefit from) prostitution. In one Beijing five-star hotel that I recently visited, the lobby was lined with glamorous-looking ladies of the evening. I can't recall the number of times I have been woken up by late-night phone calls asking if I'm interested in "massage" services.

The economic benefits of the trade are enormous—and arguably contributed to China's near-miraculous economic growth over the last decade or so. For obvious reasons, it is difficult to get reliable statistics. But there are some revealing anecdotes. Last year, I was having dinner with several Western businessmen at the Great Hall of the People and they were comparing notes on the cultural and physical particularities of *xiaojie* (hostesses) from different parts of China. One of them—a leading entrepreneur in the clothing industry—said, half-jokingly, if he's given the choice to invest and do business in China or an Islamic country like Bangladesh, where do you think he'd want to go? In Beijing, there are karaoke parlors specifically tailored for visiting businessmen of various nationalities. One club frequented by Koreans has Korean-speaking hostesses largely from China's Korean minority. The same club has a floor with Japanese-speaking hostesses for Japanese businessmen.

The government's periodic crackdowns on the trade only serve to confirm its economic importance. The economist Yang Fan estimates that with the implementation of the "Regulations on the Management of Places of Entertainment" issued by the State Council in 1999, the Chinese GDP dropped by 1 percent. Taiyuan, the capital city of Shanxi province, was known as China's karoake capital, with about seven thousand clubs in the city. In 1996, the government decided to crackdown. As a result, the restaurant and hotel business nosedived and the hostesses withdrew 400 million yuan of remittances from the local banks. The government reversed course one month later. During important government meetings, karaoke parlors in Beijing are told to expect police inspections. But the dates are carefully specified in advance, with the implication that things will soon revert to normal.

Public attitudes are also changing. In December 2006, the police officers in Shenzhen publicly paraded about one hundred women and their johns in an attempt to humiliate them and discourage the trade (or perhaps they were punished for not having paid their dues to the powers-that-be). The tactic led to a swift outcry in newspapers and on the Internet, with the police coming under a hail of criticism for violating the right to privacy of those who were paraded in public. In Beijing, an activist filed a constitutional proposal asking the National People's Congress Standing Committee to conduct a review of the constitutionality of the provisions that criminalize prostitution. Elsewhere, public authorities are taking active measures to deal with the health consequences of the sex trade. In Harbin, sex workers are given courses in AIDS education and the use of condoms. To reduce the risk of sexually transmitted diseases, every hotel room in Yunnan comes equipped with condoms.[2] There have also been national voices calling for legalization. In the 2006 annual meeting of the National People's Congress, one deputy from Heilongjiang called for legalization of prostitution in order to secure the health of workers and reduce the risks of sexually transmitted diseases. In private discussion, many intellectuals seem to endorse such views.

In sum, the gap between public morality and the social reality may not be as wide as the government may fear, and perhaps the Chinese government should now consider Singapore-style legalization of the trade. But that might be too quick. There are powerful counterarguments against legalized prostitution. Most obviously, it seems bad for women. Even relatively libertarian voices such as the *Wall Street Journal* oppose legalization of the trade because it seems fundamentally demeaning to women. And profamily voices may worry about the effect of legalized prostitution on the well-being of the family. One of the virtues of East Asian societies is that they manage to combine rapid economic modernization with relatively stable family structures, and officially sanctioned prostitution might contribute to such undesirable phenomena as high divorce rates and children growing up without supportive parents. Before we consider such arguments, however, let us try to understand the nature of prostitution in China and other East Asian societies.

The Morality of Karaoke-Style Prostitution

In northeast Asian societies—meaning mainland China, Taiwan, Hong Kong, Japan, and South Korea—the karaoke club is perhaps the most common forum for prostitution.[3] Typically, a group of male friends or business partners rents a room in a karoake bar. The "mama" (female brothel manager) then presents a group of hostesses to the men and may explain a bit about their background. Eventually, each man chooses one hostess (in South Korea and Japan, the mama often chooses for the customer). The group then engages in drinking and dice games and participates in karaoke singing (i.e., the music is played on television and the singers sing from the lyrics shown on the bottom of the screen). These activities can involve the whole group or they can involve different subgroups of customers (still in the common room). In some cases, the activities may include explicit sexual content. Some karaoke bars in Korea are known to be the particularly lascivious, involving group fellatio and cunnilingus, with the group eventually breaking up for private liaisons between customer and hostess. At the other extreme, the activities almost never have sexual consequences, as in Japanese geisha bars where the women are highly trained singers, dancers, and conversationalists. In mainland China, the karaoke room is usually reserved for conversation, singing, and drinking, and further sexual liaisons in private settings may or may not materialize depending upon the place (some karaoke bars are more open about that possibility), the customer's sexual desires (and financial position), and the hostess's needs (for additional money, mainly).[4]

The preference for karaoke-style prostitution may be partly aesthetic. In the West, the social preliminaries to direct stimulation may seem like unnecessary diversions from the task at hand.[5] As Yeeshan Yang puts it, "The western man wants to get to the dessert course quickly, and eat dessert until he is stuffed."[6] The East Asian customer, on the other hand, usually prefers "every course available."[7] Western-style prostitution tends to be cheaper and designed for the lower classes.[8] The aesthetic particularities may also be reflected in different forms of pornography. American and European porn tends to show the sex organs, and the sex acts themselves are "like a Discovery program that offers a scientific account of the mating among animals," as one Chinese friend put it. Japanese porn films, in contrast, often do not have any explicit shots, and rely more on suggestion and inference to generate sexual arousal (there is very little Chinese porn, due mainly to political controls).[9]

In any case, my aim here is to evaluate the morality of karaoke-style prostitution. It might not seem so problematic if it is compared with Western-style prostitution that involves (nothing more than) the exchange of sex for money. The typical exchange is devoid of any emotion, and there is rarely any expectation of companionship or tenderness.[10] Karaoke-style prostitution is different and involves norms of civility and deference. For starters, the male customers are supposed to be civil with each other. If a group of friends visits the karaoke bar, they will typically struggle to let others have first choice among the hostesses presented to them (analogous to mock fights over who would sit in the honored seats at banquets, with nobody wanting to take the important seat). The aim is to demonstrate one's commitment to friendship and to show that this commitment overrides the attraction to beauty (since the first pick usually gets the most beautiful hostess).[11] Such commitment is also manifested in the fact that one friend will usually pay for the cost of the karaoke room (but the private liaisons are typically paid for by the individuals involved). If it's business partners, the prospective customer would go first, but he might decline out of politeness. On the basis of field research in a karaoke bar in Dalian, Tiantian Zheng has shown that civility and traits of deference among the male clients serve to forge bonds of trust among them. The way to gain trust with the business partner is by showing self-control in the consumption of sex and thus be proven a trustworthy and responsible business partner ("Cool Masculinity," *Journal of Contemporary China*, 2006, 15(46)).[12]

Less obviously, perhaps, karaoke-style activities can lead to emotional bonding between customer and hostess. Sometimes conversation, joking, and drinking games can generate a sense of intimacy. But the real key is music. Confucians have long emphasized the moral benefits of music. Confucius himself was perhaps the first practitioner of the prelude to karaoke: "If he hears people singing well, he asks them to sing again and then joins in their harmony" (7.32). His follower Xunzi (ca. 310–219 BCE) provided a strong defense of music against Mozi, the quasi-utilitarian thinker who disparaged music because it seemed like an extravagant waste of resources. According to Xunzi, "Music is joy. Being an essential part of man's emotional nature, the expression of music is unavoidable. That is why people can't do without music" (20.1). When people listen to music together, they feel as one, regardless of their position in society: "When music is performed within the ancestral temple, lord and subject, high and low, listen to music together and are united in feelings of reverence. When music is played in the private quarters of the home, father and son, elder and younger brother, listen to it together and are united in feelings of close kinship. When it is played in village meetings or clan halls, old and young listen to the music together and are joined in obedience" (20.2). Precisely because of its effect in breaking down class barriers and generating feelings of emotional bonding, the right sort of music is essential for harmony and social stability: "The influence of music and sound on people is very profound, and the transformations they produce on people can be very rapid. Thus, the Ancient Kings were assiduous in creating proper forms. If music accords exactly with the mean and is evenly balanced, people will be harmonious and not given to dissipation. If it is solemn and dignified, then the people will behave in a uniform manner and will not be inclined to disorder" (20.5). Music, in short, "can make the hearts of the people good" (20.6).

Of course, Xunzi did not mean to imply that music in the context of the karaoke bar would have these beneficial effects.[13] But we can borrow Xunzi's insight that "when music is used to guide and regulate the desires, there is enjoyment but no disorder" (20.9). One common by-product of communal singing in the karaoke club is to tame wild sexual desires and to produce a sentiment of emotional bonding between participants. In duets involving female and male voices, the client and hostess sing together; they listen carefully to each other and must harmonize their voices, and they experience a sense of togetherness if the job is well done.[14] In the best cases, the customer develops a sense of care and concern for the well-being of the hostess (and vice versa).[15] In short, karaoke-style activities contribute not only to economic development; they may also contribute to bonding and mutual concern. At the very least, if the choice is between straightforward exchanges of sex for money deprived of any emotional bonding and karaoke-style prostitution that is preceded by social singing, conversation, and group games, it seems difficult to deny that the former is worse, morally speaking.

Well, that's the good part. We need to consider arguments that prostitution—including karaoke-style prostitution—is fundamentally demeaning to women and undermines family relationships.

Is Karaoke-Style Prostitution Bad for Women?

Whether or not prostitution is the world's oldest profession, it is certainly one of the most dangerous. Surely it is no coincidence that serial

killers often select sex workers as their victims. As the anonymous author of *Belle du Jour: The Intimate Adventures of a London Call Girl* put
it, "A finely-tuned Creep Radar is a necessary part of the business. This
is, after all, an occupation that ranks somewhere between nuclear core
inspector and rugby prop for job safety. Except I'm issued neither a foil
suit nor a pair of spiked boots for protection" (118). But some forms of
prostitution are safer than others. Singapore-style government regu-
lated prostitution is perhaps the safest form. Karaoke-style prostitution
can be dangerous because it is often controlled by gangsters (*hei shehui*), but it is still safer than streetwalking or visits to hotel rooms with
strange men. The social setting increases the likelihood that certain
norms of civility are respected. The hostesses I interviewed all agreed
that the worst customers are the ones that resort to crude and disre-
spectful behavior in the karaoke room, such as pawing the hostess in
the presence of others.[16] One hostess criticized another for tolerating
such "uncivil" behavior, saying that it should be restricted to the private
encounters rather than the group karaoke room (interestingly, she was
more critical of uncivil behavior in the group setting than of prostitution itself). Most important, the hostess can refuse further requests for
sexual intercourse if she is dissatisfied with the customer's behavior in
the group karaoke room. Depending on the karaoke parlor, the customer can ask (indirectly) the hostess if she is willing to go on to "dessert." Even hostesses who are clearly expected to go on to "dessert"
have veto power. In one notorious Beijing karaoke parlor that usually
carries the expectation of further sexual liaisons, the hostesses are fined
(by the mama) three hundred yuan (about thirty-five U.S. dollars) if
they refuse offers for paid sex with the customers: not a huge fine, given
that they can earn twenty thousand yuan per month at that high-end
parlor.

But the feminist opposition to prostitution is not only that it's physically unsafe for women. The deeper (and more common) problem is
that women are regarded as sex objects, not as fully equal human beings
with the same capacity for reason and self-direction that men are supposed to have. In the karaoke context, for example, the more beautiful
women can typically work in more exclusive establishments and earn
more money by virtue of their physical beauty.[17] One Beijing club explicitly distinguishes between relatively expensive "models" and other

hostesses (there is an extra three-hundred-yuan charge for the "models"). The issue here is not sex per se because the customer needs to pay more simply to have the opportunity to sing and converse with the "model." The cost is also related to the amount of bodily contact allowed: typically, the greater the contact, the more expensive the exchange. Again, such practices seem to reinforce the view that women are sex objects. Even some feminist theorists that do not oppose commercial sex per se (if it involves free-market exchanges between consenting individuals) object to prostitution because of the damage it does to the perception (and position) of women in society. As Debra Satz puts it, "Prostitution is wrong insofar as the sale of women's sexual labor reinforces broad patterns of sexual discrimination" (*Ethics*, Oct. 1995, 64).

But does prostitution really contribute to patterns of sexual discrimination outside the brothel and the karaoke bar? Islamic countries, with perhaps the fewest amount of prostitutes per capita, are the most oppressive societies for women. Northern European countries such as Germany and the Netherlands that legalize prostitution do well in terms of gender equality compared to the southern European countries that ban it. In the Asian context, Singapore and Hong Kong are the two societies that openly legalize prostitution, and they are also the most equal in terms of gender relations.[18] Perhaps the spillover effects of the sex trade, in terms of overall attitudes regarding women's roles in society, may not always be so worrying.

In China, the situation is quite complex. On the one hand, the economic opportunities offered by karaoke parlors can be seen as beneficial for women. It is not as if karaoke-style prostitution is the only way to escape poverty. There are many opportunities for low-paid jobs in China (Shenzhen, for example, has a labor shortage). But many women still prefer to work as hostesses over regular jobs in the "bourgeois" world. As one hostess put it, "I was working for seven hundred yuan [less than one hundred U.S. dollars] on an assembly line, twelve hours a day, six days a week. The work was tiring and very boring. My *jiejie* [literally "older sister," referring to her more experienced hostess friend] told me that I could earn that amount in one night. I took this job." Even "waitresses" (*fuwuyuan*) in karaoke parlors—pretty women who serve drinks and play dice games but do not engage in sexual relations with customers—earn much more than waitresses in ordinary restaurants. So karaoke-style jobs can be seen as an opportunity for women to make a lot of money quickly.[19] And if the comparison is with straightforward prostitution, the particular features of the karaoke-parlor may be advantageous for women. As mentioned, karaoke-style prostitution may involve group singing and emotional bonding, in which case the hostesses are not regarded purely as sex objects. Also, the "mama" may develop feelings of care for "her" hostess and treat them as something between family members and employees. The hostesses themselves often develop strong bonds: they usually share apartments and engage in common social activities.

On the other hand, karaoke-style prostitution may limit women's opportunities for prestigious and well-paid jobs in business and government. In China, doing business often means visits to karaoke clubs. The fact that social bonds among male business partners are reinforced in such settings is good for men but bad for women. In one case, I was told that a female business partner accompanied her male colleagues to a karaoke bar, but she was less than pleased by her surroundings, left in a huff, and the result was less social trust. Moreover, it is not uncommon for Chinese businessmen to invite government cadres to karaoke bars so that the officials facilitate business transactions (or overlook the legal niceties that may block such transactions).[20] Local government officials are often promoted according to the economic development in their districts, and if female officials do not have as many opportunities to forge social bonds with male businessmen that contribute to development, there may be limited opportunities for female officials to rise within the Communist Party hierarchy.

Interestingly, the past few years have been characterized by a boom in karaoke-style prostitution for well-to-do women. In Hong Kong, these developments have been described, with vivid anecdotes, in Yang Yeeshan's published research. The numbers are hard to come by (again, for obvious reasons), but my contacts tell me that there are also karaoke clubs for rich female clients in mainland China, Japan, Taiwan, and Korea. In China, the male sex workers are popularly known as "ducks" (yazi 鸭子), the complementary term to the female "chickens" (ji 鸡) (a pun upon the Chinese term for "prostitute" (jinu 妓女).[21] One notable feature of the karaoke clubs for women in Beijing is that they open late: usually starting around eleven o'clock at night, three hours later than the clubs for men. The main reason is that many of the clients are the "chickens" who go there to unwind after work.[22] If these clubs provide opportunities for ambitious women to forge the social bonds that allow them to succeed in business and politics, then such developments may not be entirely negative.

Is Karaoke-Style Prostitution Bad for the Family?

It is not just feminists who should be concerned about karaoke-style prostitution. Most of the customers are married men, and karaoke-style prostitution poses an obvious challenge to the well-being of the family unit. But the fact that prostitution is so rampant in East Asian societies may be the result of different conceptions of family values. The puritanical opposition to sex in East Asian societies—commercial or otherwise—owes more to the recent influence of Judeo-Christian values than to traditional culture. Confucius said, "I have yet to meet anyone who is fonder of virtue (德) than of physical beauty" (9.18, 15.13). He may have been expressing a moment of exasperation to his students who seemed resistant to moral improvement. But Confucius may also be suggesting that the attraction to physical beauty is a universal feature of the human condition. Rather than engage in a futile effort to eradicate it with a full commitment to leading an ethical life (à la Catholic priest), it is best to recognize its omnipresence and ensure that it does not lead to undesirable consequences. The task is not to change people to the point of extinguishing their animal desires, but rather to socialize people so that desires are expressed in forms that are compatible with cooperative social interaction.

Of course, there are similar considerations in societies with a Judeo-Christian heritage. The civilizing of desire takes place in relations between husband and wife. As Immanuel Kant famously put it, marriage is "the union of two persons of different sex for life-long reciprocal possession of their sexual faculties." Marriage is only truly realized in monogamy, and sexual relations outside of marriage are immoral. But the traditional Confucian view does not emphasize monogamy. "Thou shalt not commit adultery" (or anything referring to the badness of sexual relations outside of the husband-wife relationship) is absent from the classical Confucian texts. Mencius—held to be the most moralistic of the Confucian thinkers—criticized King Xuan of Qi for selfishly hoarding his women. It may have been legitimate for King Tai (a true king of antiquity) to love his women and concubines, but in an age when there are women pining for husbands and men pining for wives the ruler should share his fondness for sex and women (好色) with the common people. The implications may be somewhat opaque (should the ruler only take two or three concubines instead of dozens?), but the relevant point is that he does not criticize the fondness for sex and women per se nor does Mencius suggest that the king should stick to one wife (1B.5). In another famous passage that shows women in an active role, Mencius describes the shame felt by a wife and by her husband's concubine over his shameless way of earning money (4B.33). Confucian thinkers in subsequent history often seem to take it for granted that desire cannot be satisfied with one sexual partner.

I do not mean to imply that such views have direct influence upon the practices and policies regarding prostitution in East Asian societies. More recent developments (such as the encounter with the Western world) no doubt help to explain outcomes such as the fact that prostitution is illegal in most East Asian societies.[23] What I do mean to imply is that traditional Confucian values may influence accounts of what's taboo and what's not in contemporary East Asian societies.[24] It is quite striking that prostitution in East Asian societies takes *social* forms, as though there is less to be embarrassed about group participation in "illicit" sex. In Western societies, the stag party—held shortly before marriage—is often the last occasion for group display of sexual desire. To the extent there is prostitution involving married persons, it usually takes the form of private contractual exchanges between customer and prostitute in relatively secret surroundings. The john's friends and business partners are not supposed to know about it. In East Asia, groups of married men openly—shamelessly, the Christian might say—frequent karoake-style parlors.

It is also quite striking that the hostesses themselves do not seem to have moral qualms about paid sex. One successful Chinese businessman told me that he has been consistently surprised by how "shameless" the hostesses seem to be. Notwithstanding dozens of encounters, he has yet to meet any who say they experience moral qualms about prostitution per se (of course, it may be part of their job to hide moral qualms). The hostesses themselves often provide more positive moral justifications for their line of work, such as earning money for family members in need.[25] Most typical is the practice of sending remittances to support elderly parents in the impoverished countryside; as Tsinghua University sociologist and AIDS researcher Jing Jun put it, "They are absolutely moral. A lot of these women send half their income back to support their families. They're more filial than I am" (*Washington Post*, August 5, 2007).[26]

But cultures change, and today fidelity seems to be increasingly valued in East Asian societies, especially by wives. I asked the same Chinese businessman if his wife knows about his activities. He responded that she may suspect something but she doesn't ask. I noted that it's a kind of "Don't ask, don't tell policy," but he responded it might doom his marriage if he were to articulate that policy. He joked that they have a "Don't ask, don't tell" policy regarding their "Don't ask, don't tell" policy. One hostess put forward an analogous perspective. She said that she won't work as hostess for more than five years. The problem is not prostitution per se, but the fact that she hears too many married men expressing love and devotion in phone calls to wives as they are enjoying themselves in the karaoke parlor. In the long run, she said, she will think that all men are *pianzi* (骗子 "tricksters") and she might not be able to trust any of them.[27] The norms of karaoke-style encounters also point to the possible negative impact of the trade on husband-wife relations. One of the tests of a successful encounter with a hostess is that she offers to give her cell phone number to the customer so that they can chat and meet in social settings outside of the karaoke parlor (such as having meals together). But there is an implicit understanding that the customer does not give out his phone number, so as not to be surprised by a call if he happens to be with his family. If the customer does give out his number, the hostess typically sends text messages only.

Should the Trade Be Legalized?

In an ideal society, everyone would be wealthy and few (if any) would sell their bodies for money. With hundreds of millions still living in poverty, however, that day seems far off in China. From a policy stand-point, the task now (and for the foreseeable future) is to regulate the sex trade so that the advantages outweigh the disadvantages. There are three possibilities: (1) strictly enforce bans on prostitution, meaning closing down all karaoke parlors and other settings for prostitution; (2) sticking with the status quo; and (3) legalizing prostitution.

Strict enforcement would not be practicable. It would require mas-sive state intervention, and the economic costs would be huge. Nor would it be desirable. Prostitution would go further underground and become more dangerous and less profitable for sex workers.[28] And the result will be millions of sexually frustrated men (and women), with unpredictable and probably perverse political effects. Surely it is no coincidence that totalitarian societies have also tried to suppress the sexual urge and elevate worship of the political leader (during the Cul-tural Revolution, "comrades"[29] were told that they shouldn't have bour-geois preoccupations like sexual desire; instead, they should admire Chairman Mao).[30]

Sticking with the status quo is better, but far from ideal. The dubi-ous legal status of the karaoke trade means that it is often controlled by gangsters or is a "joint venture" between corrupt security officials and gangsters.[31] An account of the karaoke trade in Taiyuan reports that hostesses most dread having to deal with the local thugs that control their trade (at the lower-end karaoke parlors, the gangsters tend to be more obviously in control and ready to resort to violence). The host-esses are sometimes forced to do unpleasant sexual acts against their will. One hostess in Beijing told me that her worst experience was be-ing asked to accompany her boss's best friend for one evening.

Legalization would have many advantages. The economy would continue to thrive. Sex workers and their customers would be protected from sexually transmitted diseases and the women would work in much safer conditions. The trade could be taxed and the revenue could be used for the disadvantaged. The costs of prostitution would go down (no more bribes would have to be paid to gangsters and corrupt offi-cials), to the benefit of tens of millions of sexually frustrated migrant workers. And the karaoke business would be taken out of the hands of criminal gangs (or at least, their influence would be reduced because of competition from government-regulated prostitution).[32]

But there are also disadvantages—legalization might further increase the availability of prostitution and therefore might be bad for women and families.[33] So the government has an obligation to legalize prostitution in ways that minimize these disadvantages. One possibility is to ban Western-style prostitution that is more demeaning to women.[34] Straightforward exchanges of sex for money treat women as pure sex objects, and such relations are deprived of any genuine care and respect. Karaoke-style prostitution offers the possibility that sexual relations are preceded by group singing and emotional bonding that can mitigate, if not elevate, the purely animalistic form of interaction. Perhaps the government could also provide subsidies for women to operate their own karaoke cooperatives so that they are run for the benefit of the women involved. The government-regulated karaoke parlors could also implement less degrading ways of choosing hostesses: instead of a parade of hostesses presented to the customer, perhaps the mama could choose for the customer (as in Japan and South Korea). Or else the customer could choose from pictures that also describe some characteristics of the hostesses (home province, singing preferences, etc).

To be realistic, however, legalized karaoke-style sex work is still likely to be more expensive than straightforward "money for sex" exchanges and may be out of reach for migrant workers and others on the bottom of the socioeconomic ladder (moreover, the price of karaoke is increasing because the National Copyright Administration deems that all karaoke clubs should pay for the songs). So straightforward prostitution might have to be tolerated for the time being. It should be legalized for the usual reasons: to secure the health of the people involved and to reduce the role of gangsters in controlling the trade. As China gets richer, "sex for money" exchanges can be gradually phased out in favor of karoake-style sex work.

What about the worry that legalized prostitution would further undermine family ties? It is not obvious that legalization would increase usage, because the main constraint on usage seems to be the concern to shield wives from awareness, rather than lack of availability (weekdays are usually busier times for karaoke bars that cater to mainland Chinese, because most customers spend weekends with family members). But there is another worry: that karaoke-style sex work may actually be worse for the family than straightforward prostitution, because the customer often forms emotional ties with the hostess (or host, as the case may be). If the choice is between "pure" sex with a stranger and sex with emotional attachment, one can assume that the former is the lesser evil from the perspective of "cheated on" spouses. So if the concern is to protect family ties, then legalizing "Western style" prostitution might be preferable to legalizing karaoke-style sex work.

But the choice is not just between sex and singing plus sex. Karaoke-style activities do not always, or even usually, involve sex. One contact regularly visits karaoke bars with his colleagues because that's where they go to enjoy themselves and forge social bonds. But he always skips the "dessert," out of respect for his wife. If the choice is between singing-solidarity and straightforward prostitution, perhaps the former is more preferable from the point of view of spouses. Yes, there may be some emotional bonding between customer and hostess (or host), but such bonding is not necessarily deep or long-lasting and need not threaten strong bonds of trust and love between spouses.

But what if singing does lead to sex? And what if customers enjoy not just the sex, but also the emotional bonding? Note, however, that straightforward prostitution is not likely to satisfy the needs of customers motivated (at least partly) by emotional considerations. If customers are deprived of the opportunity for emotional bonding, they may seek out other forms of sexual liaisons in the form of consensual extramarital affairs with other adults. The more common choice, at least in the minds of customers, may be between going to karaoke bars and having an affair. One regular customer to karaoke bars told me that he would never dream of having a consensual affair—he seemed to draw a sharp moral line between karaoke-style sex and the deeper and more threatening (to his family) emotional bonds formed during extramarital affairs. I do not have the numbers, but I would speculate that the widespread availability of karaoke-style sex work helps to explain why East Asians have fewer affairs compared to, say, the French. If the choice is between the relatively brief experience of "sex, singing, and civility" and an affair with colleagues or friends, surely the former is less threatening to family ties.

I would like to conclude with perhaps the most controversial argument of this essay. One way of civilizing the sexual urge is to legalize alternative forms of marriage involving more than two persons. Again, the idea of monogamy stems from Judeo-Christian values, and societies with different cultural heritages need be bound by such ideas. Just as Islamic societies endorse polygamy, so societies with a Confucian heritage can consider such possibilities. As it happens, there is de facto polygamy in some Chinese cities. In Shenzhen—a city of seven million people adjoining Hong Kong—there are whole neighborhoods of "second wives" (er nai cun 二奶村) supported by Hong Kong businessmen. One famous businessman in Shanghai openly owns a home with twelve "wives."[35] Of course, such "wives" do not have legal protection, and legalizing polygamy might be one way of protecting their interests. If polygamy is legal, there may be less stigma attached to the practice; it may become more widespread and reduce the need for sex and bonding outside of "marriage" in such settings as karaoke bars.

What about the argument that polygamy—the concubinage system—has historically been linked with rigid patriarchal practices in Chinese history and that reviving the system would be bad for women? But the system can be revived in ways that reflect current understandings of equality between men and women.[36] For example, the modern practice of polygamy need not be restricted to "one husband, many wives" (一夫多妻): it could also allow for "one wife, many husbands" (一妻多夫). One can imagine other possibilities: the early twentieth-century Confucian thinker and political activist Kang Youwei put forward the idea of annual marriage contracts between two men and two women, with each party being able to choose not to renew. Whatever the demerits of Kang's particular proposal (for example, the constant need to reevaluate relationships might not allow for sufficient trust to develop between family members), it would be dogmatic to rule out creative adaptations of traditional practices simply because they deviate from Western-style marriage arrangements.[37]

5. How Should Employers Treat Domestic Workers?

About ten years ago, a close friend came to visit me in Hong Kong. This friend—now director of a center for ethics at a prestigious American university—seemed a bit surprised when informed that my family had hired a live-in domestic helper to help care for our child and deal with domestic chores. He had just arrived from another trip, and since he was going to stay with us for a few days I told him to put his dirty clothes in the laundry basket and our helper would take care of it. But my friend objected, saying he would do it himself. I didn't argue at the time, but after a few drinks I mentioned it again and he relented.[1]

Why would he object, I wonder? In Hong Kong, it's common for professional families to hire foreign domestic workers (the politically correct term). The workers come to make money for themselves and their families, and they are given contracts on much better terms than countries like Singapore. Their interests are represented by NGOs and their home governments (especially the Philippines), and they are free to go home when they wish. In Hong Kong, nobody thinks twice about the justice of hiring foreign domestic workers (the debate focuses on the terms of their work). But somehow it offends the sensibilities of Western liberals. Perhaps the idea of workers in the home violates the image of the family as a sphere of love and affection. Or maybe it conjures up of images of master-servant relationships from aristocratic times. There may be an element of hypocrisy—in Western countries, domestic work is often done informally or illegally by migrant workers, without contracts and without political recognition and legal protection—but few card-carrying liberals would want to admit that they hire migrant domestic workers, much less defend the practice in public.

It doesn't take too long to figure out that such attitudes, if taken seriously, can be damaging to domestic workers themselves. What if my friend had done the laundry himself, and showed himself better at washing clothes than our helper? How would she feel? She might have "lost face," and perhaps even felt that her job had been threatened. I do not mean to imply that the status quo is perfect. Quite the opposite. It can and should be improved. But we need to think of improving the status quo in ways that benefit the workers themselves—and yes, in ways, that also benefit those hiring the workers. There is obviously a tension between the interests of the two groups, but any workable policy is likely to be based on converging interests to an important extent. And it's not just a matter of figuring out the right laws and policies. So much interaction between employers and domestic workers occurs in the privacy of the home, away from the prying eyes of the state, and the informal norms of engagement within the home have great impact on the welfare of the workers. But one searches in vain within the academic literature on migration and domestic work for morally informed proposals regarding the treatment of domestic workers, as though it's immoral even to allude to that possibility. So let me begin with that topic. Yes, I confess, qua employer, part of what I'm doing is meant to make myself feel better. The vulgar Marxist might write off my views simply on account of my class position. But Marx himself set the model for transcending class position—with material support from Engels's capitalist factories, he wrote the most powerful critique of capitalism in history.[2] Of course, my own modest abilities cannot compare to those of Karl Marx. Still, I hope the reader will be willing to engage with my argument. In my view, the Confucian tradition offers moral resources for thinking about the relationship between employer and domestic worker, and I will try to spell those out. For what it's worth, my views are also informed by interviews with domestic workers in Hong Kong and Beijing and volunteer work I did with a Hong Kong–based NGO that represents the interests of foreign domestic workers.[3]

The Personal Is the Political

A basic assumption of Confucian ethics is that the moral life is possible only in the context of particularistic personal ties. For the general population, the most important relationship by far is the family. It is by fulfilling our responsibilities to family members that we learn about and practice morality. The value of caring for children is widely shared in other cultures, but Confucianism places special emphasis on filial piety, the care for elderly parents. Moreover, filial piety is not simply a matter of providing material comfort. As Confucius put it, "It is the attitude that matters. If young people merely offer their services when there is work to do, or let their elders drink and eat when there is wine and food, how could this be [sufficient for] filial piety?" (2.8). We need to serve our parents with love. Confucius also says that the way we interact with family members contributes to society at large (in contrast to the Greek thinkers writing at the same time, for whom the good life lies outside the home): "Exemplary persons focus their duties on the root. Once the root is established, the Way will flow from it. As for filial and fraternal responsibility, it is the root of humanity and compassion" (1.2). If there is harmony in the family, in other words, it is easier to establish harmony in society at large.

These Confucian values still inform people's beliefs and practices in contemporary East Asian societies. In Japan and South Korea, the duty to care for needy family members—children, elderly parents, the sick, and the disabled—is typically carried out by adult females. Wives are expected to stop working and commit themselves to the family after marriage. But Chinese societies (especially in urban areas) are relatively egalitarian in terms of gender relations (compared to Japan and South Korea) and women often work outside the home. So who should take care of needy family members? Not surprisingly, day care and nursing-home systems are relatively undeveloped, even in wealthy Chinese cities. People worry that strangers entrusted with caring duties won't show the right "attitude," hence the reluctance to commit one's children and elderly parents to state (or private) institutions. It's much better to do it oneself, and if that's not possible, to hire somebody to provide more personal care in the home. So families with the means to do so often hire domestic workers to help with caring duties. In mainland Chinese cities, middle and upper classes often hire migrant workers from the impoverished countryside, and in Hong Kong, they hire foreign migrant workers from the Philippines, Indonesia, and other relatively poor Southeast Asian countries.

Of course, one cannot easily disentangle cultural explanations from other factors such as political decisions and economic forces. For example, the preference for foreign domestic workers may be explained by the lack of quality day care in Hong Kong (on the other hand, the lack of public demand for day care, even in East Asian societies with open political systems and vibrant civil societies, is quite striking, and cultural biases against day care may be part of the explanation for the lack of demand). The role of Confucian values may be more evident in the way people actually deal with each other within the home. According to one study, Western employers in Hong Kong generally treat domestic workers differently than Chinese employers. Filipina domestic workers were more satisfied with their Western employers, who allow them more personal space and are more likely to treat them on equal terms. Respect also seems to be more important for the Western employer (Tak Kin Cheung and Bong Ho Mok, *Social Justice Research*, vol. 2, no. 2, 1998).

Respect per se, however, may not be sufficient. That is, the very best employers—only a small minority—treat domestic workers with more than respect; they also treat them as valued members of the family. Most of these employers tend to be Chinese. The same study provides a good example of family-like treatment by a Chinese employer. A Filipina domestic worker valued her employer's parents because she was treated as the daughter they never had. The ties between the employee and the employer's family was based on mutual concern and caring, not simply fairness and respect: they watched TV together, engaged in mutual teasing, and the employer showed sincere concern for the domestic worker's family in the Philippines. My own interviews with domestic workers revealed similar reactions. One domestic worker praised her former boss in Singapore for her use of affectionate family-like appellations and for including her in weekend family outings. Another domestic worker was made the godmother of her employer's child, and they would go to church together. Her family in the Philippines made regular visits to her employer's home in Hong Kong, and she hoped that her employer's family would visit her in the Philippines when she returned.

Of course, Western employers can also treat domestic workers as family members, but this is relatively rare. The Hong Kong study found that Western employers were more homogenous as a group compared to Chinese employers. My own interviewees said that Western employers often treat domestic workers with respect and tend to be fair-minded, but it typically doesn't go beyond that (an important reason may be that expatriates do not expect to stay too long and thus do not develop family-like bonds with domestic workers). Good treatment means paying beyond the minimum wage and giving more free time to employees, but the affective component may not be as prominent. Such distance has its advantages. The idea that the domestic worker belongs to the family can be used as an excuse to impose extra burdens on the worker, such as asking her to work during public holidays. This may help to explain why some domestic workers in Hong Kong will refuse to address employers by their given name, even if they are asked to do so, preferring such labels as "Sir" and "Ma'am."

Still, the feeling of being treated as a valued member of the family—of feeling loved and trusted—usually outweighs the cost. Once again, it is difficult to directly trace the influence of culture, but it is not unreasonable to suggest that Confucian ethics makes this kind of family-like treatment more likely, or at least more deeply entrenched when it happens. In Confucianism, there is a firm distinction between family insiders and nonfamily outsiders, but the concept of family is relatively flexible, and family-like concern and care is supposed to be extended to others. Mencius explicitly asks us to "Treat the aged of our own family in a manner befitting their venerable age and extend this treatment to the aged of other families; treat our own young in a manner befitting their tender age and extend this treatment of the young of other families" (1A.7). One mechanism for extending such relationships is to apply family-like labels and norms to nonfamily members. This is reflected in the Chinese language. Good friends and alumni will refer to each other as younger or older siblings, the graduate supervisor refers to his or her students as younger siblings,[4] and—in the best cases—domestic workers and their employers will also use family-like language to refer to each other.

But why are the "best cases" not more common in Chinese families? Sometimes, it's because of different languages and cultures. It's harder to forge family-like bonds with workers who speak foreign languages. In Hong Kong, many Cantonese-speaking households do not speak English well enough to converse with their English-speaking Filipina domestic workers. Yes, the employers know enough English to issue commands, but affective relationships take place when people can joke and tease each other, which requires relatively advanced language skills. Why don't the employers hire Chinese-speaking workers? In wealthy Hong Kong, few people are willing to take such jobs. More surprisingly, it's illegal to hire domestic workers from mainland China! The government fears that such workers would find it easier to blend in and thus overstay as illegals without being caught, but if the aim is to increase the likelihood of extension of family-like norms to domestic workers, then the government might want to consider modifying that policy.

In mainland China, due to shared language and culture, it may be more common for domestic workers to be treated like members of the family. But there is still a large gap between the ideal and the reality. The main problem is that city folk often look down on less well educated workers from the countryside. Here too, the government can help to remedy the problem by such means as TV programming designed to increase consciousness about the need to treat domestic workers well. Consider, for example, the fact that a television program on the eve of the Spring Festival draws an audience of roughly 500 million people. This program consists of songs and skits that convey moral messages in humorous ways (for example, one skit in the 2005 show portrayed a migrant worker who complained that his wages were not being paid on time, and the audience clapped loudly in sympathy). In future programming, perhaps one skit can depict the importance of promoting family-like relations between employers and migrant domestic workers (e.g., a humorous skit depicting employers and domestic workers teasing each other at mealtime) and refraining from abuse of the latter.

Ultimately, however, such treatment has to involve the employer's own volition. The whole idea of "enforcing" care may be incoherent: it has to come from the heart, otherwise it will be perceived as insincere and won't be effective at strengthening affective relationships. How can employers be persuaded to show more care to domestic workers? The argument from self-interest should be evident: if the worker feels cared for and loved, then she will supply higher-quality care (in Confucian terms, she will perform her duties with the right "attitude").[5] It's also worth appealing to the employer's better, other-regarding side: the extension of family-like norms promotes the well-being of the workers. Even if the employer has the right motivation, however, such extension of family-like norms to domestic workers may require active effort. They can be extended through common rituals, like eating together. So the employer can try to invite the domestic worker to dine with his or her family. The worker might resist at first, but the employer should persist in the hope that the worker will eventually join the family, eating and conversing at mealtime without being too self-conscious about it. In the Confucian spirit, the employer can also encourage joint singing as a way of generating a sense of solidarity. Again, it might seem a bit forced at first, but eventually both parties may enjoy doing it. If employer and employee do karaoke together to enjoy themselves, we can be confident that family-like norms have been extended!

The liberal may worry about the trade-off between care and rights. As Bridget Anderson puts it, "The difficulty from the migrant workers' point of view is that such relationships of kindness and gratitude leave little space for rights" ("A Very Private Business," Centre on Migration, Policy and Society, Working Paper No. 28, 2006, 19). Just as it seems distasteful (and often unnecessary) to assert rights in families governed by love and affection, so the employer seeking to promote affective ties might object to rights in the context of family-like relationships between employer and domestic worker, with the consequence that workers are more open to exploitation and abuse. In actual fact, employers have often misused the rhetoric of family harmony to argue against legislation that benefits workers. Consider the following rhetoric from the director of the Mitsubishi Shipyard in Nagasaki in 1910, arguing against a factory law that would strengthen workers' rights:

> Since ancient times, Japan has possessed the beautiful custom of master-servant relations based firmly on a spirit of sacrifice and compassion, a custom not seen in the many other countries of the world. Even with the recent progress in transportation, the development of ideas about rights, the expansion of markets, and the growing scale of industrial society, this master-servant relationship persists securely. Is it not weak like

that of the Western nations but has its roots in our family system and will persist as long as that system exists. Because of this relationship the employer loves the employee and the employee respects his master. . . . Today, there exist no evils and we feel no necessity [for a factory law]. We cannot agree to something that will destroy the beautiful custom of master-servant relations and wreak havoc on our industrial peace. (Quoted in Frank Upham, "The Japanese Experience with 'Harmony' and Law," paper on file with author)

One suspects that the workers did not share such views. We can and should be suspicious of such rhetoric. Employers themselves, if they have any conscience, should try to think from the employee's point of view and do things that employees actually care about, like paying above the minimum wage and giving them time off, whatever the impact on the development of family-like ties. Sometimes employers even need to override the worker's desire to promote relationships based on care. I need to be very careful about drawing on my own experience qua boss—I'm fully aware that it doesn't "smell" good—but let me go ahead with an example to illustrate what I mean. Once, I asked the son of our domestic worker in Beijing to help fix my computer. He came after work and eventually solved the problem, but he left before I had a chance to give him any money. The next day, I offered the money to his mother, but she refused, explaining that Westerners and Chinese are different: Westerners want to marketize everything, but Chinese value relationships based on care and emotion. My immediate instinct was to defend Western civilization, but I resisted the urge. Instead, I told our domestic worker that it would be awkward for me to ask her son for help in the future if she doesn't accept money on his behalf.[6]

Still, misuses of the rhetoric of family values should not undermine the whole ideal of promoting family-like ties between employer and employee—especially within the household, where employers interact on intimate terms with workers. Obviously it's better for the worker if the employer treats her with care and affection. And it's not just employers who say that. The interviewees in Beijing specifically noted that "being treated as a member of the family" is an important desideratum. Moreover, it would be a mistake to assume that there is always a trade-off between the protection of legal rights and family-like affective relations. In some cases, rights can actually promote affective relations. In mainland Chinese cities (unlike Hong Kong), migrant domestic workers typically work without contracts. Standardized Hong Kong–style contracts that set minimum wages and guarantee health and work accident insurance would be beneficial for the domestic workers. Less obviously, such contracts could also help to promote the development of family-like relations within the home. By specifying longer terms of engagement (say, two or three years), domestic workers would be more likely to stick with their employers, thus increasing the likelihood that family-like ties develop between employer and employee. On the other hand, an important advantage for domestic workers under the current, informal system of work is that they can easily change jobs and therefore do not have to put up with abusive employers (in contrast, foreign domestic workers only have two weeks to find new employers in Hong Kong, which means that they often must tolerate bad employers for fear of being deported). So the contract would need to allow for some form of exit, but not to the point that employer and employee do not have any motivation to deal with minor conflicts in family-like ways. Such contracts would also need to be combined with further measures that protect the domestic workers from abuse, such as severe punishments for employers who physically or sexually abuse domestic workers.

But we do need to recognize that excessive rights focus can undermine affective ties between employer and employee. Liberals seem to think that rights designed to promote equal respect and fairness should always have political (and legal) priority over concern for affective ties, but Confucians feel the tension.[7] And sometimes the latter can have priority. For example, one of my interviewees in Hong Kong praised her former Singapore employer for providing shampoo and other toiletries. Such seemingly trivial gestures were deeply appreciated because they went beyond legal obligations, and they strengthened bonds of trust between employer and employee. If the employer had provided toiletries because that obligation had been spelled out in contract form, it would not have had the same beneficial effect on their relationship.

More controversially, such considerations may bear on the issue of whether or not to legislate work hours. In Hong Kong, contracts between employers and domestic workers do not set a maximum number of work hours. There is nothing illegal about making domestic workers work sixteen-hour days. At first glance, this seems morally suspect. However, one reason for not specifying maximum work hours is that it would be difficult to enforce within the "privacy" of the home and to adjudicate cases of conflict. Another reason matters more for our purposes. The employers can offer to limit work hours to "reasonable" amounts—say, eight-hour days, with breaks in between—and this may have the effect of strengthening affective ties between employers and workers. Conversely, the domestic worker may offer to work beyond agreed-upon hours, and this will also have the effect of strengthening trust and caring relationships within the household. Eventually, the lines between economic activity and family duties may become blurred, and the process of negotiating work between employer and employee will more closely resemble the informal ways of distributing tasks between family members; put differently, it allows for the "Confucian" extension of family-like norms and practices to domestic workers. Such an outcome is less likely to develop if legal contracts specify in great detail the rights and duties of domestic workers within the family context.

The liberal may reply that the proposal not to specify maximum work hours still benefits the employer, who ultimately controls the levers of power. Why should the employer have the right to decide whether or not to exploit the domestic worker? From the perspective of the domestic worker, it might seem preferable to have the right to limited work hours, which can be invoked if need be. If the domestic worker wants to strengthen affective ties with her employer, then she can waive this right, and the employer would be grateful. In practice, unfortunately, this is not likely to happen. Once the right is formalized, there is a strong tendency to invoke it, even against "good" employers where it might not be necessary to do so. Moreover, the fact that this right is so difficult to enforce may lead to endless conflicts that could poison the atmosphere of the household.

My main point—a point that's neglected or criticized by liberal theorists—is that the Confucian concern for extending family-like relations to domestic workers should be taken seriously, both at the level of policy and the way we—bosses—actually deal with them. Ideally, legislators and employers should try to combine this concern with considerations of justice. But it may not always be possible to do so. Legal rights should protect the basic interests of workers, like the right not be abused physically or sexually. But if curbing rights doesn't lead to severe injustice and helps to promote affective ties, then the concern for the latter should have priority. In hard cases one's normative position may lead to different conclusions. The liberal individualist may prefer to err on the side of justice, but the Confucian may opt for norms and practices more likely to secure harmony and trust within the family.

The Economic Benefits of Differentiated Citizenship

But perhaps I'm missing the real problem. The whole system of migrant labor rests on the fundamental injustice of unequal citizenship: in Hong Kong, for example, foreign domestic workers cannot be put on the road to citizenship no matter how long they work in the territory. In the eyes of liberal theorists, the institutionalization of second-class citizenship—permanent unequal legal rights for a group of residents—is a violation of fundamental liberal-democratic principles and should never be allowed, no matter what the circumstances. As Will Kymlicka puts it, "It violates the very idea of a liberal democracy to have groups of long-term residents who have no right to become citizens" (*Contemporary Political Philosophy*, 2nd ed., 359). No decent government will ever compromise on these principles.[8]

In mainland China, arguably, there's an even worse injustice because migrant workers are deprived of equal rights within their *own* country! China's "floating population"—roughly 120 million migrants, mainly impoverished rural residents migrating to urban areas in search of better opportunities and higher earnings—is subject to the *hukou* (household registration) system that allows the state to control the extent of migration to urban areas and makes it more difficult for those born in rural areas to establish permanent homes in cities. The *hukou* is a politically sanctioned, hereditary distinction between those born in rural and urban areas, and migrants from rural areas must make their presence known in cities and apply for labor permits to work there. Urban household registrants are granted an extra share of rights and entitlements, and migrants are precluded from partaking of those benefits as a result of their rural backgrounds, regardless of how long they have actually lived in urban areas. From a liberal democratic perspective, in other words, the *hukou* system is the functional equivalent of a caste system that marks a group of people as second-class citizens just because they were unlucky enough to be born in the countryside.

It's worth asking what could possibly motivate what seems like a transparently unjust system. One way of answering this question is to anticipate the likely social and economic consequences of development without the *hukou* system. Consider what happened when Tibet—for Han Chinese, the most remote, inhospitable, and hostile part of the country—was exempted from the *hukou* system: "To encourage economic development in Tibet, Beijing had exempted Tibet from the general rule that one must be a permanent resident of a given area to start a business there. The result was that Tibetan cities, Lhasa in particular, were inundated with a so-called 'floating population' of Han Chinese from other provinces" (He Baogang, "Minority Rights with Chinese Characteristics," in *Multiculturalism in Asia*, ed. Will Kymlicka and He Baogang, 64). Wu Ming spells out the likely consequences of abolishing the *hukou* system in more desirable (from a Han Chinese perspective) locations such as Beijing and Shanghai:

> If the urban *hukou* is abolished, not only will this cause difficulties of technical and human management in cities, there will also be a flood of laborers from the countryside. This will lead to many "urban illnesses," particularly in developed cities on the East Coast. Perhaps we can say that there are already huge numbers of rural migrants in cities? But there aren't many "urban illnesses." That's because the urban *hukou* system has not been abolished. The rural migrants don't have a fixed residence. . . . Without the *hukou* system, they would travel in groups, if they could establish their residence [in cities], they would bring their whole families to live in the outskirts of cities and there would be a huge amount of poverty stricken people. Urbanization in Latin America is the best example of this kind of situation. (Quoted in *Xin xi bu*, November 26, 2001)

In other words, the *hukou* system has prevented the emergence of shanty towns and slums that characterize the big cities of other developing countries such as Brazil, Mexico, India, and Indonesia. The benefits for economic development of urban areas are obvious: there is more social peace and less crime, as well as a more welcoming (stable) environment for foreign investors.

Wu Ming argues that the *hukou* system also benefits the less-developed parts of the country. The medium-sized and small cities of the less-developed western part of China find it easier to retain the talent that helps to develop their economies (without the *hukou* system, more talent would migrate to cities like Beijing and Shanghai). One might add that the benefits of economic investment in relatively wealthy east coast cities can eventually be redistributed for purposes of developing impoverished regions (the Chinese government has recently announced funding for expensive infrastructure projects in the west).

There are reasons to question the empirical basis of such claims (see, e.g., Xia Xianliang and Wang Yingxi, *Urban Studies*, vol. 9, no. 4, 2002). Even if they are correct, however, the liberal would still want to abolish the *hukou* system because equal citizenship is the "mother of all values" in contemporary liberal theory. Even if unequal rights help to promote economic development, the system is fundamentally unjust and should be abolished. Here, we have a clash of fundamental values. It's not just the Chinese Communist Party that says the government should prioritize the right to subsistence over equal civil and political rights. Confucius himself was explicit that the government's first obligation is to secure the conditions for people's basic means of subsistence, and only then should they be educated (13.9). In the same vein, Mencius argued that the government must first provide for the people's basic means of subsistence so that they won't go morally astray: "The people will not have dependable feelings if they are without dependable means of support. Lacking dependable means of support, they will go astray and fall into excesses, stopping at nothing" (1A.7). In the West, theorists only began to worry about the state's responsibility to alleviate poverty in the eighteenth century,[9] whereas such concerns have long informed Chinese thinking and practice. The idea that certain rights can be sacrificed for the sake of enriching the people is not nearly so controversial in China. If there's a conflict with liberal democratic theory, the problem may lie with liberal democratic theory. At the very least, liberals should be cautious about lecturing the Chinese about the requirements of "universal" justice.

But there is one feature of the unequal rights system that should be of special concern to Confucians: the fact that migrants are often forced to be separated from family members. In the case of mainland China, migrants need to pay extra school fees if they take children with them to cities and they often leave kids behind as a result. The official newspaper *China Daily* (January 29, 2007) reports that more than 20 million Chinese children are living with grandparents or other relations after their parents left home to find work (typically, the parents return home only once a year, during the Chinese New Year). In Hong Kong, the effects of foreign migration on family life are even worse. Foreign domestic workers cannot bring family members, and they are forced to come alone, without their spouses or children.

It's worth asking why such seemingly inhumane laws are put in place. The main reason is that labor-receiving territories do not want permanent settlement by poor migrant workers, and they believe that extending equal rights to the families of migrants will encourage settlement. These views are not likely to change in the foreseeable future. Most Hong Kongers, for example, fear being flooded with poor migrants from abroad. Hong Kong is already the most crowded territory in Asia, and the last thing Hong Kongers want is massive migration by poor foreign workers and their families (even Chinese mainlanders have a hard time bringing family members to Hong Kong, though it's technically the same country). It's also worth asking what would happen if liberal theorists succeeded in persuading the Hong Kong government to change its policy. The result would almost certainly harm foreign domestic workers. Pressured by the people, the government would prevent new arrivals from coming to Hong Kong, thus depriving poor foreigners of work opportunities. The current batch of foreign domestic workers in Hong Kong—232,780 at the latest count (March 12, 2007)—may also be expelled. Many domestic helpers would be forced on airplanes, kicking and screaming, and shipped back to the Philippines and other sending countries. And many children in Hong Kong, having grown attached to their helpers, would cry themselves to sleep for a few nights. Last but not least, remittances to sending countries from Hong Kong would dry up, and global poverty would likely worsen.[10]

How does one respond to such scenarios? Over the last century of so, Western liberals have discovered the value of family ties for the good life (in comparison, it has been the central theme of Confucianism for well over two millennia), and they seek to use the language of fundamental rights to secure this value. Joseph Carens, for example, writes that "denying people the right to have their families with them for more than three months would be harsh and for more than a year would be unconscionable" ("Live-In Domestics, Seasonal Workers, Foreign Students, and Others Hard to Locate on the Map of Democracy," 7; paper on file with author). Such basic rights trump all other considerations. Even if migrant worker programs are best able to reduce global poverty,[11] the liberal theorist cannot bend such principles. For the Confucian, however, the task is to balance different values. On the one hand, the government has an obligation to alleviate poverty, and it will be prepared to consider curbing some rights if necessary to achieve this end. On the other hand, the government also has an obligation to protect and promote family values. But note that the Confucian has a different conception of family values. For the Western liberal, the family typically refers to the nuclear family, meaning spouses and their children. Hence being deprived of such relations is to be entirely deprived of family ties. For the Confucian, the concept of the family is broader; it can and should be extended to others. Most obviously, it includes the relationship to elderly parents. But it can also refer to "new" family members, once family norms and labels are extended to them. Hence the importance of promoting family-like ties between the employer and the domestic worker. To an important extent, such ties can alleviate some of the loneliness caused by separation from family members for migrant workers.

I do not mean to imply that such ties can *replace* family ties in home countries (or rural areas, in the case of migrant workers in mainland China). Mencius, for one, explicitly warns against confusing extension of family-like norms with the Mohist doctrine of impartial concern for all. For Mencius, it's natural and legitimate for a person to love his brother's son more than his neighbor's newborn baby (3A.5). And to treat my neighbor's father in exactly the same way as I treat my father, as Mozi asks us to do, would amount to a denial of my father (3B.9). So extended family-like norms cannot do all the work. Intimate family members have special value that cannot be replaced. Hence, provisions must also be made for migrant workers to return home on extended stays, at least once a year. In Hong Kong, employers are forced to pay for such visits back home, but employers can do more, say, pay for two trips back home per year. In mainland China, many employers may not have the means to pay for the home visits of their workers, but those who can help should do so (it needn't be direct help; it can take the form of bonuses during holiday seasons).

Let me conclude by emphasizing that we are dealing with hard choices in a nonideal world. These sorts of trade-offs and sacrifices should be tolerated, not celebrated. Ideally, of course, no one would be forced to travel abroad under conditions of unequal rights and deprived of key family relations simply to make a decent living. In the long term, assuming an optimistic scenario, economic necessity will no longer influence what people do. We will have overcome the problem of global poverty and nobody would need to take jobs as migrant workers in faraway lands. Even then, however, different cultural traditions may influence different ways of securing care for needy family members. Consider the issue of caring for elderly parents. In Western liberal societies, one can predict that much, if not most, of the "caring" will take place in nursing homes or by hired caretakers at home (often working below the minimum wage: see Eileen Boris and Jennifer Klein, "Old Folks at Home, *Dissent*, fall 2007). In societies with a Confucian heritage, however, the idea that care of elderly parents should be informed with the right "attitude"—particularized love—means that relatives will do the bulk of the caring.[12] Perhaps the state can provide more resources for at-home care by relatives. Just as important, let us hope that gender relations will equalize and such tasks will be distributed more equally between adult sons and daughters.[13]

6. The Politics of Sports: From the 2006 World Cup to the 2008 Olympics

China did not qualify for the 2006 World Cup, yet there was almost fanatical enthusiasm for the games in Beijing. Because the matches were played in the middle of the night, many Beijingers slept during the day. There was a brief respite from Beijing's notorious traffic jams, and the number of emergency calls to the city hotline decreased by 11 percent during the hours of the games. My son's end-of-year examinations were scheduled during the three-day interval between the two rounds. I was told the dates were purposefully chosen.

A Soft Spot for Great Historical Powers

What explains the passion that people showed for the game? It is hard to imagine Americans, say, getting so excited about victories by other nations in an international tournament for which their national team had failed to qualify. In the United States, although there is some ethnic-based enthusiasm for particular teams—Italian Americans support the Italian team, Mexican Americans support the Mexican team, and so on—the World Cup does not occupy center stage of social life. But the United States may be an outlying case. In many parts of the world—from South Africa to India to China—the bulk of ordinary citizens became crazed about soccer during the World Cup, even without any national team in the competition. This worldwide obsession can be explained by the usual commercial considerations: clever branding and marketing that tap the widespread desire to be part of a global event in countries of rising affluence.

In China, though, there may also be more particular political factors. As Yu Maochun of the U.S. Naval Academy notes, China's decision, for the first time in its history, to allow live broadcasting of the 1978 World Cup in Argentina was a turning point in China's political history because of the excitement it generated. For the first time since the revolution, the Chinese nation, exhausted by the Chinese Communist Party's incessant political campaigns, suddenly realized that the world could be excited by something other than Marxism and class struggle. Francesco Sisci, the distinguished correspondent for *La Stampa*, offers an explanation for current interest. The two best-read newspapers in China, selling well over a million copies each every day, are *Cankao Xiaoxi* and *Huanqiu Shibao*. They cover mainly international news. Many popular local papers cover local news. In both cases, the reporting does not stray too far from the facts and deals with issues that people care about. All national news, however, is official propaganda and thus uninteresting. So the Chinese develop strong local and international interests but pay less attention to national affairs than do most citizens of liberal democratic countries.[1] Educated Chinese in particular have a special interest in international affairs, including international sports.

Still, the sheer beauty of global soccer cannot be discounted as the key factor for interest in the sport. The more interesting question, perhaps, is why the Chinese support particular teams with such passion. In the 2002 World Cup, I expected that Asian solidarity would play an important role. The Chinese team had been eliminated in the first round, but the Korean team performed unexpectedly well. I watched the quarter-final match between Germany and South Korea in a Beijing bar, and to my surprise the crowd burst into applause when Germany scored and eventually won the match. I was told that support for Germany can be explained by the fact that German soccer is shown on Chinese TV and most Chinese are more familiar with German players. One friend said that Koreans (along with the Taiwanese) are known to be the most exploitative employers of Chinese workers. But I also detected a certain amount of resentment at the fact that the "younger brother" was upstaging his elders.

This year, I did not have such illusions.[2] There was enthusiasm for the Korean team in the Wudaokou area of Beijing, home to many

Korean students. But the *lao Beijing* (old-time Beijingers) I spoke to rejoiced at Korea's early exit. In the case of Japan, the antagonism is more
obvious. There were few public spaces to observe the performance of
the Japanese team during the World Cup. Most bars in the Wudaokou
area did not show the games with Japan, and there was an unusually
heavy police presence during such games, purportedly because the
government feared anti-Japanese riots that could spin out of control.
Fortunately for the authorities, the Japanese team did not win any
games and failed to advance to the next round.

My own loyalties lie with the underdog teams. In 2002, I was a big
fan of Korea. My Korean friends took great pride in what they called
the "spiritual power" of their team, which compensated for lack of talent and experience, and their enthusiasm rubbed off on me. In 2006, I
supported Ghana, the best-performing African country, which played
with such heart and excitement. Perhaps left-wing political sensibilities
naturally lend themselves to support for teams from relatively poor and
not-so-famous countries. A win would give a great boost to their national confidence, and it might have positive economic spillovers.
Surely Ghana needs more of a boost than the United States.[3] There
may also be psychological reasons to support underdogs. They appeal
to the romantic element in the soul. Think how many Hollywood movies end with the triumph of underdog athletes and teams.

There is no such preference for the underdog in China.[4] Quite the
opposite, in fact. Chinese fans support traditional soccer powers such
as Germany, England, Brazil, Argentina, and Italy. It is difficult to over-
estimate the passion for such teams. In the 2002 World Cup, the CCTV
hostess Sheng Bin wept openly at Argentina's early exit. When England
went down in defeat against Portugal in 2006, my son's piano teacher's
husband was so depressed he could barely get out of bed. Partly, the
preference for traditional soccer powers can be explained by love of the
game: Chinese fans support teams that have performed well in the past
and are likely to generate exciting games in the future. But there may
also be a special form of internationalist nationalism at work. The
support for established teams may be an expression of a more general
appreciation for nations with long and rich histories and cultures. As
director of the Institute of Italian Culture in Beijing, Francesco Sisci
could find common ground with his Chinese counterparts by appealing

to their love of history, by showing how Italy served as an important cradle of Western civilization, just as China served as the cradle of East Asian civilization.

Conversely, the Chinese won't cheer for underdogs or relatively small teams and countries without substantial talent, global impact, or long histories. In soccer, this means they won't cheer for teams like Australia ("Would you cheer for a bunch of beer-guzzling upstarts?" as one friend put it) if they're up against the more established soccer powers. In politics, it means they won't sympathize much with the aspirations of small nations or minorities, such as the Francophones of Quebec (not to mention Taiwan and Tibet). The only way to address this concern is for such small powers to show that they are worthy of global admiration. If Australia develops into a global soccer power over, say, thirty years, as opposed to scoring occasional fluke victories, it will gain the sympathy of the Chinese. If Quebec produces great achievements that the rest of the world can appreciate, it may gain the admiration of the Chinese (Even though I'm from Quebec, I'm hard pressed to explain what's great about my home province; nobody in China has ever heard of Guy Lafleur).

What's Wrong with Being Biased?

In 2006, the most striking public display of passion for a traditional soccer power occurred at the end of the quarter-final match between Italy and Australia. China's best-known soccer announcer, Huang Jianxiang, was unable to control his enthusiasm when Fabio Grosso went down in the penalty area and a last-minute penalty kick was awarded to the Italians.

It is worth quoting in full the official Chinese translation by the Xinhua news agency. Huang screamed

> Penalty! Penalty! Penalty! Grosso's done it, Grosso's done it! The great Italian left back! He succeeded in the glorious traditions of Italy! Facchetti, Cabrini, and Maldini, their souls are infused in him at this moment! Grosso represents the long history and traditions of soccer, he's not fighting alone at this moment! He's not alone! Grosso alone represents the long history and traditions of Italian soccer! He is not fighting alone!

As Francesco Totti prepared to take the penalty kick that would win the match, Huang shouted himself hoarse.

> Totti! He is about to take the shot. He shoulders the expecta-
> tions of the whole world. Goooooal! Game over! Italy wins!
> Beat the Australians! They do not fall in front of Hiddink
> again! [Hiddink, the Australian coach, had led South Korea to
> oust Italy in the 2002 World Cup.] Italy the great! Left back the
> great! Happy birthday to Paolo Maldini! Long live Italy! The
> victory belongs to Italy, to Grosso, to Cannavaro, to Zambrotta,
> to Buffon, to Maldini, to everyone who loves Italian soccer!
> Hiddink lost his courage faced with Italian history and tradi-
> tions! He finally reaped what he had sown! They should go
> home. They don't need to fly as far as Australia, as most of
> them are living in Europe. Farewell!"

As I listened to Huang's outburst, I could hear similar outbursts of joy from my neighboring flats (it was about one in the morning). I was deeply moved by this manifestation of enthusiasm for another country's triumph, for the love shown for another country's history and tradi-tions. I was also somewhat amused, because the Chinese formulation of the "Long Live" idiom—literally, "Italy, Ten Thousand Years!"—used to be invoked by enthusiastic crowds for Mao and the Communist Party ("Chairman Mao, Ten Thousand Years!").

To my surprise, Huang's comments generated a storm of controversy. Popular Chinese portals such as sina.com and sohu.com's online discus-sion forums were flooded with opinions for and against them. Beijing blogger Fly Show had a post titled "Huang 'Long Live Italy' Jianxiang, you can go home now. . . . Sorry, Australia, please forgive our crazy man!" According to an unconfirmed text circulating on the Internet, more than thirty Australian soccer supporters surrounded the Australian embassy in Beijing the next day, demanding that the ambassador make a formal complaint to the Chinese government about Huang's commen-tary. A couple of days later, Huang issued a letter of public apology:

> Dear soccer fans and TV viewers around the country. I have
> attached too much personal feeling to the match. After I woke

up this morning, I reviewed the video of the match, and I feel there is some injustice and prejudice in my comment. I will make formal apologies to viewers. I am familiar with Italian football and I hope that the Italians can gain a berth in the last eight, which will make the matches in the future more exciting, but I have mingled my feeling with . . . my job. It is not a standpoint that a TV commentator should have . . . I will draw the lesson from this case and . . . keep my personal feeling and job balanced. When we broadcast the matches, we hope referees can be just, and as a commentator, I will try my best to be fair and to do a good job.

Are announcers supposed to be neutral and unbiased? I suggest that Huang may not be drawing the right lesson from this episode (assuming that his apology was sincere; more likely, it was forced upon him). For one thing, there may be political reasons to favor passionate and controversial announcers. The key political catchword in China is "stability," and the government closely monitors the media (not to mention political organs) to ensure that controversial views are not aired. If the system fails to live up to the "ideal," then "stability" is threatened, and the government uses various carrots and sticks to restore the status quo. In this case, the government-run television station repeatedly ran footage of Australia's achievements in soccer along with the subtitles proclaiming "Australia bows out like true heroes," presumably to appease the pro-Australia contingent that may have been angered by Huang's outburst. And Huang himself was dismissed from further World Cup commentary on Italian games.[5] In my view, Huang was sorely missed. The announcer for the next two Italy games—including its win over France in the final game—was dreadfully dull, and he did not seem nearly as well informed as Huang. But the more worrisome point is that the government also invoked the sort of harsh tactics meted out to political opponents of the regime: depriving them of their jobs, public humiliation, and so on. Is that what the Australian supporters really wanted? Is this the way to deal with controversy in society, particularly in the context of a political system that frowns upon public expressions of passion and emotion?

There may also be cultural reasons to question the assumption that announcers are supposed to be neutral. Another model, perhaps more deeply rooted in Chinese culture, is that announcers should be like well-informed teachers, explaining to the viewer which players and teams express certain qualities and virtues. Announcers are not merely transmitting factual information; they are supposed to draw moral lessons for the viewer-students. It is up to the viewer-students to decide whether they agree with the announcer-teachers. And those who disagree should gently remonstrate with the teachers, not use force to show disagreement. The fact that many Chinese bloggers supported Huang suggests that the normative model of the teacher-announcer still resonates in contemporary China (according to an online survey by sina.com, nearly half the respondents said Huang's comments were not unfair; one of the most popular new cell ring phone mimics Huang's now famous enthusiasm for the Italian victory over Australia). I do not deny that there may be other explanations, such as widespread support for the Italian team in Chinese society; but it is difficult to imagine such a level of support for outwardly biased announcers in, say, Sweden or Canada. The ideal of neutrality as applied to various spheres of social life—not simply for judges and referees, but also for announcers and teachers, even friends, parents, and children[6]—seems too deeply ingrained in Western societies.

The Dangers of Self-Regarding Nationalism

The most moving aspect of Huang's outburst is the love he showed for another country. He was celebrating "the glorious traditions of Italy"! If the same outburst had been made by an Italian announcer, it would have seemed distasteful, at least to an outsider. The talk of "Italy the Great!" with the announcer almost foaming at the mouth, may have conjured up images of Italy's fascist past. Shortly after the controversial game, Huang's off-the-cuff response pointed to more dangerous manifestations of nationalism: "Australia reminded me of the lousy team that eliminated China in the World Cup qualifiers in 1981. . . . Australia will now fight for an Asian World Cup berth, and it may not be good enough to handle South Korea and Japan. But it will very likely take advantage of the Chinese team. So I don't like it." Such sentiments may be magnified when Chinese athletes achieve world-class status, say, in the Olympics, or perhaps in soccer a couple of decades from now. At that point, the Huangs will be cheering for their own team, and they may show aggressive hostility to opponents, with potentially dangerous political consequences. There was a significant wave of anti-Americanism in China when the Americans beat the Chinese in the 1999 Women's World Cup, to the point that the U.S. State Department issued a warning to Americans in China to keep a low profile (but this was also shortly after the bombing of the Chinese embassy in Belgrade during the Kosovo War).[7]

Perhaps I overstate the concern. Just as orthodox religious groups sometimes have respect for each other's religious commitments (and contempt for agnostic liberals and atheists), so soccer fans can find mutual joy in national commitments. In the lead-off to the game between Portugal and Germany, enthusiastic fans wrapped in the flags of their respective countries engaging in joint celebrations. Such fans appreciate each other's passionate commitment to their own teams; they have far more in common with each other than with those indifferent to soccer. Moreover, self-regarding nationalism can be trumped by love of the game. In the case of China, its own fans turn on the team when it performs poorly, as in the 2002 World Cup match when China was crushed by Brazil four to nothing. Even if China becomes a world power in soccer, there is no guarantee that its fans will give it unconditional support, judging by the experience of other soccer powers. When Brazil performed poorly against France in the 2006 quarter-final match, Brazilians fans jeered their own team toward the end of the game. And French fans could not muster much enthusiasm for their own team following Zinedine Zidane's vicious head-butt in the final game against Italy. Fans will often be critical if their own national team fails to display virtues that are honored by the sporting community.

Still, there are real dangers associated with self-regarding nationalism. The Chinese state's pursuit of Olympic gold medals illustrates those dangers. China's best athletes are selected at a very young age and made to undergo rigorous state-sponsored physical education, with little attention paid to other forms of learning. The athletes are used by the state to score political points, and the announcers at Olympic games make less-than-subtle claims about the greatness of the Chinese nation. As the influential Chinese journalist Sang Ye puts it, "For China, athletics has little to do with sport per se. It is not concerned with either physical health or personal wellbeing. For the Chinese, athletic competitions are a struggle between political systems. They are a heady opiate administered to salve dreams of national glory" (see Sang Ye's revealing interview with an elite athlete in *China Candid*, 166). The near-term goal is to surpass the U.S. gold medal tally at the 2008 Olympic games in Beijing.

Ironically, such an approach to sports owes its origins to ancient Greece, where city-states engaged in intense military competition, fighting for either survival or expansion. There was naturally much emphasis on the training of soldiers, and state-sponsored physical education—designed to toughen bodies and (as Aristotle puts it) to "foster the virtue of courage"—developed as a by-product. Greek states actively promoted interstate sporting competitions—most famously, the Olympics—and the main aim of such competitions was to bring glory to the state. The whole system was geared to a "winner-take-all" mentality: there wasn't even a prize for second place; only the best man won and everybody else lost. The winners were treated as conquering heroes by their home states, and they were showered with material benefits, such as free meals for life.

China's own political tradition (and, to a certain extent, earlier political practice) points to an alternative approach that may be more desirable for modern societies. The Confucian view is that physical activity should be tied to pursuit of nonmilitaristic virtues and that the test of success should be its contribution to moral and intellectual development rather than victory in sporting competitions. Such an ideal is realized by means of rituals that civilize and elevate, particularly in the context of competitive relationships that would otherwise degenerate into hostility and antagonism, if not warfare. This ideal is not entirely unrealistic in contemporary societies. Mencius's account of the archer's psychological reaction to "failure"—"an archer makes sure his stance is correct before letting fly the arrow, and if he fails to hit the mark, he does not hold it against the victor. He simply seeks the cause within himself" (2A.7)—is not dissimilar to the tennis player who graciously shakes the winner's hand after the game and pursues a rigorous self-improvement program afterward. Confucius's account of the gentleman-archer—"Exemplary persons are not competitive, but they must still compete in archery. Greeting and making way for each other, the archers ascend the hall, and returning they drink a salute. Even during competition, they are exemplary persons" (3.7)—echoes the rituals of sumo wrestlers. In soccer, the relevant rituals include helping opponents up after a fall and exchanging sweat-soaked shirts at the end of the game. These rituals need not be incompatible with passionate support for one team. In the 2002 World Cup, the Koreans were fanatical supporters of their own team. But after the team's loss to Turkey for the third-place spot in front of its home crowd, the Korean team formed a circle and collectively bowed to the audience as a show of gratitude. The crowd responded with a tremendous ovation for the Korean team and, more surprisingly, for the victorious Turkish team. There may be particular reasons for this response—many South Koreans are grateful to Turkey because of its support in the Korean War half a century ago—but such moving scenes show how Confucian-style rituals can tame the excesses of national bias. It is no coincidence that Korea is widely held to be the most Confucian country in East Asia. For the 2008 Olympic Games in Beijing, perhaps the Chinese can seek inspiration from Confucian rather than Greek athletic ideals.[8]

Postscript (January 2008): Toward Olympian Civility?

It is somewhat reckless to diagnose the psychological state of a huge and diverse country, but let me proceed. The Chinese reaction to soccer owes more to the last "century of humiliation" than to Confucian traditions. For most of the twentieth century, China has viewed itself as a weak and vulnerable country that has been denied its historical place in the sun. For a while, it looked as if the Chinese soccer team might offer something to cheer for, but its poor performance over the last decade or so has dealt a severe blow to Chinese pride. Hence, many Chinese cheer for other soccer powers with long and magnificent histories and traditions. To a certain extent, they are cheering for themselves or for China vicariously. This view can also help to explain why China cheers against Korea and Japan. In the traditional scheme of things, such neighboring countries would be somewhat subordinate to the "Middle Kingdom," and the soccer success of such countries threatens to throw the "proper" order out of whack.

In my essay, I drew the seemingly logical implication that Chinese will be cheering for their own athletes if they win competitions (there will no longer be any need to find psychological comfort in cheering for other great powers), along with the implication that they might also show aggressive hostility to opponents. I also pointed to the Chinese state's single-minded pursuit of Olympic gold medals—as opposed to the Confucian view that everyone wins when competition is fair and civil—as support for my view. But perhaps I was too pessimistic. What I failed to foresee is that Olympic success may in fact be the precondition for Confucian civility.[9] If China wins gold medals and reestablishes its "deserved" place in the sun, the traditional Confucian ways may assert themselves against—or at least mitigate—negative emotions such as resentment and aggressive nationalism. Just as China's growing political power means that it no longer has to show obsessive concern with state sovereignty, hence allowing for the projection of moral ideals abroad, so China's growing prowess in international sports competition might allow for the revival of Confucian civility.

As it turns out—to my pleasant surprise!—the past few months in Beijing have been dominated by campaigns to promote *aoyun liyi* (奥运礼仪), which can be translated roughly as "Olympic civility." Walls and overpasses have been plastered with the slogan. Over 1.5 million pamphlets on the theme have been distributed to households in Beijing (*Nanfang Zhoumou*, August 9, 2007). In various public announcements, the government is encouraging citizens to improve their behavior for the Olympics. They should queue up properly (the eleventh day of each month is set aside for this task, with the number 11 representing lining up) and spit less (even though the traditional belief of Chinese medicine is that mucus should be expelled).[10] Taxi drivers should be more courteous to passengers (even though excessive courtesy is viewed as a distancing tactic, something that intimates should not do).

The really interesting part, to me, is that spectators are being encouraged to be civil. For example, radio shows discuss the issue of how spectators should act during the Olympic Games. One common message is that spectators should refrain from demonstrating excessive enthusiasm for the Chinese athletes, and they should applaud for losing teams as well as good performances by opposing athletes. Some Confucian scholars suggest that spectators should demonstrate civil behavior by means of traditional rituals, such as bowing with hands clasped and paying obeisance by cupping one hand in the other before one's chest.[11]

Athletes are also encouraged to be civil. In a widely publicized speech to the Chinese People's Political Consultative Committee, the novelist and former minister of culture Wang Meng[12] pointedly criticized the behavior of victorious Chinese athletes at the last Olympic Games. Chinese hurdler Liu Xiang—perhaps China's best-known athlete, along with basketball star Yao Ming—was not-so-indirectly criticized for claiming that his gold medal shows that "yellow people" can also run fast. Liu's emotional after-game address was also criticized for reflecting "lack of decency and confidence. We can't always talk in the bitter manner like that of a bullied concubine." In contrast, Wang praised the black athletes who, shortly after losing the race, went to congratulate Liu Xiang for his victory. Wang also criticized a Chinese athlete who won a gold medal largely because of the misplay of another athlete from a different country. When the athlete was asked if his success depended on random factors, he replied "No, I deserve the gold medal." Wang thought the answer was too unrefined; he should have said, "Yes, the other player has the skills to win the gold medal. I feel sorry for his misplay. I hope we have more chances to learn from each other in the future. Regarding the gold medal, I don't think anyone can win it simply due to mere luck or other people's misplays." To support his views, Wang quoted Confucius's famous saying—the Chinese equivalent of the Golden Rule—"Do not impose on others what you yourself do not want" (15.24). Wang also noted the need to be friendly to one's opponents, for example by saying "Excuse me" (in English) if one bumps into an opponent, regardless of who's at fault. He emphasized that it is especially important to show civility to the athletes of countries with whom China has had unhappy histories in the past, such as Japan.[13] In an era of peace, the whole point of competition is to build character and to win together, as opposed to the "I win, you lose" mentality that characterizes wartime.[14]

To Western ears, all this might sound like yet another example of an authoritarian state telling its subjects what to think and do.[15] But that might reflect cultural differences. As P. J. Ivanhoe puts it, "The reason Westerners tend to think any campaign on the part of the state is just propaganda and mind control is that there is a deep-seated view on the part of most Westerners that no one—but God and conscience—can tell you how to make yourself better. In East Asia, most people are better oriented toward self-improvement. They don't find getting lectured a bit an attack upon their person. There is the idea that elders and wise people (at times even the state) can help to improve oneself."

And what's wrong with a bit of guidance? The Chinese state isn't forcing people what to think and do; rather, it's appealing to their moral sensibilities and urging them to act appropriately. There is no punishment attached to acting "wrongly." In this case, people do not necessarily seem to mind being "lectured to." One normally cynical driver told me that China doesn't have a long history of hosting international sporting events—for decades after the revolution, most sporting activities were viewed as "petty bourgeois" concerns—and since she personally doesn't know how to act in such events, it's good to at least discuss the issue. Athletes may feel the same way.

What's the alternative, one might ask? Should the state not try to say anything about civility and leave it up to spectators and athletes to be "natural," to follow their instincts even if it translates into arrogant and unsportsmanlike behavior and vulgar displays of national pride?[16] Should the Chinese chant "We're number one!" similar to the patriotic crowds at the 1984 Olympics in Los Angeles? To my mind, there's nothing wrong with a bit of official encouragement of civility. If China can pull off the first truly civil Olympics—where spectators cheer for opposing teams, where winning athletes go out of their way to treat losers with respect and dignity, and where ordinary Beijingers treat foreigners with kindness and civility—it will be a memorable Olympics, something that Chinese should feel proud of.[17]

PART THREE
EDUCATION

7. A Critique of Critical Thinking

In 2006, I was asked to serve as an examiner for an oral examination of a doctoral student at a Chinese university. The thesis dealt with the thought of a contemporary British philosopher, and it was an impressively comprehensive and well-documented account of his ideas. But I pointed out that the thesis had more presentation than critical evaluation, and I mentioned something I had learned from one of my teachers at Oxford: that when reading a philosophical text, we should always ask, "Is this argument true or false?" and give reasons for our views.

Another member of the examination panel intervened at this point. He said that it's hard enough for a Chinese student to engage with the thought of a difficult philosopher writing in a foreign language, that the student did an excellent job explaining the philosopher's ideas in Chinese, that his thesis in published form will be an important contribution to the Chinese academic world, and that the student should be rewarded for his effort. I agreed with this. But then the panelist said something more surprising (to me): that according to traditional Chinese ideas, the task of the student is to learn about the world until age forty or so, and only then try to critically examine that world. On the face of it, it was a preposterous statement for a university professor to make. It might seem to justify an uncritical approach to education, with the teachers seen as transmitters of "truth" and students as passive absorbers of knowledge. The political implications might seem equally ominous: that people under forty shouldn't play any substantial role in political decision-making because they're not yet in a capacity to engage in critical evaluation of policies. Upon further thinking, however, I realized that the panelist's view was not as preposterous as it seems. In fact, it may stem from a long tradition of Confucian thinking about education, and that tradition may have some merit in the contemporary world.[1] To illustrate this view, I've written a fictitious dialogue that imagines what Confucius might say if he were brought back to life (with empirical knowledge of the contemporary world) and asked to put forward his views about education.[2] In the present day, he would likely be a university professor rather than a failed politician and informal teacher, so let me preface his family name, Kong, with the formal "Professor." His interlocutor is Professor Hu, an American-trained Chinese liberal thinker.[3] For purposes of this dialogue, both professors teach at Chinese universities, and they have been asked to debate the aims, content, and methods of university education in the humanities for a one-hour televised program in Hong Kong (where people are more free to air their views without worrying about political constraints).

The Aims of Education in the Humanities

Professor Hu: We've been asked to debate different approaches to teaching the humanities in China. Let's think of it as a normative rather than an empirical task. In my view, the main aim of liberal education should be the inculcation of critical thinking skills and attitudes. Students should learn to critically reflect, debate, and challenge old dogmas. That's the key to moving forward. And there's certainly a need for more critical thinking in China!

Professor Kong: We also need to be careful about encouraging criticism. It can be an awfully destructive force. Think about what our students did during the Cultural Revolution: they criticized anything old and "feudal" and the result was a ten-year nightmare for our country.

Professor Hu: That's a ridiculous comparison. The students during the Cultural Revolution were just blindly following Mao's orders to struggle against "counterrevolutionary" views. The teaching of critical thinking is about getting students to think on their own. They should learn to evaluate and criticize traditional views, but not reject them automatically. Do you deny that students should be taught critical thinking skills?

Professor Kong: There's an appropriate time and place for criticism. We also need to inculcate what we might term "empathetic ability," the ability to understand and empathize with other people's feelings and emotions. In Western universities, there's hardly any emphasis on the affective side of education. Too often, liberal education seems to be about making people articulate in defending their own views and criticizing those of others. That may be a useful skill for lawyers, but it's not enough. Surely the proper aim of education isn't just to make people good at winning debates and "proving" that they are right. We also need to think about educating people's emotions. Being fully human is also about being able to put oneself in other people's shoes, to understand what they feel, and to sympathize with other people's needs and desires. My student Zigong once asked me if there's one expression that can be acted upon until the end of our days, and I answered: "Do not impose on others what you yourself do not want" (15.24).

Professor Hu: There are limits to empathy. I can't really know what others are thinking and feeling,[4] and it seems odd if you're suggesting that we should educate people for that purpose.

Professor Kong: There are limits, but it's still possible reflect upon the perspectives of other people. And that ability must be cultivated and nourished in the proper educational environment. Experimental evidence points to important differences between individualistic Americans and relationship-oriented Chinese in that respect.[5] But it's not enough to consider other perspectives: those lacking empathy may just want to be attuned to other people for the purpose of better manipulating them for their own ends. So people must also learn to *care* for others. I do think there's a natural tendency to seek to limit the suffering of others: only the deranged sociopath wouldn't be moved by compassion to save a child about to fall into a well.[6] But that tendency also needs to be cultivated and developed.

We do this by interacting and empathizing with one's intimates: family members, friends, schoolmates, work colleagues, and the relationship between student and teacher. Such feelings can then be extended to others, but with diminished intensity of feeling.[7] That's the key, I believe, to building a harmonious society.

Professor Hu (cringing): Harmony! Is that what you want? You sound just like the government. Their idea of the "harmonious society" seems to be a code word for conformity and loyalty to the state.

Professor Kong: That's not my view. "Exemplary persons value harmony but not conformity; petty persons value conformity but not harmony" (13.23). My ideal is a kind of harmony in diversity: a harmonious community where different kinds of people contribute to making society into a harmonious whole. The aim isn't to eliminate difference, but rather to educate people so that different roles and perspectives contribute to making a harmonious whole, similar to an elaborate dish with distinctive flavors.

Professor Hu: But we also need to encourage students to think about what they're studying, and to criticize wrong views! That's the way to improve, isn't it?

Professor Kong: I agree with the aim of self-improvement. But we should first question ourselves rather than criticize others: "Exemplary persons make demands on themselves, while petty persons make demands on others" (15.21). We can improve ourselves by learning from other people: "Even when walking in the company of two other people, I'm bound to find a teacher. Identifying their strengths, I follow them, and identifying their weaknesses, I reform myself accordingly" (7.22).

Professor Hu: But what if I'm strolling with somebody who advocates mistaken and immoral views? Shouldn't I criticize him?

Professor Kong: It depends on the context. If two enemies criticize each other, they will question each other's motives and the result may be more bad blood. Criticism may be most effective—in the sense that it leads to improvement—if it's founded on affective ties. "People who are critical and demanding yet amicable can be called scholar-apprentices. They need to be critical and demanding with their friends, and amicable with their brothers" (13.28). In a loving relationship with parents, criticism is justified: "In serving your parents, you ought to try to dissuade them from doing wrong" (4.18). But if the same criticism is made to strangers, it will likely be rejected, because it won't be seen as being motivated by affection. It's similar in politics: "Exemplary persons only criticize those above them after they've won their trust. Otherwise, their superiors will feel that they've been maligned" (19.10). And such criticisms should be expressed in the "gentlest way" (4.18) so as to maintain harmonious relationships.

Professor Hu: We're meant to be discussing teaching of the humanities in universities. It sounds like you're suggesting only friends and lovers can criticize each other in the classroom.

Professor Kong: I do think that academic exchanges are more productive if they're founded on strong affective ties between the participants. Even among strangers, however, academic rituals have evolved that help to maintain civility. Consider the academic seminar: we raise our hands, we wait for our turn, we address people by their formal titles, and we refrain from ad hominem attacks. I also think it's a good idea to make some polite points and say what's strong about the paper before launching into criticism. All these practices—more typical in East Asia, perhaps—avoid antagonisms that poison the atmosphere.

Professor Hu: You have an overly romantic view of East Asian–style critical thinking. In reality, the emphasis on "maintaining harmonious relationships"—face-saving, we might say—leads to conformity and sycophancy. That's precisely what we need to challenge in liberal education.

Professor Kong: Of course there's always a gap between the ideal and the reality, but the same is true of Western-style critical thinking: instead of advancing truth as it's supposed to do, it often degenerates into petty debating and humiliation of one's "opponents." How do we deal with the gap between the ideal and the reality? We should remind people of the ideals, and propose ways to realistically implement them while pointing to the dangers of misuse. That's what we can do with regard to teaching the humanities in East Asia. We should promote the ultimate ideal of "harmony in diversity," teach the kind of empathy that promotes harmonious relationships, and emphasize that critical thinking is best carried out in ways that don't undermine affective ties.

Professor Hu: Even if I agreed that we should teach about empathy and promote the ideal of harmony (which I don't—I think the bad consequences of this ideal far too often outweigh the good), I'm not sure why you say it needs to be promoted in higher education. Why not let families and religious authorities take care of it? Universities should focus on critical thinking; surely that's a big enough task.

Professor Kong: Well, I'm worried about the consequences of critical thinking, left alone. As mentioned, it all too often degenerates into hostility and aggression, and needlessly undermines relationships. If teachers simply improve students' critical abilities without improving their empathetic abilities, those critical abilities can be used for immoral purposes: "I detest glib-tongued talkers who overturn states and families" (17.18). In modern societies, with the atomistic pressures of global capitalism, there's an even greater need to educate people so they can nourish harmonious relationships. The family has an important role, but it won't be sufficient. We need to think about how higher education can also contribute to this task.

Professor Hu: In any case, it's not just a pedagogical dispute about how to educate people; there's also a political aim to liberal education: to make better citizens. And the two aims of liberal education go hand in hand. If people's critical faculties are developed, they're more likely to act as concerned and critical citizens who help to sustain and improve democratic political institutions. We want people to critically reflect upon and assert their legitimate interests in the rough and tumble of democratic politics, as well as respect the rights of others to do so. It's widely recognized today that liberal democracy requires a certain degree of active citizenship; otherwise democratic institutions will atrophy, and elites will manage the political process for their own political purposes.

Professor Kong: But aren't universities educating elites? Let's be frank: we're not educating common people in the art of citizenship. Only a minority of talented students go on to university, and perhaps only a minority of those actually develop their critical faculties in the way favored by democratic theorists. So I think we should admit that we're training political elites, not ordinary citizens.

Professor Hu: I don't share your elitism. I worry about this assumption that there are qualitative differences in people's political beliefs. Everyone's political beliefs matter equally and everyone should have the equal right to shape the political process. That's one reason we care about democracy, because everyone's voice matters equally.

Professor Kong: But we're talking about training an elite of students. And surely we think—we hope—that we're making them into more capable political actors, meaning that they're better at thinking about politics than the large mass of people. If my students failed to make any moral and political progress after they were done with my courses, I'd regard myself as a failure.

Professor Hu: Rather than accept the political status quo that deprives large numbers of the opportunity for a decent political education, we should try to equalize opportunities so that everybody can be educated.

Professor Kong: Agreed. "In education, there aren't any social classes" (15.39). Everybody should be given the same educational opportunities regardless of class, race, or sex.[8] As for me, "I've never denied instruction to anyone who, using their own resources, could only afford a gift of dried meat" (7.7). But that's not to say everyone has the same talent: in private, university professors often say that "student so and so is smart and talented," but they rarely come clean and admit that there may be qualitative differences in that respect. And sometimes, the students have more talent than the professors! For example, I don't measure up to my best student, Yan Hui: "From one thing he learns, he deduces ten; from one thing I learn, I only deduce two" (5.9) Nor does every student have the same level of motivation. If it were up to me, I'd "only instruct students who are driven with eagerness" (7.8). In my experience, such students are quite rare. "Yan Hui truly loved learning. He didn't take his anger out on others, nor did he make the same mistake twice. Unfortunately, he was to die young. Nowadays, there's no one—at least, I haven't come across anyone—who truly loves learning" (6.3). Besides, I'm not sure if everybody wants to be educated in the political sense. Some people prefer to stick to family matters, others to religious matters. Even if we lived in a society where nobody was deprived of educational opportunities for financial or other reasons, I suspect you would have only have a selected few with the motivation and talent to play a substantial role in their society's political affairs. And the political purpose of higher education should be to train that elite.[9]

Professor Hu: In my view, the question should be how to distribute political power to the people, not how to train an elite of decision-makers. Societies governed by elites aren't likely to do things for the people. Or perhaps you disagree that politics should be for the people.

Professor Kong: Of course politics should be for the people. "Exemplary persons should cultivate themselves by easing the lot of the common people" (14.42). But we need to accept that only a minority of people will actually govern society.

Professor Hu: Are you against democracy? Don't you think ordinary people should also be participants in the political process?

Professor Kong: Let's not get into that. We're discussing the purpose of education in the humanities for Chinese universities. We're talking about educating a minority of talented students, and we should come clean and say that we're educating future leaders, not ordinary citizens.

Professor Hu: But we also need to think about the overall political system they're supposed to fit into. If they're supposed to be educated to rule in nondemocracies, let's also come clean about that.

Professor Kong: I'm not sure if that's the key question for education. In reality, we need to recognize that people's views seldom have impact on actual policies and that modern countries tend to be ruled be educated elites—democracies are no exception. So the question is, how should we educate that elite? Political education, in my view, should stress the virtue of humility, so that elites recognize their own limits and not try to impose grand schemes upon reluctant members of the public. "Exemplary persons are distinguished but not arrogant" (13.26). The governing elites should also develop their empathetic skills, so that rulers empathize with those who are subject to the effects of policies. We want our political elite to be both intelligent and morally sensitive.

Professor Hu: A fine ideal, but difficult to realize in practice. Look at our East Asian leaders. In Singapore, the political discourse is elitist, and leaders aren't exactly known for their humility. In fact, there's nobody more arrogant than Lee Kuan Yew; he doesn't even bother to conceal his arrogance. And look at our leaders. If they're supposed to be morally sensitive, why are they so corrupt?

Professor Kong: One reason is that they weren't educated in the humanities. As you know, Lee was trained in law, and many of our leaders are trained in engineering. If political leaders only learn about the technical skills of law, engineering, management, and so on, they're missing something important, no matter how smart they may be. Future political leaders should study the great literary and philosophical texts of the past. That's where they learn about the sorts of ethical virtues—humility, sensitivity, temperance, and genuine concern for the people—that they ought to exhibit in political action.

The Content of Education in the Humanities

Professor Hu: Personally, I worry about that approach. If the aim is to teach works that promote democratic citizenship, the students shouldn't just learn about great thinkers and what they wrote. This way of teaching causes students to assume that great texts of philosophy and literature were produced by very special, unique people—the Great Thinkers. The students come to the conclusion that they could never theorize about these questions, and they often just repeat what these scholars wrote without critically examining the texts. Consider the history of our imperial examinations.

Professor Kong: The imperial examinations should have tested for both memorization and independent thinking.[10] Memorization is an important part of the learning process,[11] but at some point we must begin to think about we learned: "Learning without thinking leads to confusion" (2.15). Still, we need to recognize that the Great Works of the past serve as the foundation for future learning: don't you think we should seek out the best the past has to offer? "Loving the past, I am earnest in seeking it out" (7.20). We need to stand on the shoulders of giants.

Professor Hu: That's exactly what worries me. This idea of making students think they're standing "on the shoulders of giants" is detrimental to their potential as good citizens. Students learn the Great Works and when asked to apply the methods they've studied, they balk at the task, thinking, "Who am I to say something about that issue?" Being a good citizen involves being reflective and critical about politics, and teaching the history of Great Works conflicts with this aim. The students feel dwarfed by the stature they ascribe to the Great Thinkers, and so devalue their own abilities as critical thinkers and as critical citizens.

Professor Kong: But why should they come to that conclusion? In sports, we don't get discouraged from doing exercise by watching great athletes: quite the opposite. Usually they inspire us, especially children who dream of making it big. So why not for learning? As for me, I'm impressed by the achievements of the Zhou dynasty: "Such a wealth of culture! I'm with the Zhou" (3.14). If we learn about great minds and moral exemplars of the past, why should that discourage us from thinking further? The right response is to try to improve so we can live up to the ideals!

Professor Hu: With all due respect, that response may be atypical. In my experience, there are better ways to get students to improve than to teach them the classics.

Professor Wong: So what do you suggest instead?

Professor Hu: Rather than teach the history of ideas as the history of scholars, we should teach it as the history of issues and questions, with greater emphasis on popular sources such as newspaper articles.[12]

Professor Kong: Newspaper articles! I think students are far more likely to develop their critical faculties—if that's your aim—by engaging with the works of Great Thinkers. Again, I'm not saying students should simply be asked to memorize classic texts. They should try to understand what the Great Thinkers are saying. It takes great mental effort to grasp the ideas of Great Thinkers, to make sense of the inner logic of classic texts, and critical faculties are improved as a by-product of studying the classics. And I don't see anything wrong with the idea that such works should be approached with a certain degree of reverence and humility. As mentioned, I think it's important to inculcate the virtue of humility, particularly with regards to the future leaders of society.

Professor Hu: But don't you think students should also be encouraged to critically evaluate what the Great Thinkers are trying to say? It's rather optimistic to think that critical faculties will be improved as a by-product of the effort to understand the material.

Professor Kong: It can be dangerous to emphasize critical thinking at an early stage: "Thinking without learning leads to danger" (2.15). Learning the classics is meant to open possibilities, to teach students about what's important in life so that they have the resources to improve the way they lead their lives. Once students have a good grasp of the possibilities, then they can try to sort out for themselves what's important and what's not, to balance the different goods, and to think about the implications for the contemporary world. But if they're encouraged to criticize before they understand what kinds of things are really of value, they might come to lose faith in the possibility of any kind of good life. That's why there's a kind of vulgar relativism—any perspective is as good as any other—so prevalent among university students these days. Or else they might develop an inflated sense of their own capabilities. An all-too-common flaw of students these days is that they jump to conclusions too early, without having an adequate grasp of the depth and complexities of the ideas of the Great Thinkers.[13] That's the sort of intellectual arrogance I'd worry about, both in students and in political leaders. In my view, we need to understand the Great Works and then we can innovate: "Reviewing the old as a means of realizing the new: that's what it means to be a teacher" (2.11). What's the big hurry with critical evaluation? Why should we ask students to do it early on, when they haven't properly understood the texts?[14]

Professor Hu: So it's just a question of staging. We agree upon the end—to further critical thinking—but we disagree about how to implement that end. You think it's best implemented by saving it till the end of the learning process, whereas I think critical skills are best developed if they constitute every stage of the learning process. Certainly at the university level, it's absurd to tell students they shouldn't think about critical evaluation until they've mastered the texts!

Professor Kong: I didn't say "master the texts." My point is that effort should first be directed at understanding the material, rather than evaluating it. I'd say university students should also approach texts that way, especially if it's their first encounter with the texts.

Professor Hu: It still seems like we agree upon the end: to further critical thinking. Our dispute is just about how to get there.

Professor Kong: That's not all. Remember, my view is that critical abilities should be developed only if they contribute to harmonious development, and we need to structure the educational curriculum with this end in mind. An important reason for teaching the Great Works of the past is that they offer insights that can help us to improve our social lives today.

Professor Hu: I wonder if you're overestimating the power of Great Works. Not only do you think they can improve critical abilities, but you also seem to think they can lead to moral growth and social harmony if taught in the right way.

Professor Kong: Reading books is important, but it's not sufficient. Moral education is key, and for that purpose we need to consider the role of poetry and art. Most important, arguably, is musical education. "Be stimulated by the songs, take your stand on the rites and be perfected by music" (8.8). It's by participating in musical activities that we come to feel part of a harmonious community: "Music begins with playing in unison. When it gets into full swing, it's harmonious, clear, and unbroken" (3.23). The right kind of music can bring people together and they will experience a sense of togetherness.

Professor Hu: Yes, that's what happens at rock and roll shows I've attended. But once the music stops, what happens then? The sense of togetherness doesn't last.

Professor Kong: There's music and there's music. "The *shao* music is both superbly beautiful and superbly good. . . . Once I heard the *shao* music, and I couldn't appreciate the taste of meat for three months after that. I had no idea that music could reach such heights!" (3.25, 7.14).[15]

Professor Hu: Perhaps the animal rights activists should play more of that music.

Professor Kong: My point is that musical performers, and maybe even audiences, often undergo more long-lasting moral transformation. If I hear people singing and they sing well, I "ask them to sing again and then join in their harmony" (7.32). Performers try to be sensitive to other people's styles while being aware of their own roles, and together they create beauty and harmony beyond the capacity of any one individual. The ideal of "harmony in diversity" is like an orchestra, where each player contributes to the whole.

Professor Hu: Are you suggesting that musical education should be part of the university curriculum?

Professor Kong: That's exactly what I'm saying! Studying music well requires years of diligent practice. People become experts in their own areas, and when they play together, they gently criticize each other so as to improve the common good. Those musical virtues are the same ones we should encourage if we're training political leaders: diligence, hard work, self-improvement, innovation, and gentle criticism designed to improve the harmonious whole. The performers who master an instrument and perform well in groups are more likely to have the sort of traits that contribute to "harmony in diversity."

Professor Hu: U.S. Secretary of State Condoleezza Rice is an excellent pianist and plays with an ensemble in her spare time.

That didn't stop her from campaigning for the invasion of Iraq. Harmony isn't the first word that comes to mind if we want to describe the results of that invasion.

Professor Kong: Musical education is important, but it's not sufficient. As mentioned, we also need to devote years of study to the Great Works to get the right kind of moral education.[16] If it were up to me, I'd choose political leaders well versed in the classics who also have musical ability, especially the ability to perform well in groups. And I do think universities should promote both traits. We should regard musical education as contributing to moral growth, and it should be taken more seriously as part of the educational curriculum.[17]

Professor Hu (shaking his head in disbelief): I think it's absurd to think that musical education can help to train political leaders.[18] Politics is about the distribution of scarce resources, and politicians must make hard choices between winners and losers. We hope they will make those decisions in principled ways, but whatever they do, it can't be compared to playing in an orchestra and creating a harmonious whole that's greater than the sum of the parts.

Professor Kong: We have different ideas about politics. As I see it, the aim is to balance different goods in appropriate ways so as to produce a more harmonious outcome.[19] It might be tempting for politicians to sacrifice some goods for others—particularly if those goods do not serve their interests—but if our leaders are trained in music, they may be more inclined to think in terms balancing different goods that contribute to the harmony of the community.

The Methods of Education in the Humanities

Professor Hu: Well, I agree that learning isn't just about reading books. But I wonder about your emphasis on music. If we want to promote critical thinking, the Socratic method is more appropriate for higher education in the humanities. The teacher should ask questions, rather than providing the answers and telling the students what to think. The student will eventually realize his or her errors and be open to new ideas. There's no better way to improve critical thinking and prepare the student for democratic citizenship.

Professor Kong: I'm not sure if Socrates should be emulated. He neglected his family so that he could pursue the good life, but my view is that the family is an important part of the good life. "Filial and fraternal responsibility is the root of humanity and compassion" (1.2).

Professor Hu: Whatever. My concern isn't the historical Socrates, it's the method that bears his name. And if the aim is to promote critical thinking, then we should adopt his method in higher education.

Professor Kong: I worry about the Socratic method. Too often, the student can be subject to ruthless scrutiny. The aggressive questioning techniques often lead to the shaming of students and an adversarial approach between teacher and student. As mentioned, we should try to promote critical thinking in a harmonious context, not critical thinking that undermines affective ties. If Socrates had been more concerned with harmony, he wouldn't have made so many enemies, nor would he have paid with his life to defend his ideals.

Professor Hu: But don't you realize the emphasis on harmony undermines the aim of critical thinking? East Asian students in American universities are often very reluctant to express their own views, not to mention criticizing the views of others. In my case, it took several years of immersion in Western liberal universities before I could shed my cautious ways.

Professor Kong: I'm not sure if caution is a bad thing. As I see it, "Exemplary persons should be slow in speech but quick in action" (4.24). Yan Hui, my best student, rarely spoke: "I could speak with Yan Hui for an entire day without his raising an objection, as though he were not very bright. But when I looked into his private conduct after he withdrew, it illustrated perfectly what I'd been saying. Indeed, there was nothing slow about Yan Hui!" (2.9). It's puzzling to me why some teachers seem to emphasize class participation, as though students must be able to immediately grasp and engage with the material being taught. Surely what matters is that the students reflect upon the material and manage to understand it in due course, as well as live their lives in accordance with their new understandings. Why should we encourage students to speak up if they haven't developed good understanding of the material?[20]

Professor Hu: It seems like you're encouraging students to be passive recipients of the teacher's knowledge. They should follow the teachings and never criticize their teachers in class.

Professor Kong: With all due respect, that's not my view. "In striving for humanity and compassion, do not yield even to your teacher" (15.36). The student should try to learn from the teacher, but not at the cost of pursuing humanity and compassion. If the student really thinks the teacher is espousing mistaken or immoral views, he or she can say so.

Professor Hu: I doubt the students will dare to criticize the teacher if they're supposed to stand in awe of the teacher's superior knowledge and not participate in class until they have a good grasp of that knowledge.

Professor Kong: The student shouldn't stand in awe of the teacher. Rather, "The younger generation should be held in awe. After all, how do we know that those yet to come will not surpass our contemporaries? It's only when one reaches forty or fifty years of age and still has done nothing of note that we should withdraw our sense of awe" (9.23).

Professor Hu: Fine words, but how can we encourage students to develop their critical skills if they're supposed to promote harmony and refrain from putting forward uninformed views?

Professor Kong: It's possible. For example, the classroom can be divided into groups. The teacher can pose a question, let the students debate among themselves, and then group representatives can present their conclusions to the whole class. The teacher can then evaluate the various conclusions in front of the whole class. No individual student need take responsibility for uninformed views if the teacher criticizes the conclusions of the whole group. Students' critical skills are improved when they debate among themselves, and they can also learn from the teacher's evaluation of the group conclusions. All this can be done without undermining group harmony.

Professor Hu: The Socratic method needn't undermine group harmony. If teachers are sensitive, they can criticize the students' views without embarrassing them, for example, by praising their effort and guiding them toward the answer by different questions. What's distinctive about the Socratic method is that knowledge is elicited by means of the teacher's questioning—the teacher questions the student rather than asserts and defends his or her own views—but such questioning need not be rude or unpleasant. More than that: the teacher can model "modest" questioning. If that's the way to improve critical thinking, then that's the way to go.

Professor Kong: In your view, the main task of the teacher is to improve the student's critical abilities. The teacher is like a technician—

Professor Hu (interrupting): Now you're being unfair. I recognize that the teacher has more experience and insight than the student. If the teacher didn't have more expertise than the student, then he or she wouldn't be a teacher. And during the learning process, the students learn knowledge as well as improving their critical skills. They may also learn certain "thin" virtues like tolerance as a by-product of watching the teacher in action. But teachers should refrain from espousing their own views to the extent possible; they should let students make up their own minds and settle difficult questions without being told how to do so.

Professor Kong: We have different conceptions of the role of the teacher. In your view, the teacher is supposed to be an intellectual authority, but she should transmit knowledge and promote critical thinking while trying to be as neutral as possible. In my view, the teacher is supposed to be an ethical model, not just a source of intellectual wisdom. "Being strong, resolute, honest, and reticent is close to compassion and humanity" (13.27).[21] When teachers present material, they should do their best to tell students what they take to be correct understandings, and they should try to steer students on the right path. We need to be concerned about the moral character of students. It's not just a matter of improving their critical abilities and knowledge of the world.

Professor Hu: And the teacher should require the student to hold the moral views of the teacher.

Professor Kong: No. "Exemplary persons make demands on themselves, while petty persons make demands on others" (15.21).

Professor Hu: But professors must make demands on students! We're supposed to evaluate what they do.

Professor Kong: It's also the other way around. Once they have good understanding of the material, the students should evaluate the teacher. They should raise objections so that teachers can improve. Admittedly, they don't always do that. Even Yan Hui didn't question me as much as he should have: "Yan Hui was of no help to me. There is nothing I said that he didn't like" (11.4). Of course, he died young; he was only thirty-one. He would have been more helpful had he lived longer. He was so modest (*voice begins to crack*) . . .

Professor Hu: I'm sorry.

Professor Kong: I can't get over his death. My students ask me, "Sir, why do you grieve with such abandon?" I reply, "If I don't grieve for him, then for whom?" (11.10).

Professor Hu: I'm really sorry . . . (*waits a few seconds*) But the point I was trying to make, if you'll allow me, is that we need to evaluate students in the sense that we need to grade what they do. And it's unclear to me how we can grade "improvement of moral character."

Professor Kong (*regaining composure*): Here's what I do. On exams, I pose an ethical dilemma and ask the student to think about implications from different points of view. Those who do this well are more likely to have empathetic ability. At the very least, I can filter out the dogmatic and demagogic personalities—the "petty persons"—who seem congenitally unable to understand moral complexities and consider matters from other points of view, traits that are crucial for the pursuit of harmony. Mao, Hitler, and Stalin would have failed such questions.

Professor Hu: OK, you'd filter out some, but not the very clever candidates who have the intellectual ability to consider matters from different points of view without the motivation or desire to do so in real life. So I don't think examination questions can test for "character" in ways that matter.

Professor Kong: Again, music is crucial. As I say to my students, "Why don't you study the songs? Reciting the songs can arouse your sensibilities, strengthen your powers of observation, enhance your ability to get on with others, and allow you to express your grievances" (17.9). If my students do well in musical performances, I think it reflects well on their moral character.

Professor Hu (*incredulous*): So you think students in the humanities should be graded according to their musical ability?

Professor Kong: At the very least, we should value musical ability when we're choosing which students to admit to university. We can also do encourage students to participate in group musical events; that's an important way to instill the motivation to pursue harmony. And we have other ways of judging the student's moral character, such as letters of recommendation.[22]

Professor Hu: You're assuming teachers are good judges of moral character. That's a bit of an arrogant assumption, don't you think?

Professor Kong: Yes, well, when I teach, I appeal to the examples of the great teachers of the past.[23] I try to avoid talking about myself; that would indeed seem arrogant.

Professor Hu: But *you're* the one doing the evaluating. So there's an assumption that you're a good judge of moral character; you can't always hide behind others. So how do we know that you're a good judge of moral character? How do we measure that?

Professor Kong: The best measure is the way I'm actually leading my life: It needs to reflect the moral ideals I espouse in the classroom. At the very least, there shouldn't be a radical inconsistency: If an authority leads an ethically problematic life, we'd wonder about the validity of the ideas expressed by that person. That's why teachers should be held to higher moral standards than common people. I regret to report I still have a long way to go: "As far as realizing the life of the exemplary person, I have accomplished little" (7.33). But I won't give up trying: "To quietly persevere in storing up what is learned, to study without flagging, to instruct others without growing weary—is this not me?" (7.2)

[*Director of television program informs participants that the taping is over.*]

Professor Hu (*looking at his watch*): I'm growing a little weary, I must confess. Perhaps we should retreat to our quarters.

Professor Kong (*surprised*): What! We haven't started yet! I'm inviting you for drinks. Let's have a real conversation! After that, we'll go for karaoke.

8. Teaching Political Theory in Beijing

Few Western academics would aspire to teach political theory in an authoritarian setting. Surely the free, uninhibited flow of discussion is crucial to our enterprise. When I tell my Western friends that I gave up a tenured, high-paying job in relatively free Hong Kong for a contractual post at Tsinghua University in Beijing, they think I've gone off my rocker. I explain that it's a unique opportunity for me: it's the first time Tsinghua has hired a foreigner in the humanities since the revolution; Tsinghua trains much of China's political elite, and I might be able to make a difference by teaching that elite; the students are talented, curious, hardworking, and it's a pleasure to engage with them; the political future of China is wide open, and I'll be well placed to observe the changes when they happen. Still, I do not deny that teaching political theory in China has been challenging. This has to do partly with political constraints. But it's not all about politics. Even if China became a Western-style liberal democracy overnight, there would still be cultural obstacles to deal with. In this chapter, I will discuss some of these political and cultural challenges.

The Political Challenges

The willingness to put up with political constraints depends partly upon one's history. In my case, I had taught at the National University of Singapore in the early 1990s. There, the head of the department was a member of the ruling People's Action Party. He was soon replaced by another head, who asked to see my reading lists and informed me that I should teach more communitarianism (the subject of my doctoral thesis) and less John Stuart Mill. Naturally, this made me want to do the opposite. Strange people would show up in my classroom when I spoke about "politically sensitive" topics, such as Karl Marx's thought. Students would clam up when I used examples from local politics to illustrate arguments. It came as no surprise when my contract was not renewed.

In comparison, China is a paradise of academic freedom. Among colleagues, anything goes (in Singapore, most local colleagues were very guarded when dealing with foreigners). Academic publications are surprisingly free: there aren't any personal attacks on leaders or open calls for multiparty rule, but particular policies such as the household registry system, which limits internal mobility, are subject to severe criticism. In 2004, state television, for the first time in history, broadcast the U.S. presidential elections live, without any obvious political slant. (I suspect that the turmoil surrounding the 2000 U.S. presidential elections, along with the 2003 U.S.-led invasion of Iraq, discredited U.S.-style democracy among many Chinese, and the government has less to fear from the model.) More surprisingly, perhaps, I was not given any explicit (or implicit, as far as I could tell) guidance regarding what I could teach at Tsinghua. My course proposals have been approved as submitted.

In spring 2005, I offered one graduate course titled Topics in Contemporary Political Philosophy. It was a small seminar, and students freely drew upon "sensitive" cases such as Tibet to illustrate theories about self-determination and multiculturalism. My experiences of political constraints came outside the classroom. One was self-imposed. A student asked me to address a "salon" at Tsinghua on the topic of democracy. I consulted some trusted friends, who suggested that I stay away from it. I found out later that the salon was just a discussion group among graduate students in philosophy, not a trap, and that my fears were likely ungrounded.

I did have one experience with censorship imposed from outside. I gave an interview to a Chinese newspaper that is widely read in intellectual circles. The interview dealt with China's role in international affairs, and I made some critical comments about the U.S.-led invasion of Iraq that were published. However, I also made some comments about the ancient thinker Mencius—I argued that he justified "punitive expeditions" that were functionally similar to modern-day humanitarian interventions—that were not published. The Chinese government does not support any infringements on state sovereignty, and the newspaper probably worried that readers would draw implications for contemporary debates. To my surprise, the editor of the newspaper phoned me to apologize, explaining that the article was "reviewed" by a party cadre and that he had no hand in the matter. He also offered to publish the interview in full in an academic publication that would not be subject to the same sorts of constraints. In Singapore, by contrast, it is hard to imagine that the editor of the progovernment *Straits Times* would apologize to contributors whose views were censored: public humiliation is a more common tactic for dealing with those who do not toe the party line.

I presented the same argument about Mencius and just war in extended form at an informal seminar at the headquarters of one of China's main computer manufacturers. An interesting feature of China's academic scene is that some prominent reformist intellectuals obtain material support from sympathetic capitalists to organize seminars outside the formal university structure. These seminars are meant to be relatively free-flowing and less subject to political constraints. However, I was advised to delete the part of my paper that drew implications for the mainland's relations with Taiwan (I argue that Mencius would justify armed intervention against Taiwan only if its government systematically deprived people of the right to subsistence). I agreed to do so, thinking that the benefits of exchanging ideas on the topic of just war with a group of influential Chinese intellectuals outweighed the cost of censorship. Besides, the full, uncensored version of my article was to appear in my forthcoming book (*Beyond Liberal Democracy*, published in the fall of 2006). It seems that the Chinese authorities rarely care about English-language material, which allows more scope for intellectual freedom.

In fall 2005 I taught two courses. I was invited to co-teach a course on contemporary Western political philosophy at Beijing University, China's other prominent university (located next to Tsinghua). It has a history of political turmoil, and one might expect political constraints to be more severe: after the student-led political uprising in spring 1989, the government forced Beijing University students to undergo one year of compulsory military training.[1] Once again, however, I could teach anything—with one exception: Marxist thought. I was told that this area is still too sensitive, the government won't welcome foreigners putting forward alternative interpretations of Marxism. I was also told that students won't welcome Marxist teachings under any guise: they've been subject to enough, and they want to learn something else (a former student at Beijing University told me how she used to reserve her seats in the library by putting her Marxist philosophy lessons on her chair, secure in the in knowledge that no one would bother to steal her books; two decades later, I'm told, the practice has not changed).

After the first class, a student stayed behind to ask, in fluent English, if he could audit the course. He introduced himself as a graduate student at the university that is administered by the Central (Chinese Communist) Party School. I asked (half jokingly) if I could give lectures there, and he said that foreigners weren't allowed. Then I said he'd be welcome to audit my course if he was interested in the material. He did seem genuinely curious, though I wondered why he would tell me his party affiliation. The next class dealt with Jeremy Bentham's utilitarianism, and I found myself scanning for his facial reaction when I mentioned Bentham's disillusionment with benevolent despotism (he could not find monarchs to adopt his Panopticon proposal) and subsequent "conversion" to democracy. After the lecture, I asked an academic friend if the party would send spies to my classroom. He laughed and told me that it was normal for students from the party university to audit classes at Beijing University, that I'm regarded as an academic and nothing else. He also told me not to be so paranoid and reminded me that China's totalitarian days are long gone.

At Tsinghua, I teach a graduate seminar on Just and Unjust War. The "realist paradigm"—the idea that states are motivated by nothing other than self-interest in international affairs and that morality is not and should not be used to judge the international behavior of states—seems to be dominant in China, and I think there's a need to consider theories that allow for moral evaluation of wars, especially as China becomes a more dominant power in the international arena. After the first class, the same student from the party school stayed behind to ask if he could audit that class too. I agreed.

The second session dealt with the topic of humanitarian intervention. It is hard for many Chinese to believe that any sort of intervention might be justified on moral grounds. I asked how they would feel if a massacre occurred in their neighbor's home—say, a father killing his children—and they had the power to make a difference. Most agreed they would intervene. I drew a comparison with massacres in other states, asking if it would make a moral difference if it were a neighboring state. Most agreed there could be a moral case for intervention, even for a nonneighboring state. Then I discussed the case of the Rwanda genocide, noting that Bill Clinton says his greatest regret is that he did not intervene to stop the genocide. So far so good.

Next, we moved on to a discussion of Kosovo. Not a single student seemed to believe that NATO's intervention was justified. "Only" a few thousand had died before the intervention; it wasn't anything like a Rwanda-style genocide. I tried to explain the context, that Europeans had been watching the Serbs carrying out ethnic cleansing for several years, and most thought they were prepared to do it again. But I doubt that anybody was persuaded. Then the student from the party school raised questions about sovereignty. He noted the Chinese view that human rights should not have priority over sovereignty. I replied that human rights—or at least, the functional equivalent of human rights, whatever we want to call it—is what gives the point to sovereignty. Sovereignty only has moral value because it serves (usually) to protect the fundamental human rights of people in the state, and it loses its value once the state infringes upon, or fails to protect, those rights. I asked the student whether I, as a leader of a sovereign state, could kill millions of my people, then be justified in telling you not to intervene because you'd be trampling on my sovereignty. He agreed that I could not do so. I then asked him what moral value sovereignty could have if not its contribution to securing the fundamental rights of people in the state. He seemed genuinely puzzled, and then repeated out loud, to the whole class, "What you're saying is very different from what we've learned."

The student noted that my view on justified intervention is also espoused by defenders of the U.S.-led invasion of Iraq. I had been discussing Michael Walzer's theory of just war, and I noted that Walzer's theory would bar intervention in this case, because there was another alternative to war (the UN inspectors), and war should not be launched unless other alternatives are seriously pursued. I reminded him of the other conditions of just war, and I noted that in most cases today measures such as economic sanctions might be more appropriate to deal with injustices in foreign lands.

He then asked me if I thought economic sanctions should have been used in China after June 4, 1989. I was shocked. It was the first time any student had mentioned that fateful day in a classroom setting (as opposed to private discussion). I couldn't ignore the question; neither could I answer it directly. I mumbled a bit, until finally I thought of the "right" answer: that our seminar deals with the morally justified use of violence, and that nobody argues that foreign powers should have intervened militarily after June 4, because the costs of intervening against a nuclear power would likely outweigh the benefits. It's the same reason no sane person calls for military intervention against Russia to protect the people of Chechnya. Another student intervened and noted people weren't killed on June 4 for ethnic or racial reasons, so the case doesn't compare to most cases of humanitarian intervention. I wanted to respond that the moral case for foreign intervention turns more on the number of people killed than on the reason they were killed,[2] but I held my tongue. The seminar ended, and on the way out, I thanked the visiting student for his contributions to making the discussion more interesting. He said, "You're the one we should thank. We hope for more debate, and we want to hear more of your own views."

The next day, I sent an email to the whole class that included the following paragraph:

> Next Monday, we will pursue the discussion of Walzer's views on the conditions for just war. For discussion, we will debate the following hypothetical issue. Assume you're advising the leader of a state. In your neighboring state, one million people (members of a vulnerable minority group) are at serious risk of being massacred. Your country probably has the power to intervene to protect the minority group and prevent the genocide. However, the UN would not support intervention. What do you do? We can split the debate into two halves, and the students will switch positions at the halfway point. This way, you

will be able to look at both sides of the question. Remember, this is an academic seminar, the aim is to learn and critically evaluate arguments, not to defend particular political positions.

In the debate, the students raised an interesting argument not covered in the reading: namely, that most soldiers sign up to defend national interests, and it would be hard to justify putting their lives at risk in another country if the intervention does not benefit their own country in any way (in other words, the convergence of national and humanitarian interests makes the moral case for humanitarian intervention stronger, not weaker). Of course, I was also curious about the performance of the student from the party school. He did well representing both sides of the debate, including a defense of the view that human rights abuses can justify infringements of sovereignty. He also steered clear of provocative comments.

In subsequent classes, I learned to relax with the students and to go over the material without worrying about sensitive political implications. We discussed Christian, Realist, Confucian, and Islamic perspectives on just and unjust war, with the students doing presentations and debating more issues among themselves. The student from the party school did an excellent presentation on the Maoist perspective. In debate, he made thoughtful and constructive comments, as one might expect of a talented student. To the extent he had a political motivation, it seemed to be the desire to learn theories that may be useful for China's future reform.

Let me sum up these reflections on the challenges of political constraints. Constraints on writing are easier to tolerate if censorship is carried out in an open and apologetic manner and if there are alternative opportunities for publication within one's country and outside. Constraints on teaching are easier to tolerate if one has the experience of more severe constraints, but it is difficult to prevent students from steering discussion into precisely those sensitive areas that may lead to trouble. The constraints on political talk may also lead to unjustified paranoia, particularly for new arrivals uncertain of the boundaries of political correctness. Perhaps I should be more positive. The very fact of operating in a restrictive political environment does have some psychological benefits. If political authorities care about what I do, then I do not have to worry about the practical utility of my work. It is commonly remarked that Russian intellectuals felt somewhat demoralized after the Soviet Union collapsed, because people seemed to have lost interest in their work. If their dreams had been realized, then they should not have felt demoralized. But there usually remains a large gap between one's ideals and the reality, even after the revolution, and it is something to worry about if political freedom means that critical intellectuals begin to feel irrelevant.

The Cultural Challenges

It's not all about politics. With or without political constraints, there will be cultural particularities in different settings to which the foreign teacher needs to adjust. I will set aside such philosophical issues as the commensurability of terms to focus on the personal issues. I've had to adjust to the Chinese language as well as to different methods of teaching and ways of dealing with colleagues and students. These challenges require strategies that are not necessarily specific to teachers of political theory.

The first question I'm usually asked is "What language do you teach in?" I wish I could say that I lecture in Chinese, but I use mainly English. The proportion of Chinese is increasing as my academic oral Chinese improves, and I set aside time for discussion in Chinese. I also take questions in Chinese (usually answering in English) because I can understand most of them. The key word is "most." If the questioner has a heavy regional accent or gives a long speech on a topic only distantly related to the teaching material, then I may not be able to catch everything. What do I do in such cases?

Sometimes, I ask the questioner to repeat the question. Occasionally, however, even that doesn't work. Then I answer the part of the question that I understood. Or I make inferences and answer what seems like a pertinent question. At Beijing University, I co-teach the course with a Chinese professor, and I may let him take the question. Of course, there's a risk of missing interesting details,[3] but relying on a translator would be too disruptive of the ebb and flow of discussion. The challenge of lecturing in a foreign language environment also affects my syllabus.[4] In my first term, the course was an exercise in comparative political philosophy. I took certain themes—such as utilitarianism, liberalism, and communitarianism—and discussed both Western and Chinese thinkers who shed light on those themes. But my lectures on the Chinese thinkers did not go well. I could tell that many students felt they weren't learning much. Some of the students had memorized the classics, most were familiar with the history of interpretations, and they probably felt that a Western political philosopher should be teaching Western thinking.[5] So I've changed my approach. At Beijing University, I use the excellent Chinese translation of Will Kymlicka's *Contemporary Political Philosophy* as the main text.[6] And to fill in some of the required background, I lecture on Western historical thinkers before discussing Kymlicka's themes (for example, I lecture on Mill and Bentham before looking at Kymlicka's chapter on utilitarianism). I draw some comparisons with Chinese thinkers along the way (for example, comparing Mozi's ideas with utilitarianism), but less than last term. For my seminar on just war at Tsinghua, I do not spend time introducing the thoughts of well-known Chinese thinkers. I dive right into comparison and critical evaluation, on the assumption that most students are familiar with the basics.

One of the benefits of being a teacher in China—and even more so, a professor at a well-known university—is the relatively high social status that one enjoys. The Cultural Revolution's antipathy to intellectual elites seems to be long forgotten. Tsinghua, once the bastion of ultraleft politics, now has a statue of Confucius on campus. The state officially recognizes the social importance of teachers by means of such policies as travel discounts for teachers.

The high social esteem translates into understandings of the teaching profession that have challenged my prior ways of doing things. In the past, I've tried not to let my own views color my presentation of the material (though a certain bias always shows through). I've tried to present the ideas of various thinkers in their best possible light, then let students debate and make up their own minds. In China, however, such an approach invariably disappoints students. I've been told over and over again to state my own views. Students want their teachers to present and defend their own outlooks, perhaps because they are supposed to serve as exemplars to follow (or reject) in the traditional Confucian mode. In my class on Mill's utilitarianism, for example, a student asked me whether the government should promote higher or lower pleasures or both. Normally, I would have asked him for his own views, but that would have made him unhappy. So I said any decent government should try to enact measures that provide means of subsistence for the poor as well as policies that allow for a flourishing intellectual life. I didn't elaborate, and I avoided hard questions about limited resources and trade-offs between values.

The high social status of professors also translates into distinctive ways of dealing with students outside class. For one thing, the professor is supposed to be both an intellectual authority and an ethical person who cares about the student's emotional development. Thus, my one-on-one encounters with students typically begin with questions about the student's well-being and that of family members. At the end of term, I invite the students to my home, and they pepper my family members with questions. The students, for their part, sometimes bring gifts from home after long vacations. It would be the height of rudeness to refuse a gift. In early September, the whole country celebrates Teachers' Day, and students often present their teachers with flowers. On that day, the side streets of the Beijing University campus are lined with flower sellers.

The boundaries between private and public are challenged in other ways. Graduate students do much more than help with research. They also help with personal tasks: in my case, the department appointed a graduate student to help me with my visa and settling-in procedures. On the other hand, the boundary between economic and academic spheres is more rigidly enforced. I've asked graduate students to help me with classical Chinese. We do regular tutorials, going through the classical texts slowly and carefully. No matter how much I try, they refuse to be compensated. So I've had to exchange their work for work of my own, such as help with their English studies. The truth is, that what I do for them rarely matches what they do for me. They claim that they're also learning during the tutorials, but they're probably just being polite. I'd almost prefer a market relationship that would be fair for both sides, but perhaps the idea of the teacher paying the student to teach the teacher is just too far removed from ordinary conceptions of proper roles.

This is not to deny that graduate students need money. They are paid a stipend of US$50 or so per month by the university. Not surprisingly, they don't buy English-language books. I was shocked at first by the unabashed flouting of intellectual copyright laws: students openly sell or distribute photocopied versions of whole books. But it's unrealistic to expect them to pay for English-language books (Chinese-language books, in contrast, are much cheaper, typically around US$2 or $3 per book). For what it's worth, fellow authors, I lend my own books to students so that they can be photocopied.

Lest there be any misunderstanding, I would like to emphasize that norms of respect and cordiality and the concern for affective well-being do not necessarily mean sacrificing intellectual rigor. True, aggressive debate in seminars is frowned upon. I was invited to present a lecture on communitarianism last year, and the host professor proceeded to comment on my views, noting that Western-style communitarianism should be seen as an extension of Western-style liberalism. He hit a sore spot. I've made a (not-very-successful) career of trying to distinguish communitarianism from liberalism, and I jumped in, arguing that he was "wrong." I felt bad after. The professor is a kind and polite elderly scholar. I was not invited again.

I've since learned to observe norms of cordiality during the course of debate. In my political theory class at Beijing University, my co-teacher might claim that he needs to "supplement" some of what I've just said. He goes on to criticize my views and defend his own preferred alternatives. I then reply that I need to "supplement" some of what he has just said. This way, we can argue without, Oxford-style, tearing each other to shreds. And I refer to my fellow teacher as "Teacher,"[7] never using his full name in class.

The students also raise questions in class. They are no slouches: it's probably harder to be admitted, statistically speaking, into Tsinghua and Beijing University than into leading American universities. My students are supposed to be leaders of society: I'm told that the Communist Party student members at Tsinghua prepare the educational curriculum for all the young Communists in China. They are intellectually confident and often well versed in the Chinese and Anglo-American (if not French and German) philosophical traditions.

Nonetheless, they often communicate their most critical comments via email, not in the classroom. Of course, the e-mails are cordial, but the substance is often harshly critical of what I've said in class.

There are other out-of-classroom settings for debate. To promote affective ties between students and professors, my department at Tsinghua organizes weekend excursions. This term [fall 2005], thirty-five graduate students and four "young" (under fifty) professors took a three-hour bus ride to the foot of the Great Wall. We climbed the "wild" part of the Wall and settled down for an excellent dinner of local produce. The dinner involved lots of drinking, with the professors going from table to table to toast the students.[8] To my surprise, the group then proceeded to debate the merits of Alasdair MacIntyre's critique of liberal modernity. Two graduate students had prepared papers, which they read before discussion. Another group of tourists was engaged in Dionysian revelries just outside our dining-seminar room, and some students could not help glancing over, but it was an otherwise orderly debate. I was grilled with questions about communitarianism, even though I had consumed my share of spirits. The next morning, I told our team leader that I was surprised that such a serious debate had taken place after so much drinking. He responded, "It's because of the drinking that we could have this kind of debate."

Let me sum up these reflections on the challenges of cultural difference. Teaching in a foreign language environment is perhaps the biggest challenge of all. Ideally, the foreign teacher would converse in the local language that best lends itself to critical exchanges, but this may require years of immersion. In the short-to-medium term, there may be less-than-ideal compromises, such as the "passive bilingualism approach" (each speaks in the preferred language) that also characterizes some European Community meetings. In China, the long tradition of high esteem for learning is an obvious blessing for the teacher, though it means that teachers (and students) have nonacademic obligations that go beyond the usual Western ideas of teacher-student relationships. But these obligations can also be a source of emotional gratification. And intellectual activity doesn't stop at the classroom door: fueled by the right sorts of rituals, critical debate with teachers and students can take place in various settings without anybody losing face.

Postscript: A Talk at the Party School (October 2005)

A few weeks into term, the student from the party school phoned to ask if I'd give a talk there. I thought you said foreigners can't go there, I responded. He said that they were trying to change that policy and he thought that students from the school should be exposed to the ideas of foreign professors. He then asked if I could do it the next day. I said sure, I'd love to, but what should I talk about? He said I should give a lecture on how to improve one's English. I laughed and said I know nothing about the topic, I learned English as a kid, that's not a very useful lesson for Chinese students. He responded, come on, you're a professor, you'll think of something. I'll pick you up tomorrow at 5:00 p.m.

The next day, we took a taxi from Tsinghua and he told me it was the first time that the students had invited a Westerner to give a talk at the Central Party School.[9] It took much effort to get me invited; he had to get approval from the vice-president of the school. We'd have to proceed slowly, by beginning with a less controversial topic than political philosophy. I asked about his family, and he said that he was from Qufu, Confucius's hometown. I said I'd been there, and he nodded: "Yes, I know, we checked on the Internet and we saw pictures of you addressing the Confucian university." He also told me that one of his professors had read my book *East Meets West* (the last chapter puts forward a constitutional proposal for post-Communist China). When I showed my surprise, he told me that their classes are very open at the party school; they can talk about anything without restrictions, even more so than at Tsinghua University.[10]

When we arrived at the school, he took me on a tour. He told me that the university is directly administered by the Central Committee of the Communist Party. It is Beijing's most beautiful university campus, with an unnamed lake in the middle.[11] One of the buildings once housed the Japanese military's headquarters during the occupation (now it houses a party periodical). We encountered a group of Tibetan-speaking young women, and my student noted, "Those are the future rulers of Tibet." As I waited in line at the student cafeteria, I received the sort of looks—half bemused, half curious—that I had encountered only in the most remote parts of the Chinese countryside.

The university has about six hundred graduate students (no undergraduates), and several have experience serving in government. My student, for example, worked in the economic affairs bureau of a local government and had traveled abroad extensively. About a hundred students came to my talk. As I walked in to the hall, the largely female audience giggled, and my student informed them that I was married to a woman from China. The student—now I call him my friend—introduced me as a political philosopher and said I'd talk about learning English. My presentation consisted of tips I'd learned during the ongoing process of learning Chinese, and I just substituted "English" for "Chinese" in my mind. I explained the need for a Middlebury College–style language school in China, where students would be forced to speak English during a period of at least two months.[12] I said that if I were a capitalist—"which I'm not"—I would invest money to build that kind of school in Beijing. I also said that it helps to have an English-speaking boyfriend or girlfriend. I noted that advanced students should not simply learn about economics and politics, but also literature, poetry, and philosophy, in order to develop appreciation for the culture that is expressed in the language.

The discussion period began with some questions about learning English. One student asked whether she should listen to the British Broadcasting Channel or Voice of America. I replied that because VOA is American government propaganda, she would enjoy the learning process more by listening to the BBC. Another student asked which social science book she should read to improve her English. I replied that she should read what she enjoys, and improving her language skills would be a by-product. I asked her major, and she said "party-building", to some laughter in the crowd. I suggested that she could read some of Marx's works in English. (Only a fraction of Marx's works have been translated into Chinese.) A female student then asked for more practical tips on learning English. Having run out of ideas, I repeated my point about finding an English-speaking boyfriend. My host interjected that the young man (in military garb) sitting next to the questioner is her boyfriend.

To my relief, the questions then shifted to political philosophy. I was asked about communitarianism, Marxism, and Confucianism, and I did my best to provide academic responses, steering clear of overt political content. The discussion took place in a mixture of English and Chinese, and it was a genuine pleasure to discuss ideas with such curious students. After the lecture, a couple of female students stayed behind for further discussion. One student criticized Westerners who read Sunzi's *The Art of War* to get ideas for defeating China in war. I said of course that's not a good reason to read the Chinese classics. Then she asked the other student if she would leave the country and find an English-speaking man and not return to China. I interjected with the thought that she might find a man and return to China with him, as in my case.

My student/friend (along with two other students) accompanied me by taxi back to the Tsinghua University campus. We had the usual argument about whether the Beijing haze was fog or pollution. They dropped me off, and I asked how they would be getting back to their campus. They said they'd be taking public transport. I felt guilty, saying there was no need to accompany me all the way back to Tsinghua. But deep down, I was grateful that my hosts had been so gracious.

Another Postscript (January 2008)

I wrote the preceding for *Dissent*, a small, socialist, U.S.-based periodical that is read mainly by academics and left-wing intellectuals. Partly, I wrote it to let my Western friends know what I was doing and partly, I guess, to justify what I was doing. China is not as totalitarian as it may seem, I meant to argue, and there are other positive reasons for teaching here. I worried a bit that word of the article would leak back to China and get me in trouble (the main fear is that the authorities won't renew my visa and I'd have to leave the country), but I didn't really expect anything to happen. As far as I know, nobody reads *Dissent* in China.

What I didn't anticipate was the power of the Web. As soon as the article was put on *Dissent*'s website, it generated a flood of responses. I was getting several emails a day from students, academics, journalists, and diplomats. Some had questions (e.g., how can I get a teaching job in China?), some related similar experiences (e.g., teaching political theory under the constraints of apartheid in South Africa), and quite a few wanted to meet me (including one "diplomat" from the U.S. embassy who was "interested in gaining a better understanding of the overall experiences and trends related to American foreign experts living and working in China"; I told him I was Canadian and he didn't pursue it). Encouraged by the enthusiastic reaction to my article, I decided to write a whole book that combines the personal with the theoretical, drawing on my experience living and working in China (hence this book).

Even more surprising, the article was translated into Chinese (without my permission) and posted on major Chinese language websites, some of which register more than one million hits per day. Some parts were left out—such as the line "the political future of China is wide open, and I'll be well placed to observe the changes" and the anecdote about the student at Beijing University who reserves her seats in the library by putting her Marxist philosophy books on her chair—but most of it was faithfully translated, including the discussion about June 4 in the classroom. Overnight, it seems, my colleagues, students, and family members (including those living outside of Beijing) had heard about the article. The article also led to interviews in the Chinese press, including a long article about my experience that was published in *Bingdian* (Freezing Point), the influential weekly that had sacked its liberal editor a few months earlier. The article was titled "Foreigner Teaches Politics at Tsinghua," and it was a surprisingly frank account of the challenges I've faced teaching here.

I regret to report that my article and the subsequent publicity was not always favorably received by my Chinese colleagues and students. I was told that I'm being manipulated by the Chinese media, that I'm being used as an example to trumpet the "new freedoms" in China and that I shouldn't talk to the press. They told me that I have more breathing space as a foreigner teaching in China and that I shouldn't make it seem that China is a "paradise of academic freedom." One of my students said something a bit intimate about me, and he explained, "See, we also talk about you behind your back." It seemed, for while, that students were more cautious when they were around me, perhaps worried that I'd write about them in the press. More worrisome, I was told that I might get the party school student-friend in trouble once the authorities find out about him.

Of course, I tried to defend myself. The line about academic free-dom clearly refers to the comparison with my previous experience in Singapore (my article was picked up and distributed on some opposition websites in Singapore). And the article discusses my own experiences with censorship; obviously my intention isn't to glorify Chinese-style aca-demic freedom. Perhaps I should have noted that foreigners have more freedom in China, but some Chinese scholars like He Weifang and Liu Junning have taken courageous public stances on controversial issues, in fact, far more daring than anything I've done. Most important, I had shown the article to my student-friend before it was published in order to get his OK. If he had refused, I wouldn't have published the article.

I've also had to be cautious in my dealings with Western journalists. Unlike Chinese journalists, they do not always check quotes before they are published, which has led to some mistakes. And their favorite topic (understandably, perhaps, given their trade) seems to be censor-ship in China; what I say about the need to humanize China rarely seems to get published in the Western press.[13] Of course I've had con-tinued run-ins with the Chinese censors. Anything concrete about re-forming political institutions—such as the proposal to select deputies for the Chinese People's Political Consultative Committee by means of meritocratic examinations—gets shot down. But there are ways around the restrictions. The Internet is much more free than the published page: for example, an earlier version of chapter 1 published in *Dissent* was translated and distributed on several Chinese websites without any changes,[14] even though it touches on many sensitive issues.[15] Some-times, one can express the same critical point using more indirect lan-guage (this practice goes back hundreds of years in Chinese history). Or else, it's just a matter of being patient. The few months before the Party Congresses held every five years are traditionally characterized by political infighting and the rest of us keep our heads down during that time. So it came as no surprise that the Chinese translations of two of my books have been put on hold until the end of the Seventeenth Party Congress, held in October 2007. My books should be out shortly there-after, so what's the big deal?[16]

What about the cultural challenges? The good news is that my aca-demic Chinese has improved. At conferences, I present papers and comment in Chinese. At Tsinghua, I usually teach small seminars, and we do that in Chinese. The discussion, as one might expect, flows much better if it's done in the students' native tongue. If I have to prepare weekly lectures, I'd still use mainly English, but with lots of translation, it seems to sink in. The bad news is that I realize I'll never be as good as my students in terms of Chinese language expression. In fact, it's a humbling experience, and I'd recommend teaching in a second (or third) language to professors that become too complacent or arrogant. It might also be more consistent with Confucian injunctions against "eloquent speech." Other than the occasional joke, one necessarily focuses on the substance without too many embellishments or digressions.[17]

Perhaps the biggest challenge I continue to face is my inability to sing in Chinese (or English). When I go out with students, they often end up singing, and I'm the mute one. My colleagues go out to sing karaoke and I can't join them. At the end-of-year party, the students and professors sing karaoke and beautiful duets, often requiring days of preparation. Every year, I need to prepare new excuses (last time, I said I had planned to sing with a female colleague who was ill that day and that we'd do it the following year). Let me emphasize that my inability is not simply regarded as a technical problem. It's a moral flaw. It reflects my inability to contribute to a sense of harmony and well-being among intimates. It really hurts me to say this.

Oh, yes, I should mention my second visit to the party school. A few months ago, my student-friend phoned me and asked me if I could return to his school to lecture students about improving their English. This time, I really laughed. How can you expect that excuse to work? My article explained what happened last time, they know we're going to talk about politics. My student-friend said that was a long time ago, and people have short memories, don't worry. But why can't we just tell them we want to talk about politics? We need to do it this way, he said, please, don't be upset. I then told him I had nothing new to say about learning English, and that the students would be bored. "Please, don't worry," he said. "It's a different set of students; they don't know what you said last time, and some of them really do want tips on improving their English."

At that point, I suggested that I bring along my wife, a Chinese lawyer who speaks fluent English. She'd have a lot more to say regarding the official topic of the lecture (moreover, she was curious to see the party school for herself). He agreed, and we showed up later that same day.[18] I had since learned that several foreigners had previously spoken at the party school. What was distinctive about my first visit was that it was organized by a student; there was nothing special about me per se. Needless to say, some of the magic had worn off and I wasn't so enthusiastic this time.

It was already dark when we arrived. The gate was open and we didn't have to register. I know it's irrational to feel this way, but I was somewhat disappointed at the lack of security.[19] We walked straight to the classroom, and I noticed another foreigner lecturing on the topic of improving one's English who really was talking about learning English. My heart sank. The classroom was hot, crowded, and nearly all-male (there were no female Tibetan Communist student leaders, as far as I could tell). Finally, it was our turn. I repeated the same obvious points I had made two years ago, but my wife offered more useful ideas for improving English. Then it was question period.

First question: How many years does it take before one can speak English fluently? Second question: Is it better to read English books or watch English movies with subtitles? I struggled hard to conceal my boredom, but my wife valiantly answered the questions. Then I was asked to tell the story of our romance. I laughed and evaded the question, not because I didn't want to answer, but because the answer might be too politically sensitive (we met in May 1989, in the midst of student uprisings in Beijing, the romance being energized by the political ferment).[20]

At last, the questions took a political turn: How can we have democracy if we don't have a history of freedom? A deep and important question, I said. In the West, the development of democracy was informed and constrained by the liberal tradition's emphasis on individual freedom. But democracy can take different forms in non-Western societies. It will likely be shaped by nonliberal traditions such as Confucianism, with its emphasis on social relationships as the key to the good life. Whether that's a good or bad thing is for you to think about. Another question: What is the relation between democracy within the party and democratization in society at large? That's a tough one! The party has seventy-three million members—more than twice the Canadian population—and obviously democratization within the party is bound to have some social impact. But the truth is that I hadn't thought about that question, and I struggled to answer it. An easier question: What are the main ideas of your book, *Beyond Liberal Democracy*? I talked for a few minutes. And then there was time for one last question: Is it true that all English exams in Western countries are multiple choice?

9. On Being Confucian: Why Confucians Needn't Be Old, Serious, and Conservative

The editor of an English-language periodical once asked me to write an article titled "On Being Chinese" as part of a series on identity. I laughed, and said, sorry, I can't do that. Why not? There's the obvious physical difference: it's not uncommon for Chinese kids to point to me and say *waiguoren* (foreigner).[1] There's the fact I don't hold Chinese citizenship. Language is another issue: it wouldn't take too long for native speakers of Chinese to notice I'm not one of them. And let's not forget that identity depends partly, if not mainly, on how others perceive us: unfortunately, perhaps, few Chinese would ever view me as Chinese, even if I want to define myself as Chinese. Finally, I don't really view myself as a Chinese—I sometimes wish I'd act more "Chinese" so as to better fit with my surroundings, but deep down I know it's a pretty fruitless task.

Still, we were having a good talk, the wine was beginning to take effect, and I did not want to turn him down. So I paused a bit and came up with another idea: what about writing something titled "On Being Confucian"? For one thing, Confucius himself was a teacher, and that's what I do. Confucianism is mainly an ethical philosophy, and identification with central values in the Confucian tradition rather than ethnicity or language seems to count as the main criterion for being Confucian: South Korea is perhaps the most "Confucianized" society in East Asia, and there is a school of "Boston Confucians," so why not a Canadian Confucian living in Beijing? Moreover, I have been identified as a promoter of Confucian values, so my article might not seem so implausible to the outside world. Most important, perhaps, I generally sympathize with Confucianism. On the one hand, it's an

ethical philosophy that makes sense of most of my preexisting ethical
commitments: that the good life involves rich family ties and affective
relations between friends, that morality develops from intimate ties and
spreads to strangers, and that we should be committed to the well-being
of our communities and the world at large. I like the idea that early
Confucianism has vague metaphysical commitments and may be compatible with diverse religious beliefs. Confucius's idea that educators
and legislators should rely on moral power before legal punishment
seems attractive, as does his idea that first task of government is to provide for the well-being of the poor. I also like Mencius's idea that humanitarian intervention abroad should be justified with reference to
alleviating the material suffering of people, not the promotion of democracy. And I'm consoled that some feminist scholars have reinter-
preted Confucianism to show it's compatible with gender equality.

On the other hand, my engagement with Confucianism seems to
have challenged some of my preexisting moral commitments.[2] It's not
just a matter of seeking more ammunition for what I already believe;
I've also learned new and better ideas. By reading Xunzi, I've learned to
appreciate the moral value of hierarchical rituals—they can actually
contribute to material equality—and I no longer raise my eyebrows
when subordinates bow to social superiors. I've learned that singing can
contribute to social harmony, and I'm more sympathetic to karaoke
than I used to be. I've learned that there should be limits to critical
thinking, and I won't blindly encourage my students to criticize texts
they have yet to understand. And I've learned to question that most sacred of modern Western values—rule by the people in the form of one
person, one vote. I now think that other ways of choosing rulers, such
as an examination system, are more likely to ensure quality rule, and I
freely confess it's the sort of argument I would have found deeply dis-
turbing before my engagement with Confucianism. In sum, Confucianism coheres with many of my preexisting moral intuitions while
allowing for moral growth. Isn't that a good reason to identify with
Confucianism, and to write about what it means to be a Confucian?

Satisfied with myself, I reported to my (Chinese) wife that I've been
commissioned to write an article titled "On Being Confucian." She
laughed—just as I had laughed when the editor asked me to write an
article "On Being Chinese"—and implied it was a ridiculous task. But

why, I asked? She looked me up and down and said, "Come on, you're not Confucian," and then she switched to another topic. Why would she be so dismissive, I wondered? Is it because I'm not leading the life of a Confucian? Because I'm not serious enough? Because I'm not sufficiently conservative? Let me try to respond to some of the objections. If I succeed, then I'm qualified to write this kind of article. I probably won't convince my wife, but perhaps the reader will be willing to engage with my argument.

Confucianism as a Way of Life

Liberalism is mainly a political philosophy rather than an all-embracing ethical philosophy.[3] Instead of trying to provide detailed judgments about how to lead this or that form of life, liberals aim to defend political principles applicable to the basic structure of society. In their private lives, people can do what they want so long as they respect the basic rights of others. Consequently, liberal thinkers needn't worry too much about practicing what they are preaching.[4] For example, they can defend the rights of others to engage in wild sex acts even though they might lead very conservative family lives. Or they might defend the right of women to have abortions while never dreaming of doing it themselves. Even politicians should be given more leeway to do what they want in their off-hours: it is at least arguable that Bill Clinton's political performance should be evaluated separately from his private life. Such divergence between "the political" and "the personal" needn't raise too many question marks because liberal philosophy itself aims to leave ample room for diverse private lives without state interference. The political principles of liberalism are not supposed to be undermined by the way that the defender of those principles leads his or her life.

Confucianism is different. There is infinitely more pressure to "walk the walk," not just "talk the talk." It's not sufficient to read and write about Confucian philosophy: the Confucian is also supposed to try to lead a life inspired by Confucian values. That is, he or she must aim to become an exemplary person (*junzi*) who sets a good example for others. But what does that mean? At minimum, it means being a good family person. If I neglect my parents or refuse to even try to educate my child, then I'm not doing my duty. No matter how beautiful my writings may be, it would undermine my credibility if it turns out there's substantial divergence between my personal life and my theoretical commitments. Nobody would listen to the Confucian philosopher who seems to lead a personal life that's radically inconsistent with central Confucian values.

But I don't think my wife laughed because she thinks I'm bad to family members. Yes, I'm far from perfect and there's substantial room for improvement, but arguably I'm not beyond redemption.[5] I think she laughed because of certain stereotypical images that seem to characterize Confucian philosophers. They're supposed to be old. They're supposed to be serious, not jokers. They're supposed to be politically active, usually aligned with the conservative camp. And I may not be sufficiently "Confucian" in those respects. But perhaps those really are just stereotypes, meaning common misunderstandings of what Confucianism as a way of life actually requires. If so, then I may still be considered eligible to write this kind of article. So let me proceed.

Does Morality Improve with Age?

One of the most widely quoted sayings from *The Analects of Confucius* is the brief account Confucius gives of his own life: "At fifteen, I set my mind upon learning; at thirty, I took my stance; at forty, I was no longer perplexed; I fifty, I realized the "ways of the universe"; at sixty, my ear was attuned; at seventy, I followed my heart's desire without overstepping the boundaries" (2.4). In contemporary China, the saying has become somewhat distorted: for example, thirty-year-olds take Confucius to be saying that they should be established in their careers. Whatever the merits of such interpretations, there's one thing that cannot be argued: Confucius is tracing his own process of moral growth. As he gets older, he improves morally: his capacity for moral judgment improves and he can act better, morally speaking. Elsewhere, Confucius presents the process of moral growth as a more general process: at the age of forty, for example, a person should have learned enough to be liked by others, and if not, he or she is a hopeless case (17.26).[6] But what are

Confucius's reasons for thinking that morality improves with age?[7] Unfortunately, the text itself is not so clear, but we can consider some possibilities.

The most obvious reason why the capacity for moral judgment might improve with age is that morality can improve with education. Learning is a never-ending process of accumulating knowledge: as Confucius puts it, "A person who is constantly aware of what has yet to be learned and who, from month to month, does not forget what has been learned, can be said to truly love learning" (19.5). From a moral point of view, we need to study, to learn what others have thought and said, in order to get ideas to improve the way that we lead our lives. And the more we read, the more ideas we can have. Since reading and studying is a time-consuming process, the elderly are more likely to have had the time to read and study with a view to improving their lives.[8] Hence the elderly are more likely to have the store of knowledge that allows for better moral judgment.

Equally if not more important, the elderly are more likely to have *experienced* different roles and forms of life that increase the capacity for moral judgment. Confucianism in particular is an action-based ethics: one learns by participating in different rituals and fulfilling different responsibilities in different roles, and the wider the life experience, the greater the likelihood that one has developed the capacity for good moral judgment in this or that particular situation. On the one hand, it's a matter of deepening experience in particular roles: for example, the teacher concerned with self-improvement should get better as she learns from her mistakes and deals with a wider range of students and teaching materials. On the other hand, it's a matter of learning from new roles, some of which can only be undertaken later in life. A key aspect of the learning by doing process is filial piety, caring for elderly parents: as Confucius puts it, "Filial and fraternal responsibility is the root of humanity and compassion" (1.2). But the young can rarely practice filial piety: the parents care for the children rather than the other way around. Parents are more likely to need care as they get older, so it's usually adults that can really begin to seriously practice filial piety. And filial piety extends to caring for parents after they have already died, both in the sense of caring for the dead bodies (as Xunzi notes) and by means of various ancestor worship rituals defended by neo-Confucians.

What this means, at the very least, is that young people are not likely to have the necessary experience that allows for the development of humanity (ren), meaning love and caring for others.

Another reason for believing that the elderly have greater capacity for moral judgment is that they are less enslaved by sexual desire.[9] At seventy years old, Confucius notes that he can give free reign to his heart's desires, meaning that there is less of a conflict between what he wants to do and what he should do. Why would Confucius say that? Elsewhere in the *Analects*, Confucius notes despairingly that he "has yet to meet anybody who is fonder of virtue than of sex" (15.13). But Confucius is addressing his students, and he may not say the same thing to an older crowd. That is, as sexual desire diminishes with age, there may be less conflict between the desire for sex and the desire to do good (at the very least, the older crowd may not waste so much time thinking about sex). So one reason why moral judgment improves with age is that the elderly do not typically experience conflict between sexual desire and the desire to do good to the same extent as younger people.[10] This is not to imply that the desire for sex needs to be entirely extinguished for elderly people, but it is easier to control and subordinate to moral principles (compared to male adolescents!).[11]

So let me return to my case. I do not mean to sound self-indulgent, I'm just trying to figure out if I'm qualified to write an essay titled "On Being Confucian." As mentioned, it's not just a matter of learning about Confucian texts, for my life should also reflect the Confucian values I'm espousing. And there seem to be very good reasons for believing that only the elderly—those over seventy—can really instantiate Confucian values, hence my lack of qualification for this exercise. But perhaps it's not an all-or-nothing question. When I mentioned to an immensely well learned colleague that I've been commissioned to write an essay "On Being Confucian," he suggested that it should be titled "On Becoming Confucian." The point he was trying to make, I gather, is that the quest for self-improvement is never-ending, there will always be better people and better ideas worth learning from, there is no "end point" or "Confucian destination." That's why, perhaps, Confucius himself claimed that he hadn't become an exemplary person (7.33) and he didn't even mention the possibility of achieving sagehood.[12] In other words, nobody can really instantiate Confucian values. Some people might be better than others, but it's impossible to really become a "Confucian" in one's lifetime. In the contemporary world, the task may be even more daunting: there are too many books to read, too many diverse roles to experience, too many cultures to learn from. So even the elderly can't really be considered eligible to write an article on being Confucian.

But let's not play with words. The fact remains that the elderly may still be in a better position to exercise moral judgment than the young. In Confucian terms, they may have experienced enough roles and read enough books to make informed judgments that won't be obstructed by sexual desire. So am I old enough to write this kind of article? I'm forty-three and still, I confess, often perplexed. But perhaps the stages take longer to experience now that life expectancy has been extended since the days of Confucius. And I've experienced various family roles, including taking care of elderly parents. I've done a fair amount of reading. Theoretically speaking, I've passed the stage where I need to guard against uncontrolled manifestations of sexual desire.[13] So perhaps the gap between Confucian values and my actual life may not so wide as to disqualify me from writing an article titled "On Being Confucian."

What's Wrong with Making Jokes?

There is another image of Confucians: that they are boringly serious moralizers. In that sense, it's hard for me to write about what it means to be a Confucian: as I see it, a life without humor and laughter would hardly be worth living. But perhaps the image is wrong. Or at least, there are good Confucian reasons to think that there is nothing incompatible between making jokes and defending Confucian values. More than that: there may positive reasons to think that humor contributes to key Confucian values.

Confucians value relationships between intimates informed by trust and love. And humor often works best among intimates. A Chinese friend once told me that I should start to worry about my relationship with my wife when she stops teasing me. As far as I can tell, he meant that intimates tease each other because they care about each other. Joking and teasing can also *contribute* to trust that underpins intimate ties. Relationships with colleagues often change from collegiality to friendship at the point that they start teasing each other. It's worth asking why intimates would want to tease each other. One reason is that they care about improving each other, and putting forward criticisms in a joking spirit is more likely to be effective. When Confucius tells his students that he "has yet to meet anybody who is fonder of virtue than of sex," he may be teasing them and urging them to guard against the temptations of lust in their quest for self-improvement. His students are more likely to listen—to really change their minds—if Confucius makes them laugh than if he sternly announces the (moral) truth that they're supposed to follow. And Confucius is more likely to invite gentle teasing and implicit criticism from his students—hence allowing for his own improvement—if he creates an informal, joking atmosphere with them.[14]

Humor can also be used as an indirect tool for social criticism. For example, Sacha Baron Cohen—who pretends to be Ali G. and Borat in his interactions with unsuspecting people—uses crude and "politically incorrect" humor as a way of exposing racist and sexist values in the people he deals with.[15] If there was no political commentary implicit in Cohen's humor, we—at least educated, politically progressive people—probably wouldn't be laughing at his jokes.[16] The ultimate point of Cohen's humor is to shed light on racist and sexist practices in contemporary society as a way of improving the society. I cannot confirm this, but Cohen would probably agree to live in a world without racism and sexism even if it meant that his brand of humor would be rendered superfluous.

But this seems too "serious" a defense of humor. Is humor to be valued just because it's a tool for improvement of self and society? Sometimes we appreciate jokes without any moral content (though I can't think of any offhand). If Confucians only value humor because of its moral purpose, it seems like an impoverished view of humor. But that may not be Confucius's own view. Perhaps an analogy can be drawn with music. Confucius appreciates music for its moral effects (it contributes to harmony) and also because it can induce joyful states.[17] Consider Confucius's own reaction to *shao* music: "The *shao* music is both superbly beautiful and superbly good. . . . Once I heard the *shao* music, and I couldn't appreciate the taste of meat for three months after that. I had no idea that music could reach such heights!" (3.25, 7.14). Confucius is suggesting that this music made him happy, happy to the point that he didn't have as much of a need for other typical sources of happiness, such as eating meat.[18] The same can be said of some jokes: they make us happy, and that's it, there's no need for further justification.

So how did Confucians develop this reputation for being so serious and humorless? One reason, I would surmise, is that Confucius's most influential followers—Mencius and Xunzi—seem so morally earnest, with hardly any trace of humor or self-deprecation in their writings. But there may be good reasons for that. Mencius and Xunzi were writing in the midst of the most bloody part of the Warring States period, and it might be inappropriate to make jokes in the midst of such evil (one doesn't make jokes in the immediate aftermath of a suicide bombing).[19] More prosaically, I should not tease my enemies, or even strangers, because there isn't the foundation of trust that allows for teasing to serve its critical function. Confucius himself seemed to recognize the limits of humor:

> When the Master went to the town of Wu, he heard the sound of stringed instruments and singing. He said with a gentle smile, "Why would one use an ox cleaver to kill a chicken?"
>
> Ziyou responded, "In the past I heard you say, Master, 'Exemplary persons who study the way love others; petty persons who study the way are easier to employ.'"
>
> The Master replied, "My young friends, what he says is quite true. Just now I was only making a joke." (17.4)

This passage is hard to interpret. The joke itself doesn't seem particularly funny, for one thing (perhaps, like many jokes, "you had to be there"). According to Arthur Waley, what Confucius meant, in effect, was that teaching music to the inhabitants of this small town is like "casting pearls before swine." The joke is somewhat cruel: Confucius is implying that the inhabitants of this remote town are too culturally backward to appreciate and be elevated by beautiful music. And Ziyou picks up on the cruelty, quoting his teacher about the need to love others, even culturally backwards people. Confucius notes that it was just a joke, but he seems to regret having made the joke. If teasing isn't founded on intimate ties, it will be taken as an insult, and such jokes should not be made.

So let me modify my initial claim, that a life without humor and laughter would hardly be worth living. In the presence of truly great evil, humor is inappropriate. In such contexts, the moral task is to improve society so that it becomes more peaceful and informed by ties of mutual trust and love. Once societies pass this minimal threshold, then humor can play an important role in further strengthening affective ties, allowing for further progress, and contributing to enjoyment. Even then, however, humor, especially of the teasing sort, works best with intimates. Let me then conclude that Confucians can and should make jokes, but they should be sensitive to context. Just because I've made an odd joke doesn't disqualify me from writing this article.

Confucianism and Political Participation

Another common stereotype of Confucians is that they are politically conservative. I'd like to think of myself as politically progressive—as a "man of the left"—so does that mean I can't be Confucian? Again, the stereotype may be mistaken. If conservative means support for the political status quo, there's plenty of evidence that Confucians haven't been conservatives. Confucius, Mencius, and Xunzi were all radical critics of the status quo. Once Confucianism became the official ideology of imperial China, there may have been more support for the status quo among Confucian scholars. But there are also many counterexamples. As Theodore de Bary shows in his book *The Liberal Tradition in China*, the institution of the Censorate allowed Confucian scholars to criticize the government, though several paid with their lives for doing so. And some Confucian scholars used their writings to put forward radical criticisms of the status quo. The seventeenth-century scholar Huang Zongxi is one famous case. He opens his book *Waiting for the Dawn: A Plan for the Prince* with a radical attack on the government of his day: "In ancient times, the people were considered the master, and the ruler was the tenant. The ruler spent his whole life working for the people. Now the ruler is the master, and the people are tenants. That no one can find peace and happiness anywhere is all on account of the ruler."[20] Huang's critique was circulated "samizdat" among sympathetic intellectuals for two and a half centuries, finally seeing the light of day in the latter part of the Qing period, with the dynasty in disarray.

Perhaps "conservative" means that Confucians tend to look backward for inspiration—to the Western Zhou dynasty, in the case of political ideals—rather than forward. But such appeals to golden ages of the past may be more rhetorical than real. There is very little historical knowledge of how things actually worked in the ancient Zhou dynasty, and social critics may be invoking past ideals rather than their own ideas simply because it's more likely that powers-that-be will listen if calls for reform seem to be sanctioned by "sages of the past." At the very least, the social critics must have realized that they were drawing upon their own imagination to fill in the historical gaps. How could they not have been aware of what they were doing?

There is, however, one sense in which Confucians can uncontroversially be said to be conservative: to a certain extent, they do seek inspiration from the past. The idea is that we should learn from past thinkers and exemplary rulers and seek moral inspiration from them. It's a much more effective way of moral learning than trying to create everything oneself: as Xunzi put it, "I once spent a whole day in thought, but it was not so valuable as a moment in study. I once stood on my tiptoes to look out into the distance, but it was not so effective as climbing up to a high place for a broader vista" (1.3; see also the *Analects*, 15.31). As ethical practice, it means being open to the possibility that the past can offer useful moral lessons for the present. As political practice, it means that change must be based, at least partly, on past practices and traditions. The alternative—to criticize and attack all forms of old thought—was propagated during Chairman Mao's Cultural Revolution. The result, of course, was disaster. As Confucius had warned, "Thinking without studying leads to great danger" (2.15). So, yes, Confucians are conservative if that means being averse to utopian political projects that owe nothing to the past. But who can object to that?

The key question, in my view, is not whether Confucians should necessarily be viewed as "conservative." If anything, the question should be the opposite, whether Confucians have a moral obligation to be social and political critics. Given the inevitable gap between the political reality and ideal values and forms of government, do Confucians have an obligation to engage in political debates of the day in order to try to improve the reality? Ever since the decline of the golden age of Zhou, argued the eighteenth-century Confucian thinker Zhang Xuecheng, history repeats itself as a never-ending series of ages in which different intellectual tendencies are overemphasized, and the task of the morally committed individual is to resist the excesses of the dominant fashion in order to bring things back into balance.[21] Hence, according to Zhang, the Confucian will (should) always be a social critic.

Confucius himself may be more nuanced. On the one hand, there is a moral obligation to deal with social and political problems: "We cannot join the world of birds and the beasts. Am I not one among the people of this world? If not them, who should I deal with? If the Way prevailed in the world, I wouldn't be trying to change it" (18.6). But if times are really bad without any serious hope of reform, then it may be legitimate to withdraw from political affairs until things improve: Confucius praises the exemplary person Qu Boyu for rolling up (his talent) and tucking it away when the Way does not prevail in the state (15.7). During the Cultural Revolution, one might imagine that Confucius would have chosen exile over trying to persuade a group of sadistic Red Guards. But what about in nonchaotic societies, where the social critic doesn't have to worry about being subject to violent death at the hands of others? Does the Confucian need to play an important political role?

It depends partly on one's stage in life. If one is engaged in a period of study, it makes sense to stick to study: only "students with a surplus of energy should devote their services to the state" (19.13). Moreover, Confucius himself does not take a narrow view of politics as direct engagement with the representatives and institutions of the state. Positive interaction with family members is also a political contribution, both in and of itself and because it sets an example for others:[22]

> Someone asked Confucius, "Why are you not engaged in public service?" The Master replied, "The *Book of Documents* says 'It's all about filial piety. Just being filial to your parents and friendly to your brothers is contributing to public service.' In

doing this I'm carrying out the work of government. Why must
I be employed in government?" (2.21)

In fact, family obligations are necessary conditions for the good life,
and they sometimes need to take priority over obligations to the public.
As Confucius (in)famously noted, the care owed to elderly parents
could justify breaking the law: "The Duke of She told Confucius, 'In
my country there is a man called Upright Kung. When his father stole
a sheep, he bore witness against him.' Confucius said, 'In my country,
the upright people are different from this. A father covers up for his
son, and a son covers for his father. Uprightness lies in this'" (13.18).[23]
On the other hand, one's public responsibilities can also set constraints
on family obligations. For example, Confucius notes that he could not
provide his deceased son with an outer coffin because "I could not go
on foot in order to give him one—in my capacity as a retired official, it
was not appropriate for me to travel on foot" (11.8). The task is to balance family and social responsibilities, and the proper balance depends
on the context.

In any case, what seems clear is that Confucians are supposed to
think about the social and political implications of their way of life.
Perhaps the best way I can make a contribution to improve the world is
by engaging with my students and help them to improve themselves.
But I need to be conscious of that aim as well as to think of appropriate
means of realizing that aim. If the result of my teaching is that my students go on to serve evil rulers, I need to reevaluate what I'm doing.[24]
Such questions are not simply limited to those in the teaching profession. If a medical practitioner devotes his energies to performing plastic
surgery for the rich and spends all his income on luxury goods, then he
should not be viewed as "being Confucian," no matter how well versed
in the Confucian classics he may be.

I would like to conclude that the Confucian need not be politically
conservative, nor need she be politically active in the sense of serving
or criticizing the government. But the Confucian needs to be conscious of the importance of family obligations as well as engage with
the broader social world for the purpose of improving it, all the while
trying to minimize the tension between the two kinds of responsibilities. I may not be living up to that ideal, but arguably, qua family mem-

ber and teacher of political theory who tries to think normatively about contemporary social and political controversies, it may not be completely implausible to suppose that I can write an article titled "On Being Confucian." So let me proceed.

Confucianism and Chineseness

I would like to return to the question of whether Confucians need to be Chinese. Perhaps things are not as straightforward as I implied earlier. Yes, it's true that Confucians, like liberals and Christians, have often shared the aspiration to universalize their values and have rejected the assumption that their values should be restricted to one particular ethnic group or cultural context. It's also true that Confucianism has spread beyond China to such countries as South Korea and Japan, and that several philosophers of Western descent have also embraced Confucian values. But Confucianism is closely tied to the Chinese *language.* The fact is that most of the texts in the Confucian tradition have been written in Chinese, and consequently most adherents of Confucianism have the ability to read Chinese. The early Confucian classics have been translated, but even the best translators such as Roger Ames recognize that deeper engagement with the tradition requires reading knowledge of Chinese. Key Confucian terms such as 仁, 诚, 天, 道, 心, 礼, and 让 are almost impossible to translate into English with the right nuances.

I've spent several years learning classical Chinese, but my knowledge of the language is still not sufficient. I've concentrated my efforts on learning the classical Chinese that would allow access to the early classics. I've also read many works on Confucianism written in modern Chinese by contemporary thinkers. But I've only read a small proportion of what comes in between, the thousands of original and commentarial works written by Confucian scholars during imperial China. One important obstacle is that classical Chinese has evolved differently at different times, and I need to improve my knowledge of the language as well as put in the time to read the texts. That's what I plan to do the next twenty or thirty years.

Why does it matter? Because I'm writing an essay titled "On Being Confucian" and I'm not yet in a position to know all, or even most, of what the Confucian philosophers have written about their tradition. Perhaps I'm not saying anything that hasn't been said better by earlier thinkers. Or perhaps the tradition is so diverse that it makes no sense at all to even think about "Confucian values."[25] I suspect that the first claim might be correct and the second one might be wrong, but I'm not yet in a position to evaluate either claim.

So I need to apologize to the reader. My wife was right after all: I should not be writing this essay. How can I write an essay about what it means to be Confucian without knowing what others have said about the tradition? In thirty years, perhaps, I will be in a position to do so, and I beg the reader to ignore what I've written so far. It was irresponsible—no, impertinent—for me to consider writing this essay now. I must first return to my books to improve my knowledge of the Confucian tradition. And I should also learn to sing properly.

Appendix 1:

DEPOLITICIZING THE ANALECTS

In China, Yu Dan's *"Lunyu" Xin De* (Reflections on the *Analects* of Confucius) has become a publishing sensation. At the latest count, it has sold about ten million copies (including six million pirated copies). The rest of the world is also paying attention: major newspapers and media outlets have reported on the Yu Dan phenomenon. Such headlines as "Confucius Makes a Comeback" in *The Economist* are typical. The last book out of China to attract so much attention has been, well, let me think . . . Mao's *Little Red Book*. If Mao's book erred on the side of excessive politicization of our everyday world, however, Yu Dan's book has the opposite problem.

Why So Popular?

It's worth asking why Yu Dan's book has become so popular. It's actually quite a thin book, and much of it consists of quotes from the *Analects* followed by translations into modern Chinese, the kind of work that has been done dozens of times. So why did Yu Dan's work stand out from the others? One reason, of course, is that Yu Dan's book started out as lectures on state television. She was given prime time, with an audience of millions, to discuss the *Analects*. In that sense, she had government support. But that can't be the main explanation. In most cases, it would be quite boring to hear a forty-something university professor expounding her theories on classical works in philosophy, and one wouldn't expect such an enthusiastic response.

So an important reason for Yu Dan's popularity is Yu Dan herself. She is obviously very intelligent, and, speaking for myself, I can only admire her facility with classical Chinese, as though she has memorized the whole corpus of Chinese classics. Her gender is also important.

The domination of men over women seems to be one of the defining characteristics of Confucian theory and practice—one might even say that patriarchy is the "Achilles heel" of Confucianism. In response, several contemporary theorists have tried to argue that Confucianism can take on board modern ideas about gender equality without altering its major values. But the best argument against the view that Confucianism justifies patriarchy, perhaps, is for an impressive female intellectual to show that she takes Confucianism seriously. Yu Dan fulfills that role. Still, that can't really explain her popularity among ordinary people who may not worry about such theoretical problems. I would surmise that the force of her personality is what does the trick. She projects charisma and moral engagement—what classical Confucians called 德, or "moral power"—and clearly seems to believe what she is saying. To the Western observer, the closest parallel would be a religious evangelist who discourses on the meaning of the Bible for contemporary life with passion and commitment. To be fair to Yu Dan, however, there are important differences. Unlike the firebrand evangelist, she doesn't terrify those who disagree with the threat of eternal damnation. And her rather eclectic references express an open-mindedness that is rare among religious preachers. She peppers her book with references to other religions and philosophies: Daoism, the Bible, Hegel, and so on. In the American context, it would be like Billy Graham invoking Buddhist, Islamic, Confucian, and Marxist ideals in his sermons. Not surprisingly, Yu Dan doesn't defend Confucianism as a religion. She steers clear of transcendental claims, nor does she explicitly reject the possibility that Confucianism as an ethical and political philosophy is compatible with diverse religious foundations. That's the kind of Confucianism I find attractive (as opposed to, say, the view that Confucianism needs a strong metaphysical foundation to combat religions such as Buddhism and Christianity). In that sense, all the more power to Yu Dan!

Yu Dan's book also came at the right time. As we know, China is a rising economic power, and with economic might comes cultural pride. The Weberian view that Confucianism is not conducive to economic development has come to be widely questioned in view of the economic success of East Asian countries with a Confucian heritage.

Unlike Islam, Hinduism, and Buddhism, there has never been an organized Confucian resistance to economic modernization. And now, with China poised to become a global power, it's China's turn to affirm its cultural heritage. Yu Dan's book does the job; she makes people feel proud about China's heritage while showing that it's compatible with the requirements of modern life.

But modernity also has a downside. With economic progress come higher expectations. One friend who spent time in a Chinese jail said his guards all dreamed of opening a business and making tons of money. My friend felt sorry for the guards, because most of them were bound to be disappointed. In cities, it's becoming harder and harder to find good jobs, even for graduates of top universities, and the competition for social status and material resources is becoming fiercer by the day. What can be done about the rising gap between such expectations and the social reality? One solution is to reduce the expectations, and that's what Yu Dan counsels. Don't worry so much about your car, your house, or your career. Don't worry about what other people think of you. What matters is your inner heart. So long as you have confidence and a strong sense of self-worth, you will be happy. Your happiness doesn't depend on the external world.

But it doesn't end there. Another downside of modernity is that people become more atomized and more individualistic, with declining social responsibility and other-regarding outlooks. But most people—in China, at least—do not want to be viewed as individualistic. The idea of simply focusing on individual well-being seems too self-centered. To really feel good about ourselves, we also need to be good to others. Here too, Yu Dan provides a soothing message. And best of all, it doesn't require much effort! All we have to do is focus on our own inner happiness. If we do that, others will also benefit and the world will be better for everyone!

So the real secret of Yu Dan's success, in my view, is the content of her message. She diagnoses the malaise in modernizing China and tells people there's an easy way of dealing with their problems. It just takes some introspection. She also appeals to people's desire to be good. If I'm happy, then others will be happy too!

Distorting the *Analects*?

Yu Dan's book has been subject to scathing criticisms by several experts on Confucianism. My academic colleagues tend to be dismissive of her work. The main accusation is that she has simplified the *Analects*. In the context of a discussion on the relation between words and actions, for example, Yu Dan says that "an exemplary person must always do something before talking about it" (63–64). Some passages in the *Analects* may seem to lend themselves to that interpretation (e.g., 2.13), but surely not *every* word needs to be preceded by an action. If that were the case, it would be hard to run seminars. Nor would it be possible to articulate plans to other people. Rather than make an appointment in advance, I would just show up somewhere and then tell others to meet me there. Is that really what Confucius meant to say?

But we shouldn't be too pedantic. What she means to do is counsel against immodesty and words that cannot be backed with actions, in line with the everyday understanding of the *Analects*.[1] There's no reason to expect very nuanced and qualified interpretations, original scholarship, or deep awareness of the commentarial tradition. Yu Dan is addressing a popular audience, not experts. Let me be more positive. There's a kind of division of labor between experts and popularizers, and the division can be mutually beneficial. Popularizers can learn from and incorporate the insights of experts, and experts can learn from attempts to show the value of the classics for the contemporary world. We—meaning those of us teaching and writing on the classics—should be grateful for Yu Dan's contribution. She shows that our work can and should have relevance beyond academic circles. It will be harder to question the value of our own work!

The more serious accusation is that Yu Dan has *distorted* the *Analects*. If she misreads and mistranslates the *Analects*, then we need to worry. It would mean she is using the authority of China's most influential thinker to propagate her own views. If it's done intentionally, we can question Yu Dan's academic integrity. If not, her competence. But there are no obvious mistranslations, as far as I can tell.[2] At most, there are contestable interpretations. For example, Yu Dan says that everybody can become an exemplary person (66), but she downplays the elitist dimension of the *Analects*.[3] Yes, it's true that everybody should have an equal opportunity to become an exemplary person (15.39). But it's a bit of a stretch to believe that Confucius believed everybody can become an exemplary person. Quite the opposite, in fact. He takes it for granted that a minority of exemplary people can and should rule over common people (e.g., 12.19, 14.42). Confucius clearly seems to believe that some people, such as Zaiwo, have moral limitations that cannot be overcome (5.10). He also suggests that common people have intellectual limitations (8.9). Nor does everyone have the same level of motivation, and Confucius says that he only instructs those with who are driven with eagerness (7.8). Yu Dan doesn't mention such passages, perhaps because such views wouldn't play well with her intended readership. But she may be deviating substantially from Confucius's original views.[4]

Does it matter? Confucius was writing in times of low economic development, and his views may reflect those times. Perhaps he couldn't conceive of a society where the large majority of people might be able to receive a decent education and develop their inner happiness rather than slaving in the fields. Thus, Yu Dan's more egalitarian views may be more appropriate for modern-day societies. If that's the case, however, she should be more explicit that she is changing (if not overturning) Confucius, not simply interpreting him.

More serious, perhaps, Yu Dan's views may not be as appealing as they may seem at first glance. In her egalitarian vision, we can all be exemplary people if we focus on our inner hearts and develop inner confidence. But how do we do that? She calls on us not to treat material goods as the end of life and to limit our desires for such goods. Nothing particularly controversial so far: not many philosophers or theologians would disagree with that. But then what do we do? By what mechanism do we actually develop our inner happiness? Anybody looking for practical guidance is bound to be disappointed. Some of her advice is downright contradictory: for example, she says that those with the correct professional attitude should not surpass assigned tasks at work (42) and also that exemplary persons should not be fixed upon the goals of their profession (64). It's far from obvious how both attitudes can coexist. Beyond that, the way to inner happiness is somewhat mysterious. Yu Dan doesn't say anything about mechanisms from other traditions, such as prayer or meditation. More surprisingly, she downplays the importance of Confucian mechanisms. Clearly for Confucius, lifelong study is an important and necessary means for self-cultivation (see, e.g, 7.2 and 19.5). In the last chapter of her book, Yu Dan insightfully discusses the process of growth that Confucius lays out in his famous account of the stages of his own life (2.4). She discusses the importance of study in Confucius's early life, but minimizes the effort involved. For Confucius, learning is a never-ending process of accumulating knowledge. Why doesn't she mention this? Again, I would surmise it fits uneasily with her egalitarian desire to point to an effortless way to enlightenment. For Confucius—and, arguably, what he says remains true today—only a tiny minority of people will have sufficient motivation and talent to devote themselves to constant study. After all, Confucius himself denied that he had realized the life of the exemplary person (7.33)![5] If Yu Dan were to make that explicit, it may put off some of her readers. But what can she offer instead? She doesn't provide any alternative path to self-cultivation, other than peering into one's soul.

Even more surprising, she downplays the importance of *practice*. For Yu Dan, the inner life is key, and the right kind of courage can overcome lack of technical expertise, as in the example of an amateur swordsman who defeats an expert simply by virtue of mental traits he had learned as a tea-maker (30–33). But Confucianism is an action-based ethics: one learns by participating in different rituals, learning different technical skills like archery and music, and fulfilling different responsibilities in different roles. A key aspect of the learning by doing process is filial piety, caring for elderly parents: Confucius says, "Filial and fraternal responsibility is the root of humanity and compassion" (1.2). In other words, one cannot become a fully moral human being without having practiced filial piety. So that seems to rule out many people: in today's China, it's often elderly parents who care for grandchildren rather than adult children caring for elderly parents, at least until the parents get very old.[6] Again, Yu Dan would lose many readers if she were to make such views explicit. But she doesn't offer any alternatives. It's fine to have the right inner attitude, but how exactly do we get there?

The relatively concrete advice Yu Dan does offer seems inconsistent with Confucius's own views. For example, she tells a story with the lesson that we should help people nearest to us, and we should do so immediately, without any delay (17). But that's closer to the Bible's idea of the Good Samaritan who helps the total stranger. For Confucius, what we do depends on the roles we occupy vis-à-vis the people we're dealing with. I owe more obligations to my father than to total strangers (Yu Dan doesn't discuss the infamous example of the son who covers up for his thieving father, 13.18). And we should reflect upon such differential obligations, it's not just a matter of plunging into action regardless of circumstances. What Yu Dan says also seems inconsistent with Confucius's own personality, with the kind of model he sets for others. For example, she quotes Confucius' student Ziyou to counsel that we should not get too close to people, including our friends (39-40, 42). But Ziyou is notorious for emphasizing formality at the expense of human warmth; that may not be Confucius's own view. Confucius himself was deeply emotional, if not passionate. He burst into song when he heard a good tune (7.32) and grieved with abandon over the death of his favorite student Yan Hui (11.10). Is it any wonder that people from Shandong (Confucius's home province) who take pride in their Confucian heritage emphasize codes of brotherhood and personal loyalties (讲义气)? Yu Dan's words about the need not to "waste one's heart" (38) over excessively intimate social engagement may owe more to Zhuangzi, who seemed indifferent to the death of his own wife (chap. 18; see also chap. 3). On the Daoist view, it's best to "go with the flow," to submit to fate in a calm and steady way rather than lettting loose intense emotions. To be fair, Yu Dan does explicitly mention Zhuangzi several times in her book, so she's not covering up that fact that her interpretation of the *Analects* has Daoist characteristics. Nor is she necessarily wrong in advocating Daoist-inspired responses in modern society. People are different, depending on their background and personalities, and different things work for different people. Some of us may experience more genuine happiness from interaction with the hard-drinking and singing crowd, from self-sacrifice, and from unquestioned loyalty to friends, even if such behavior may not seem completely rational. Others may prefer the somewhat cold and distant self-regard that Yu Dan seems to advocate. That's fine. But the deepest problem with Yu Dan's book is the Daoist-inspired effort to depoliticize Confucianism.

Depoliticizing the *Analects*

Confucius was a radical social critic. He had a very low opinion of the rulers of his own day (13.21) and wandered from state to state, hoping to find a ruler more receptive to his ideas about good government. Note that he was offering *political* criticisms: Confucius aimed not just to develop individual character, but also to encourage those who hold authority to rule in a competent and compassionate manner. Unfortunately, Confucius failed in his political aspirations, and he was forced to settle for what we would now call a teaching career. But it wasn't *only* a teaching career. He continued to criticize political authorities, pointing to the gap between the reality and the ideal, and laid the foundations for subsequent political reformers inspired by his views of humane government.

Of course, Confucianism became more conservative once it became official state orthodoxy. But the critical implications of Confucius's ideas were rarely far from the surface, and courageous Confucian thinkers such as Huang Zongxi were severe critics of the political status quo, sometimes paying with their lives. For the eighteenth-century Confucian thinker Zhang Xuecheng, the Confucian thinker should always be a social critic, no matter what the circumstances: he argued that history repeats itself as a never-ending series of ages in which different intellectual tendencies are overemphasized, and the task of the morally committed individual is to resist the excesses of the dominant fashion in order to bring things into balance. Unfortunately, Yu Dan does not discuss such views. The whole thrust of her book is to depoliticize the *Analects*.

When Yu Dan does discuss political passages, they are denuded of political content. For example, in the famous passage where Zigong asks about politics, Confucius replies that the government should secure sufficient arms for defense, sufficient food, and also that the common people should have confidence in their rulers (12.7). Confucius is then asked to rank those desiderata in order of importance, and he says that sufficient arms comes last and the people's confidence is most important. Yu Dan takes this passage to mean that the state should look to the people's happiness rather than the size of the GNP (10). But how can we tell if the people are happy and thus have confidence in the government? Yu Dan implies that it's about inner happiness, rather than anything the government has to do for its people. To illustrate her view, she points to the example of Yan Hui, who was happy in poor surroundings (11). But Yan Hui is a particularly bad example for Yu Dan's case. For one thing, he didn't *aim* at being happy: he aimed at following the Dao, at being a good person and making the world better. This commitment gave him the strength to live in want without become depressed or losing his moral compass, but personal happiness only emerges as a by-product, not the end. Nor does Yu Dan mention that Yan Hui was an exceptional student (Confucius says that he himself doesn't measure up to Yan Hui, 5.9). Yan Hui may have had to fortitude to be good (and happy, as a by-product) in miserable circumstances, but most people are not capable of such heroism. It is highly unlikely that Confucius could have conceived of the possibility that the bulk of common people could be happy, or could act morally, without sufficient resources.[7] Why else would he say, elsewhere, that the first task of the government is to provide for the people's basic means of subsistence, and only then to educate them (13.9)? So the key condition to gain the confidence of the people is to provide for their means of subsistence. Once the trust is there, then, in exceptional circumstances (e.g., war), it may be justified and feasible to deprive them of food. But they have to be made happy first!

I don't want to be unfair. Yu Dan would probably agree that the government has an obligation to secure the basic means of subsistence. What she is criticizing is the blind worship of GNP growth, implying that things besides money matter for people's happiness. But the passage itself points to the relation between the people and the government, and she could—should—have said more about how the government is supposed to secure their trust. It is a question worth asking, especially if the economic situation turns sour. Here Yu Dan could have mentioned Confucius's emphasis on morally upright leaders who inspire the rest of the population (e.g., 12.19), perhaps adding a criticism of rampant official corruption in contemporary China. Or she could have

suggested other means of gaining political legitimacy, such as meritocratic examinations or democratic elections. But going that route may
have led to political trouble, or at least, it's hard to imagine she could
have used prime time television to utter such views. The cost, though,
is that she has betrayed Confucius's own political vision.

Other passages are denuded of their critical potential. Yu Dan notes
that exemplary persons should be concerned with broader goods, not
just the good of their own home and situation. Fair enough. But then
she says that this view became transformed into the Confucian idea
that "the flourishing or destruction of all-under-heaven is the responsibility of the common people" (天下兴亡, 匹夫有责, 57). This phrase
is known to most high school students in China, and it is used almost
interchangeably with "all-under-heaven" or "state" at the front. Either
way, it seems to support the idea that ordinary citizens should serve and
care about the well-being of the state. But Yu Dan doesn't mention that
the phrase comes from the seventeenth-century Confucian social critic
Gu Yanwu, who had more subversive implications in mind. Gu Yanwu
explicitly distinguished between the fall of the state (国家) and the fall
of all-under-heaven (天下), arguing that common people's obligation is
to the latter but that securing the state or dynastic polity is the concern
of rulers and officials (see the Ph.D. theses by Tom Bartlett at Princeton
and John Delury at Yale).

Yu Dan also discusses the famous line from the *Analects* that exemplary persons should pursue harmony but not conformity (13.23) to
emphasize the importance of tolerance and respect for different views
in personal interactions (60-61). Fair enough. But Yu Dan also trivial-
izes this idea, as when she says that being a good party host means paying attention to all the guests rather than simply the usual set of friends
(60). But that line also has political implications. The contrast between
harmony and conformity owes it origin to the Zuo Zhuan, where it
clearly referred to the idea that the ruler should be open to different
political views among his advisers. Contemporary social critics have
often drawn on the phrase to urge the government to be tolerant of different views and not simply enforce one dominant state ideology on the
whole population. Of course, Yu Dan does not discuss such views.

Perhaps Yu Dan is not simply motivated by political caution. Her
commitment to Daoism, I would surmise, also skews her interpreta-

tions. There is one seemingly puzzling passage in the *Analects*, perhaps the longest passage in the whole text, that seems to lend itself to an apolitical (or antipolitical) interpretation. Not surprisingly, Yu Dan devotes several pages to this passage. In this passage—which she quotes and translates in full—Confucius is sitting with four of his students, and he asks them about their different ideals (11.26). The first student, Zilu, says that he wants to run a state with a thousand chariots and that he would defeat foreign armies, conquer famine, and imbue the people with courage within three years. Confucius responds with a skeptical smile. Ranyou then says more modestly that he could govern a smaller state but that it would take an exemplary person to promote higher civility and music. Zihua then says, even more modestly, that he could serve as a minor protocal officer. The seemingly puzzling part is Zengxi's response and Confucius's response to it. Zengxi says that he would like to bathe with his friends and then return home singing. Confucius's response is to express approval. As one might expect, Yu Dan takes this passage to mean that personal attitude is more important than commitment to politics (90). She invokes the authority of Zhu Xi (the one and only time she does so) to argue that Zengxi's ideal seems minor in comparison, but that it's actually superior to the others because Zengxi aims to develop his inner attitude and self-cultivation rather than having concrete plans (91). Later on, she again discusses Zengxi's ideal, using Daoist language to point to the importance of appreciating nature (93) and then mentioning Zhuangzi's idea of "individual contact with the forces of the universe" (独与天地精神) to explain Confucius's approval of Zengxi's ideal (99).

But it would be odd if the passage were really about pursuing individual happiness, harmony with nature, and individual contact with the universe. What would that kind of view be doing in a book that stresses the importance of social relations and political commitment?[8] In my view, the passage is about political commitment, but Confucius means to stress that political commitment isn't just about governing the state. Consider the end of the passage, where Confucius, conversing with Zengxi, explains his reaction to Ranyou and Zihua. Confucius says that they're still thinking about important forms of social and political commitment even though they're not pulling the highest levers of state power (Yu Dan cannot make sense of this further discussion; if her interpretation is correct, the passage would have ended with Zengxi's ideal, with no need for anything further). What about Zengxi's ideal? It makes sense in the context of other passages in the *Analects*, where Confucius points to the importance of singing and informal social inter-action among intimates as crucial for forging the bonds of trust that underpin social harmony. What Zengxi describes—singing and playing with friends—contributes to the social trust (social capital, to use the language of contemporary social science) that underpins the harmoni-ous society. Confucius endorses that activity because it's foundational, the necessary context for "higher" forms of morally defensible political activity. Zilu thinks he can govern a state and change it just by the force of his personality and correct policies, but he ignores the necessity for social trust that can render those policies effective, and that's why Con-fucius is most dismissive of his ideal. If we interpret Zengxi's ideal (and Confucius's response to it) that way, the passage as a whole makes more sense: political commitment involves everything from governing the state to informal interaction among intimates, and the latter is, in some sense, more foundational.

　We can argue over interpretations, of course. That's an academic task. But there's also a political reason to be concerned about Yu Dan's efforts to depolitize the *Analects*. Her account isn't as apolitical as it seems. By telling people that they shouldn't complain too much,[9] that they should worry first and foremost about their inner happiness, by downplaying the importance of social and political commitment, and by ignoring the critical tradition of Confucianism, Yu Dan deflects at-tention from the economic and political conditions that actually cause people's misery, as well as the sorts of collective solutions needed to bring about substantial improvement to people's lives.[10] In actual fact, her account is complacent, conservative, and supportive of the status quo. Confucius must be turning in his grave.

Appendix 2:

JIANG QING'S *POLITICAL CONFUCIANISM*

It is an honor to comment on Jiang Qing's work. Professor Jiang has written the most systematic and detailed defense of political Confucianism since the establishment of the People's Republic of China. It also requires a great deal of courage to put forward such views in present-day China. I share his view that political transitions must draw on already existing cultural resources if they're to achieve long-term political legitimacy (P, 39).[1] In the case of China, it would mean drawing on the tradition of "political Confucianism"—the most politically influential of China's traditions—and Jiang offers an interpretation of this tradition meant to be appropriate for China in the future. The tradition offers relatively concrete ideas for social and political reform, and it is a clear alternative to the political status quo as well as to Western-style liberal democracy. In this comment, I would like to discuss the actual political recommendations that Jiang derives from the tradition. I will begin by explaining Jiang's methodology and justification for his recommendations, and then I will move on to critical evaluation of his recommendations. My view is that Jiang's recommendations hold much promise, though they would need to be modified somewhat in order to better suit China's social and political context.

Reviving the Gongyang (公羊) Tradition

China

Jiang's ultimate aim is to put forward political ideas for dealing with China's current crisis of political legitimacy. The current political system is not stable for the long term because it rests (too much) on coercion and fails to engage people's hearts and minds. There may be a case for the current system of economic liberalization combined with tight political control as necessary in the short term to avoid chaos during the highly unsettled period of economic development, but the system lacks legitimacy and there is a need for an alternative that can provide long-term stability. For this purpose, we need concrete ideas of social practices and political institutions inspired by Chinese cultural resources that are best able to remedy the crisis of political legitimacy. Jiang argues that such ideas are most likely to emerge from the Gongyang Confucian tradition. The Gongyang tradition is closely associated with Dong Zhongshu (179–104 BCE), the Han dynasty scholar who successfully sought to promote Confucianism as the official ideology of the imperial state, and it was revived centuries later by Kang Youwei (1858–1927), the Confucian reformist who championed what he saw as the antitotalitarian message of the Gongyang. Both messages also form part of Jiang Qing's work. Jiang contrasts the Gongyang with the Xinxing (心性) Confucian tradition, with its emphasis on self-cultivation. The Xinxing tradition inspired Confucian thinkers in Chinese imperial history who engaged with Buddhism as well as twentieth-century thinkers who sought to promote Confucian values in politically unpropitious times. Jiang argues that both traditions are necessary, but the most pressing political task now is to revive the Gongyang tradition because it offers more resources for thinking about reform of Chinese social and political institutions. To the extent that contemporary scholars inspired by the Xinxing ("mind and nature") Confucian tradition think about social and political institutions, they tend look to Western-style liberal democratic models.[2] But following this road, according to Jiang, would lead to the obliteration of Chinese culture and would not help to resolve the crisis of political legitimacy. So we should look to the Gongyang tradition to deal with the current crisis.

In his book *Political Confucianism*, Jiang does not discuss his actual political recommendations in any depth. I would surmise that the main reason is political: in order for the book to be published in mainland China, Jiang could not discuss ideas for political institutions that substantially diverge from the status quo. However, he does discuss alternative ideas for institutions in his unpublished (Chinese language) book 生命信仰与王道政治—儒家文化的现代价值 (2004) (A Faith in Life and the Kingly Way of Politics: The Modern Value of Confucian Culture).[3] This book consists largely of lengthy interviews with Professor Jiang on topics related to the contemporary value of political institutions, and I've been sent a copy by email.

Jiang argues that the current political system is not stable for the long term. That argument per se may not be radical because it is implicitly put forward by the Chinese Communist Party. According to the CCP's own formulation, the current system is the "primary stage of socialism," meaning that it's a transitional phase to a higher and superior form of socialism. The economic foundation, along with the legal and political superstructure, will change in the future. Where Jiang parts with the government is in rejecting any substantial role for Marxist ideology in shaping China's future. He does not make it explicit—again, no doubt due to political constraints—but he rejects the possibility that Marxist ideology should underpin the next phase of China's political development. The main reason, one would surmise, is that Marxism is mainly a foreign ideology and hence cannot underpin political legitimacy for the long term. Marxist ideals may coincide with Confucian political values—and in fact, Jiang argues that the two traditions have much in common—but the main source of legitimacy must come from Chinese cultural resources. And since the Gongyang tradition is best suited for thinking about political institutions (among the various Chinese traditions), then it—in revived form—should underpin China's political institutions for the future.

Why, one might ask, do ideas for political reform need to come from only *one* Chinese tradition? I don't think Jiang provides a good answer to that question. For example, the Xinxing Confucian tradition may have more to offer than Jiang suggests. Jiang criticizes it for the assumption that social and political change comes mainly from transformation of the ruler's heart-mind (L, 225). But few representatives of that tradition seriously held that view. Zhu Xi put forward, and tried to implement, many ideas for reform of community-level social and political institutions that do not depend solely (or even mainly) on the emperor's change of heart-mind (心). The same goes for twentieth-century Confucian scholar-activists like Liang Shuming. Some passages in the Mencius seem to suggest the ruler's moral power is sufficient to change the world, but Mencius also puts forward ideas for social and political reform such as the well-field system that do not depend solely on the ruler's virtue.

Nor is there any particular reason to be restricted to the Confucian tradition. If Legalism, Daoism, Mohism, and other Chinese traditions offer possibilities for thinking about potentially stable and legitimate political institutions, then it seems dogmatic to refuse to consider those possibilities. Even "foreign" traditions, once implanted in Chinese soil, can take on Chinese characteristics and may be able to provide ideas for reform. In one widely circulated essay, the "new leftist" thinker Gan Yang, for example, has put forward the idea of "Confucian socialism" as the way to think about China's future political ideology.[4] He argues that there are three main traditions in Chinese history—the Confucian tradition, Maoist egalitarianism from 1949 to 1979, and the free market ideas that have emerged from the post–economic reform period. The surprising part about the essay is that Gan Yang recognizes the political importance of reviving Confucianism (most new leftists have tended to disparage Confucianism according to the stereotypes of the May 4, 1919 activists: it encourages blind subservience to rulers, it is rigidly patriarchal, it is incompatible with modern science, etc.). He doesn't say much about the content of Confucianism, but, like Jiang Qing, he invokes the Gongyang tradition. But it's only one source of inspiration, not *the* source. To the extent Confucianism will be appropriate for the modern world, it needs to be reconciled with left-egalitarian values. It may be possible to plumb the Gongyang tradition for similar ideas, but why should we not make use of the socialist tradition that offers rich resources for thinking about social solidarity and material equality? To my mind, and here I agree with Gan Yang, the future lies in some sort of "left Confucianism" that combines Confucian and socialist values. However we term this revived tradition, it would need to be sufficiently inspired by traditional Chinese cultural resources so that it can be viewed as legitimate by the Chinese people. But it need not be exclusively Confucian, and even less so exclusively inspired by the Gongyang Confucian tradition. Confucianism can be enriched by engaging with socialism, and vice versa.

The Political Implications of Three Types of Legitimacy

Be that as it may, the actual political recommendations put forth by Jiang do not turn on the validity of his critique of the Xinxing Confucian tradition, or even on the tenability of the distinction between the two main Confucian traditions he identifies. If the aim is to resolve China's current crisis of political legitimacy, the key question is whether the political institutions he proposes can do so. So let us return to Jiang's actual account of the Gongyang tradition, focusing specifically on political implications said to derive therefrom. This tradition is characterized by 王道政治 (the kingly way of politics). The main content of the "kingly way of politics" is that there are three types of legitimacy for political power (L, 156-57). One type of legitimacy is "heavenly" (天) and it refers to the legitimacy that comes from sacred sources (超越神圣的合法性). The second type is "earthly" (地), and it refers to the legitimacy that comes from historical continuity. The third type is "human" (人), and it refers to the legitimacy that comes from people's endorsement of political power and makes people willing to obey their rulers (L, 157). The last type of legitimacy is more familiar to Western ears—it seems similar to the democratic idea that government is legitimate to the extent that it derives from people's support—but Jiang warns over and over again that democratic sources of legitimacy should not have superiority over the other two forms. A political system is legitimate, according to the Gongyang tradition, if and only if all three types of legitimacy are properly balanced (L, 157-58, 167), with no one type being superior to the others.

One reason democratic legitimacy should not be superior is that democratic majorities may favor policies that are harmful to those not able to exercise political power, like children, ancestors, future generations, and animals. For example, Jiang notes that the Bush administration did not ratify the Kyoto accord on global warming partly because the current generation of American voters did not view it in their interest to do so (L, 162). Hence, there is a need for a balancing force of morally superior decision-makers able to take into account of the interests of all affected by policies, including future generations.[5]

Another reason democratic legitimacy should not be superior is that it won't be stable without historical roots. In a Western context, it may be stable because democracy has a long historical tradition, and people will stick with the system even during hard times. Moreover, they will fight to defend democratic values when they are threatened, as happened during World War II. But in non-Western societies, democracy lacks historical roots, and people may not stick with the system when it no longer suits their interests. If democracy leads to economic decline and political instability (at least, if it is perceived as being responsible for bad consequences), then "the people" may opt for other nondemocratic forms of government, such as fascism (L, 168).

So it is not sufficient to seek legitimacy via the people's support. A fully legitimate government should be legitimized to a certain extent by the people's support, but it also needs to be balanced by legitimacy that comes from decision-makers concerned with the interests of all those affected by the government's policies as well as legitimacy that comes from historical continuity. Only this kind of balanced government can be legitimate for the long term.

Jiang's proposals for institutionalizing the three types of legitimacy seem to owe more to his political imagination than to ancient texts. Such creativity is necessary, because any morally defensible attempt to revive traditions will involve putting forward new ideas and proposals. There may be good political reasons to appeal to past authorities to justify one's proposals—for example, they are more likely to be taken seriously if they are seen as coming from the minds of ancient sages—but fortunately Jiang does not merely recycle old ideas. He has thought hard about how to make real the three types of legitimacy in the Chinese context.

In the past, the three types of legitimacy took the form of autocratic rule (君主制) along with associated local, educational, and religious institutions (L, 169). In modern China, however, the old system has collapsed, the historical context has changed, and there is a need for new institutions appropriate for modern times. More concretely, Jiang argues that the three types of legitimacy should take the form of a tricameral legislature, with each house of government representing one type. The 通儒院 (House of Exemplary Persons) represents the legitimacy of the sacred sources, the 庶民院 (People's House) represents the legitimacy of the common people's endorsement, and the 国体院 (House of Cultural Continuity) represents the legitimacy of historical legacy.[6] The particular way of choosing the leaders and representatives of each house of government is quite complex. The members of the House of Exemplary Persons are chosen by nomination and appointment by Confucian organizations in civil society as well as official Confucian institutions. Regarding the latter group, they should be chosen on the basis of political experience as well as tested for knowledge and training in the Confucian classics (四书五经). The members of the People's House are chosen by elections and functional constituencies, and the members of the House of Cultural Continuity should be representatives of religions (including Buddhism, Daoism, Islam, and Christianity) and descendants of great sages and historical figures, including the descendants of Confucius himself (L, 170).

The key to balance is that none of the houses of government has more power than the others. Unlike Western democratic countries where the democratic house has ultimate power, and unlike Iran, where the Council of Guardians has ultimate power (L, 165), each house would have roughly equal power. In concrete terms, it means that no bill could be passed, no policy enacted, unless it has the support of all three houses. No part (or parts) of the system should dominate the other(s). That way, the three types of legitimacy could be balanced, and the ideal of the kingly way of politics could be realized.

An Evaluation of the Proposal for a Tricameral Legislature

The key to evaluating Jiang's proposal is whether it is likely to address China's current crisis of political legitimacy and to provide a long-lasting and stable political alternative. In Jiang's terms, the question is whether it is likely to secure the three kinds of legitimacy that ought to be secured. It's difficult to answer that question, because the political institutions Jiang proposes do not owe anything to actually existing political institutions. Although Jiang defends the Gongyang school of interpretation partly because it is concerned with actual historical experience rather than metaphysical speculation (P, 32), his actual political proposals do not seem to owe much to history, other than being inspired by a reading of the moral ideas put forth in "sacred" texts. If Jiang had been more concerned with historical continuity, he could have pointed to similar political institutions in past China—or, ideally, in contemporary China—that seem to have a certain degree of political legitimacy, then suggest how they can be reformed in ways that make them even more legitimate. Or perhaps he could have drawn on social science research showing that his recommended political institutions are more likely to be legitimate than others. In the Chinese context, he could have pointed to actually existing social groups more likely to support his proposals because it corresponds to their interests and aspirations. But Jiang does not do any of that. He seems rather pessimistic that his proposals could be implemented in contemporary China, and he pins his hopes on convincing the intellectual community of the merit of his proposals (L, 225-26). But if there's one thing we learned from the Chinese revolution, it's that the large majority of Chinese—namely, the farming class—must perceive political change to be in its interest. Unfortunately, Jiang does not try to put forward that kind of argument.

Of course, the farming class is likely to endorse the democratic house since it will be viewed as a way for its interests to be represented in the political process. In that sense, it will be easier to satisfy the type of legitimacy that comes from people's endorsement of political power. But Jiang says that the People's House should also be composed of deputies chosen by functional constituencies, meaning that different professions and social groups vote for their own representatives in the assembly. Again, this proposal doesn't seem to come from mainland China's historical experience (or from sacred sources), so we have to look elsewhere to evaluate the likelihood that functional constituencies are likely to secure the support of the people (hence satisfying the criterion that legitimacy comes from people's endorsement of political power).

The idea for "functional constituencies" can be traced to Hegel's proposal for a lower house of corporations and social guilds (as put forward in *Elements of a Philosophy of Right*). He worried that individuals not tied to any groups or organizations would be, in his words, "elemental, irrational, barbarous, and terrifying" (sec. 303; see also sec. 308). According to Hegel, individuals come to take an interest in common enterprises and to develop a certain degree of political competence only by joining and participating in voluntary associations and community groups, with the political implication that the lower house should be composed of corporations and professional guilds (the upper house should be composed of the landed propertied class).

In the modern world, the closest approximation of Hegel's ideal is the Legislative Council of Hong Kong. In 1985, the British colonial government decided to institute elections for a number of seats in order to represent more authoritatively the views of Hong Kong people. But it disparaged the idea of introducing direct elections for universal suffrage on the grounds that this might lead to instability. So the government decided that a large number of seats should be allocated to functional constituencies based on various interest groups, a system that still exists, with the largest block of seats assigned to business groups and professional associations. The problem is that it's the least legitimate part of Hong Kong's political system: most functional constituency representatives are perceived as serving the narrow concerns of the richest and most privileged sectors of the community, and there are endless disputes over how to draw the lines within and between the various voting blocs. In poll after poll, the large majority of Hong Kongers prefer to replace this system with directly elected seats. And yet Jiang proposes to implement functional constituencies in the house that's supposed to be the most democratic among the three legislatures! If the house is to have any hope of securing political legitimacy that comes from people's endorsement of political power, the Hong Kong experience suggests that the lower house would have to be fully democratic, meaning that deputies would be selected on the basis of one person, one vote.

It would be even more of a challenge to secure the other two types of legitimacy in the other two houses. The problem is that it's hard to tell—to measure—the effectiveness of legitimacy that comes from sacred sources and historical continuity. The only real way to test the legitimacy of political institutions is whether the people governed by the political institutions endorse them. At minimum, it would mean refraining from rebellion, and at maximum it would mean showing willingness to sacrifice for the political community in various forms, such as paying taxes, participating in the political process, and sacrificing for the country if it's threatened by outsiders.

The problem is that it's against most people's interest to support institutions that curb their own political power. In theory—and here I agree with Jiang—there is a good case to constrain the power of the majority. If majorities vote to oppress minorities, or to sacrifice the interests of future generations by pushing for rapid economic development regardless of the environmental consequences, or to vote for policies that impose substantial costs on disadvantaged outsiders (like agricultural subsidies from rich countries that penalize farmers in poor countries), or to support bloody unjust wars against other countries, then majorities *ought* to be constrained. The question is, how can we persuade most people that their power ought to be constrained? Jiang recognizes that true political legitimacy cannot rest on force or coercion, so at some level, "the people" need to endorse political institutions like the House of Exemplary Persons and the House of Cultural Continuity that constrain their own power. Under what conditions are they likely to do so?

The most obvious answer—one supported by mainland China's post-reform experience, as well as the experience of other economically successful East Asian states—is that states derive an important measure of political legitimacy if they manage to be effective in implementing policies for the people, meaning that they provide the goods that most people care about. What do most people care about? First and foremost, economic growth that provides the foundations for material well-being, employment, educational opportunities, and decent health care. If nondemocratic states can deliver economic growth, then they will have substantial political legitimacy. At the very least, they will avert rebellions. At most, they may cause some people to defend nondemocratic models as morally superior to democracies, as when Lee Kuan Yew praises less-than-democratic states that secure goods like economic growth and social order over democratic states (like the Philippines) that seem to do the opposite.

So let us turn to Jiang's model of a tricameral legislature. Is it likely to lead to effective policies that lead to economic growth while minimizing bad consequences of development such as economic inequality and environmental degradation? Here one has doubts. The main problem arises from Jiang's argument that the three houses of government, each securing a form of political legitimacy, should be "balanced," with no one house having more power than the other. Concretely, again, that would mean bills must be passed with the accord of all three houses. But what if the houses don't agree? What if the People's House favors no-holds-barred economic development, whereas the House of Exemplary Persons favors expensive measures that deal with global warming in the name of protecting the environmental well-being of future generations? Or what if the House of Cultural Continuity favors massive restoration projects for Qufu (Confucius's hometown) whereas the People's House prefers using those funds to provide for hospitals in poor areas? Such conflicts are bound to occur, and Jiang does not provide any mechanism for dealing with them. The likely result will be political gridlock, with the country unable to put forward policies that can provide for economic well-being and other desired goods that underpin political legitimacy in the real political world. The people won't put up with constraints on the democratic process if the government doesn't provide the goods, and there will be intense pressure to abolish, or at least to dilute the power of, the two nondemocratic institutions.

In short, there is a need for a constitutional framework that provides guidance for dealing with conflicts between the three houses of government. But no matter what the framework, it seems unlikely that three houses of government with decision-making power can ever function effectively together.[7] The risks of disagreement and consequent political paralysis are just too great. So the key political requirement for nondemocratic legitimacy—effective decision-making that provides the goods most people care about—would seem to require simplifying Jiang's proposal.

In my view, the most promising way to simplify the proposal would be to forgo the plan for a House of Cultural Continuity. For one thing, it can be viewed as a temporary political institution, according to Jiang's own logic. He notes that democracy is more deeply rooted in Western countries, so the legitimacy that comes from historical continuity can be secured by democratic institutions (L, 164–65). But Jiang's proposal has an important democratic component—the People's House—and if it becomes institutionalized in China's political future, then democracy would eventually become rooted in China, and there would be no need for an institution meant to safeguard historical continuity.[8]

Moreover, the actual political function of the House of Cultural Continuity can be secured by other means. Jiang says that the task of this institution would be to deal with such matters as the state religion, language, and territory (L, 170), but such matters could be put forth in a constitution, along with mechanisms for change that would involve deliberations in the other two houses. Most serious, perhaps, it is doubtful that the House of Cultural Continuity could ever be viewed as legitimate by the public at large. According to Jiang, this house would be composed at least partly of descendants of great leaders and cultural authorities of the past. But it would seem hard, if not impossible, to persuade contemporary Chinese that people are owed extra shares of political power due to their bloodline. Whatever plausibility such proposals may have had in the past has been undermined by the egalitarian ethos of the Chinese revolution. Such proposals are complete nonstarters, in my view, no more plausible than proposals to reinstate hereditary aristocrats in the British House of Lords.

What does have deeper roots in Chinese culture, in my view, is the idea of meritocracy: the idea that the most talented and public-spirited members of the political community should rule, or at least should be given extra shares of political power. The idea is that everyone should have an equal opportunity to be educated (in Confucius's words, "in education, there are no social classes," 15.39), and those with sufficient talent and virtue who succeed in open competition should be given extra shares of political power. This idea, of course, was institutionalized by means of the civil service examination system in imperial China,[9] and Jiang's idea for a House of Exemplary Persons, with deputies selected (at least partly) by examinations that test for knowledge of the Confucian classics, may well receive substantial support, particularly given what seems to be renewed interest in reviving Confucian education in contemporary China. Moreover, the revived civil service examination system is one way of maintaining historical continuity with the past, so the House of Exemplary Persons could simultaneously secure two types of legitimacy: the legitimacy that comes from sacred sources and the legitimacy that comes from historical continuity.

There are still some questions to be raised about the House of Exemplary Persons. First, it may be misleading to refer to the source of legitimacy as "sacred sources from Heaven." Confucius himself, for one, did not regard himself as a sage. Moreover, few Chinese today treat the texts as "sacred" in the same way that, say, Islamic people treat the Koran as the word of God.[10] And the effort to promote them as sacred texts is not likely to succeed in contemporary China. Just as it's difficult to "reenchant" the monarchy once it loses its magic, so it's difficult to "resacralize" books once they lose their magic. More importantly, perhaps, does it really matter if the texts being used are viewed as "sacred sources"? For educational purposes, what matters is that they can teach deep ethical ideas that provide guidance for the good life. For political purposes, what matters is that the texts offer guidance to members of the House of Exemplary Persons, meaning that those trained in the classics are more likely look out for the interests of those likely to be neglected in the People's House: future generations, minorities, disadvantaged groups, foreigners, animals, that is, all those affected by the state's policies who are likely to be neglected by democratic majorities. To my mind, what's good about the classics is that they teach people about the virtues that exemplary persons are supposed to exhibit, such as empathy, reciprocity, humility, and the ability to think as generalists. Such virtues should also be exhibited by political rulers entrusted with the task of looking out for the interests of all those affected by the state's policies, and that's why they should be studied by decision-makers. Ideally, the revived examinations would also test for other abilities and virtues more appropriate for modern-day decision-makers, such as basic knowledge of economics, science, and world history, as well as knowledge of a foreign language. There are many other questions to be answered, such as how to grade the exams in an impartial way, how to filter out clever but amoral (or immoral) exam takers, how to ensure representation by minority groups, and whether the decisions of the House of Exemplary Persons or the People's House should have priority in cases of conflict, but I shall leave these questions aside here.[11]

I suspect that Jiang will think that his proposals have been watered down to the point that they are not sufficiently Confucian, that without more state and institutional support for Confucianism, in particular, his interpretation of Confucianism, such proposals will not be sufficient to address the moral vacuum in contemporary China as well as the attendant crisis of political legitimacy. Hence, I would like to end by considering his proposal for enshrining Confucianism as China's state religion. Jiang is careful to distance himself from authoritarian views. He argues that state support for Confucianism might translate into resources for Confucian educational institutions, but that it would not mean prohibiting other religions.[12] He compares his proposal to state religions in the United Kingdom and Sweden, where other religions can and do flourish without fear of persecution. Still, the proposal to enshrine Confucianism as a state religion is deeply unpopular in mainland Chinese intellectual circles, even by some thinkers otherwise sympathetic to Confucianism. Qin Hui, for example, says that "it is fine to study and promote Confucianism, but setting up Confucianism as the national doctrine seems to imply treating opposition to Confucianism as heresy. . . . I am very much against it."[13] The main question is whether the Chinese state can be trusted with the task of promoting Confucianism without acting against other religions. The history of imperial China offers some hope in this respect. Typically, the state officially sanctioned Confucianism while tolerating competing religions or doctrines such as Buddhism and Daoism (the worst persecution of Buddhism was actually carried out by the Tang dynasty Emperor Wuzong who was a devout Daoist). But the history of the Chinese state since 1949, to say the least, does not inspire confidence in this respect. In the future, perhaps, it will demonstrate more tolerance to opponents of official ideologies and doctrines. Until that time, however, we need to be very cautious about proposals to implement an official religion in China.

Postscript (September 2007)

I wrote the preceding comments for a conference on Jiang Qing's thought held in June 2007. Jiang kindly offered detailed comments on each paper, including mine. I've also met Jiang at another conference last month. Let me report my personal impressions first. Jiang's moral integrity should inspire other innovative thinkers in China, whether or not they agree with his views. He clearly puts forth and defends an alternative to the political status quo, seemingly without fear of the consequences. He himself recognizes that it may take years for his ideas to have substantial political impact (he says twenty years, at least). Meanwhile, he has left his formal academic post and established a *shuyuan* (Confucian academy) in remote Guizhou province with the support of sympathetic businessmen. The academy is modeled on Confucian academies in the Song and Ming dynasties that were located in outlying parts of China so as to minimize the likelihood of political interference. The aim is to educate a community of friends and scholars in the

Confucian classics and to plant the seeds of political Confucianism. They read classic texts in the morning, discuss in the afternoon, and sing together in the evening.[14] One Beijing University philosophy professor told me that participants are particularly moved by the evening's activities. With his deep and lovely voice, I can imagine Jiang makes quite an impression.[15]

At first sight, Jiang lends support to the view of his critics that he is an anti-Western "Confucian fundamentalist." He wears the traditional Ming dynasty clothing of the Confucian intellectual and often greets people with hands clasped rather than the "Western" handshake. But when he greeted me, he shook my hand. As we parted, I tried to reciprocate by clasping my hands, but I put the "wrong" hand on top and he smiled, saying there was no need to worry about such things. This good cheer and openness also informed his response to my essay. He is not against Western ways. But the question is why they should be dominant in China. In personal life, why should Western clothing be regarded as "universal," as the only acceptable form of clothing? In politics, why shouldn't Confucian values inform political institutions? What he repudiates is the tendency to completely—blindly—repudiate the Confucian political tradition, in the manner of many twentieth-century Chinese intellectuals (whether liberal or Marxist).

Does he go to the other extreme? Not in my view. He argues that Confucianism should form the moral and political framework and that learning from other traditions can and should take place within that framework. But what's wrong with that? It's no more dogmatic than Western liberals who show openness to other traditions, but only within the framework of liberal democracy. Institutionally, he says (in his response), it means that the House of Exemplary Persons should have priority over the more democratic People's House. Ideally, the houses should try to agree on policy. But if they don't agree, the House of Exemplary Persons should have veto power of the decisions of the People's House.

What about the worry that the People's House would thus be marginalized from the political process? Jiang proposes to limit the power of the House of Exemplary Persons by limiting its veto power to three vetoes every five years. I'm not sure that would work in terms of Jiang's goal of securing the dominance of the House of Exemplary Persons: the People's

House might just force vetoes from the House of Exemplary Persons on relatively trivial matters in the first year or two, with the consequence that the House of Exemplary Persons would not able to get its way on important issues later. But it's an interesting proposal and less convoluted, arguably, than the complex formulas for determining priority of political institutions in some Western constitutions.

Regarding the House of Cultural Continuity, Jiang concedes that it has been the most controversial of his political proposals, but he insists that it's necessary for a political institution to secure such goods as the protection of the Chinese language. I'm still not persuaded, but there's something neat about the idea of three political institutions that reflect the intergenerational outlook of Confucianism, and one might imagine another variation: one institution with the task of securing the interests of ancestors, one for present-day people, and one for future generations.

Perhaps the key issue isn't legitimacy but stability. I still have trouble grasping what it means to secure legitimacy from "history" and the "sacred sources of Heaven." What is clear, however, is that the nondemocratic political institutions won't be stable for the long term if they don't secure the people's support. In his response, Jiang argues that "the Confucian House and the House of Historical Continuity that limit the power of the people do not need the people's agreement, because it is impossible to get people to agree to arrangements that limit their power." But that seems too pessimistic. Even countries with liberal-democratic frameworks have institutions that limit the people's political power, and such institutions are often widely respected. In the United States, for example, the Supreme Court, the armed forces, and the Federal Reserve Bank—all appointed rather than elected bodies—score highest in surveys asking Americans which institutions they most respect. In the Chinese context, with its tradition of benevolent rule and respect for educational achievement, it may be even easier to secure support from the people for political institutions that limit their power. Obviously, such support would also be desirable. As Chinese history shows, "the people" will rebel against political institutions they object to. Perhaps that's why Confucius himself argued that the most important task of government is to secure the "trust" of the people (12.7).

Jiang notes another problem: that it is difficult to persuade ordinary people on rational grounds since they may not understand the issues at stake. His solution is to ignore the uneducated masses. But perhaps he underestimates the political intelligence of ordinary people and overestimates that of intellectuals.[16] Jiang is surely right that political capacities vary—not everyone has the same capacity to make sensible and morally informed political judgments—but that capacity doesn't always correlate with educational levels and other standard measurements. Hence, it's still worth talking to people who might not seem initially receptive to reasoned political argument. What about those—the majority, perhaps—who are mainly moved by narrowly self-interested or emotional concerns? For the purpose of stabilizing the political system, it is still necessary to secure their support at some level. Hence the need for political practices and social rituals that include the people and make them feel part of the system. The real magic of elections, arguably, is that they seem to empower the people without really doing so. Meritocratic examinations open to all also make the people feel part of the system. There may be other possibilities. At any rate, the question of how to persuade those inclined to selfish or emotional political judgments of the merits of political institutions designed to empower exemplary persons should not be swept under the carpet. Jiang needs to win the people's hearts and maybe even their minds.

Notes

Introduction

1. I've also added two appendices—critical discussions of influential Chinese-language books on the contemporary relevance of Confucianism—that may be of interest to those who are reading this endnote.

Chapter 1: From Communism to Confucianism

1. What's temporary for Chinese leaders, however, may be longer than what others may have in mind (recall former premier Zhou Enlai's famous joke: asked what he thought about the French Revolution, he replied, "It's too early to tell"). In February 2007, Premier Wen Jiabao said: "We are still far away from advancing out of the primary stage of socialism. We must stick with the basic development guideline of that stage for one hundred years."

2. Marx rushed to write and publish *Capital* because he thought the communist revolution was about to occur in his day and thus feared his writings would be overtaken by events.

3. The aspiration to emulate Scandinavian welfare states is somewhat misplaced, in my view. The differences in history, population, level of economic development, and natural resource endowment make comparisons with China difficult, if not impossible. There may be more to learn from the experience with social welfare of other East Asian states such as Japan and South Korea that have similar traditions and economic trajectories, but national pride and memories of recent historical conflict often get in the way. At a recent conference on social justice organized by leading Chinese intellectuals, the attention seemed to be almost exclusively on learning from Scandinavian welfare states.

4. With the exception, of course, that most social democratic theories also defend, if not give priority to, civil and political rights. The CCP aims to secure the interests of the disadvantaged while maintaining tight curbs on the freedom of the press and the freedom to participate in the political process.

5. Cui's views have had political impact. In 1994, he wrote an article arguing for the preservation of the shareholding-cooperative system (SCS), which is a kind of labor-capital partnership. A leading official in the government read the article and decided to allow the SCS to spread in rural China. The centralized decision-making of the one-party state has many disadvantages, but one advantage is that it may be easier to implement radical (but defensible) ideas if the top leadership is convinced.

6. I would like to note that the argument regarding the end of ideology by the distinguished American sociologist Daniel Bell (no relation), has been widely misunderstood. The main argument in his influential 1960 book *The End of Ideology* is that Marxism has been exhausted as an ideology in the United States, not that all normative ideologies have been, or should be, replaced by nonideological commitment to technocratic decision-making.

7. As Peter Hays Gries has noted (conference in Beijing, October 2006), many Chinese intellectuals call on the state to deal with extreme forms of nationalism (rather than viewing the state itself as part of the problem).

8. Yes, there is a huge gap between the reality and the ideal—corruption is rampant among government officials, and those at the wheel of government vehicles in Beijing often drive like maniacs, as though they're above the rules that others are supposed to follow. In one important respect, however, government officials are forced to lead by moral example: the one child per family rule is rigorously implemented for the seventy-three million members of the party, whereas the rules are often more lax for nonmembers, especially in rural areas.

9. Hu Jintao's only recorded joke came when he was visiting the United States five years ago. The then-governor of New Jersey, James McGreevey, told Hu—whose hair is jet black—that he did not look his fifty-nine years. Hu replied: "China would be happy to share its technology in this area" (*The Australian*, September 2, 2007).

10. Some secondary schools in Beijing are replacing the works of the "anti-Confucian" writer Lu Xun with the works of Jin Yong.

11. Of course, such practices are not distinctively Chinese. But there are other relevant differences. One former student who went to the United States for overseas study told me she was shocked when her host family's elderly parents paid separately in restaurant outings with their adult children: that would be the height of immorality in a Chinese context.

12. The use of Confucianism in Chinese prisons is not so unusual. Changchun Beijiao prison in Jilin province has a "Confucian classroom" and closed circuit TVs that send Confucius's sayings into cells. Warden Yang Mingchang explains: "The study of traditional Chinese culture can help inmates cultivate virtue and promote good behavior."

13. In Beijing, for example, I've "asked" my son to attend weekly tutorials at a privately run school that focuses on the teaching and memorizing of Confucian classics. The teacher—an admirably gentle and patient graduate from Tsinghua law school—also questions the students and helps with interpretation. Why memorize the passages? The idea is that the students will have ready access to the relevant values and stories of exemplary behavior that can be applied in different ways at different stages of life.

14. Interestingly, some academic conferences and websites use Confucius's alleged birth date as "year zero," followed by the Western (Christian) calendar date.

15. The Central Party School in Beijing now teaches the Confucian classics and seems to be moving toward the mission of promoting both Marxism and traditional Chinese culture. Such a change in approach has been made official in the party-run

Socialism College (*zhongyang shehuizhuyi xueyuan*) designed to train overseas Chinese, Taiwanese, Hong Kongers and "friendly foreigners": it has been named the Chinese Culture College (*zhonghua wenhua xueyuan*). Both names are used in the official literature.

16. Civil service examinations have been revived in China, with thousands of people competing for top spots. These exams are largely meritocratic (meaning that the successful candidates are the ones with the top scores), but they test for political ideology in ways that reward conformity rather than political ability. More pertinently, the successful candidates are theoretically supposed to implement policy, not make it (unlike the successful candidates of the imperial examinations, who occupied posts of political power). Internal party advancements have been made more meritocratic of late, but political advancement is still limited to party members, and those who reach the top spots do so at least partly (if not mainly) due to their ability to outmaneuver political opponents and refrain from taking unpopular positions (not the sort of traits that would be valued by a system designed to reward ability and public-spiritedness). The reform-minded members of the CCP seem to favor intraparty democratic elections for leaders (similar to political reforms in Vietnam) rather than emphasize more meritocracy within the party.

17. In South Korea, perhaps the most Confucian-influenced country in East Asia, Confucian intellectuals played an important role in the prodemocracy movements that eventually led to the establishment of electoral democracy in that country.

18. In Chinese, it is common to comment on the "quality" (*suzhi*) of the people. Nor is it just a matter of educated elites looking down on the *hoi polloi*. The migrant-worker waitresses at the Purple Haze restaurant in Beijing, where I am part owner, complain about the "quality" of customers who bark commands, show disrespect, and act in a selfish manner (e.g., four customers reserved a table for ten on a busy night, spread newspapers, and read for a couple of hours).

19. Lee claims to be inspired by Confucianism, but he is trained in law rather than philosophy and the Confucian classics. Not surprisingly, the political system he has put in place owes much more to Chinese-style Legalism than Confucianism: the heavy reliance on fear and harsh punishments for social control in Singapore is far removed from Confucian ideals that emphasize rule by moral example and informal norms and rituals (with legal punishments as a last resort). Had Lee been actually trained in the Confucian classics, it is hard to imagine he would show the same lack of humility and vindictiveness toward political opponents.

20. I do not mean to imply that there are no good arguments for justifying constraints on the democratic process in Singapore. One of the virtues of Lee Kuan Yew is that he has publicly attempted to justify Singapore's regime without being constrained by Western-style notions of political correctness. I try to evaluate his arguments in my book *East Meets West*.

21. It is worth recalling that the spring 1989 prodemocracy demonstrators were led by student elites from China's most prestigious universities. Even the anti-intellectual Cultural Revolution was led (initially) by students from China's most prestigious universities (including Tsinghua).

22. The examinees for the all-important *gaokao* (college entrance examinations) are sequestered during the examination process and prevented from communicating with the outside world so as not to leak the answers. And no matter how corrupt things are in contemporary China, the *gaokao* examination process is relatively clean.

23. Such fears are widespread among intellectual elites in China, but they are not absent in other contexts: Bryan Caplan, an economist at George Mason University, has written a provocative book titled *The Myth of the Rational Voter: Why Democracies Choose Bad Policies*. Caplan argues that "voters are worse than ignorant; they are, in a word, irrational—and vote accordingly" (2), and he favors tests of voter competence, or "giving extra votes to individuals or groups with greater economic literacy" (197). The book has been widely discussed (see Gary Bass, *New York Times Magazine*, May 27, 2007), but the chances of his proposals being adopted in the American context are roughly zero. In China, however, he may get a better reception.

24. The symbolic leader of the state—perhaps the eldest member of the meritocratic house—could also be selected from the meritocratic house. One of the problems with democracy in Confucian-influenced Taiwan and South Korea is that excessive faith is placed in elected leaders who are expected to manifest the traits of Confucian morally exemplary leaders. The leaders are then given strong executive authority, leading to abuse of power, corruption, and nepotism. Naturally, disillusionment soon sets in, there is a popular backlash, and the leaders end their days in disgrace (see Randall Peerenboom's impressively researched book, *China Modernizes*). If the symbolic leader is chosen from the meritocratic house, there would be less of an expectation of morally exemplary leadership on the part of democratic leaders, the people would be more rational in evaluating their elected leaders, and the democratic system itself would be more stable.

25. In the sobering documentary *An Inconvenient Truth*, Al Gore notes that he has been hammering away about the dangers of global warming for decades and he expresses frustration at the lack of interest among democratically elected decision-makers in the United States. China will soon be the largest contributor of greenhouse gases (in terms of new contributions; the United States will still be far ahead in terms of total and per capita contributions) and the imperative to limit these emissions should be obvious to anyone who has seen the movie. The question is, who is more likely to enact laws that limit greenhouse gases in China: political leaders chosen by poor farmers who understandably worry first and foremost about short-term economic development in their districts, or deputies in the meritocratically chosen legislature?

Chapter 2: War, Peace, and China's Soft Power

1. Kang Xiaoguang, "Zhongguo roan liliang jianshe yu Rujia wenhua fuxing de guanxi" (China's Soft Power and Its Relation to the Revival of Confucian Culture), www.tech.cn/data/detail.php?id=12170, visited July 3, 2007.

2. The English translation is adapted from *Sources of Chinese Tradition*, ed. Wm. Theodore de Bary and Irene Bloom, 2nd ed., 343.

3. Interestingly, the Chinese government refers to the current stage of economic development as striving toward the *xiaokang shehui* (society of moderate prosperity). As noted in the previous chapter, it is vague about what is supposed to come afterward.

4. Quoted in Shi Ping-hua, "Chinese Utopianism in Political Discourse: Comparing Japan and the Former Soviet Union in Social Reforms (1898–2000)," http://new.china-review.com/article.asp?id=16705, visited June 27, 2007.

5. Quoted in Joseph Chan, "Territorial Boundaries and Confucianism," in *Confucian Political Ethics*, ed. Daniel A. Bell, 67.

6. For an English translation, see http://new.china-review.com/article.asp?id=17048, visited June 27, 2007.

7. Note, however, that China is one of the few countries to have territorial boundaries within its country: the borders to Macau and Hong Kong are functionally equivalent to international borders, and the *hukou* (household registration system) imposes more restrictions on labor mobility than, say, workers in the European Union. I do not mean to imply that such restrictions are necessarily illegitimate—they are mainly explained by the huge differences in wealth within China, and the fact that rich regions fear being overwhelmed by poor immigrants—but the ideal of Tian Xia can serve to remind us that they are temporary, less-than-ideal solutions to difficult circumstances and that boundaries should be done away with at the earliest opportunity.

8. The twentieth-century Confucian scholar Mou Zongsan (1909–95) responded to such concerns by rejecting the superiority of Chinese culture, but he went to the other extreme of affirming a diversity of cultures that are worthy of *equal* respect. Other cultures may be worthy of respect, but it seems dogmatic to affirm that they are worthy of equal respect prior to detailed engagement and understanding of those cultures. And the way that Mou Zongsan goes about his cross-cultural comparisons suggests that Confucianism may still be doing the work—he claims that the four basic ethical instincts of human beings identified by Mencius (the heart of compassion, of shame, of courtesy and modesty, and of right and wrong) are the same for everyone, but their concrete norms and modes of expression may vary from culture to culture (Chan, "Territorial Boundaries and Confucianism," 79). It is highly unlikely that, say, a devout Muslim would view her moral commitments as mere variations upon Confucian themes.

9. I do not mean to imply that Confucian thinkers are unique in this respect. If anything, the messianic impulse—the view that the state can and should embody universal principles to be promoted abroad—runs much deeper in American political discourse. And it's not just religious fanatics. The liberal *New York Times* columnist Thomas L. Friedman writes that Americans "need to find a way to reknit America at home, reconnect America abroad and restore America to its natural place in the global order—as the beacon of progress, hope and inspiration" ("The Power of Green," *New York Times Magazine*, April 15, 2007).

10. There may be brief, euphoric moments in history (e.g., shortly after the revolution) when such feelings may have been widespread, but it is difficult to sustain regimes premised on the extinguishing of self-interest and particularistic attachments.

11. Chinese intellectuals also debate whether Chinese can and should become a more global language and whether more efforts should be spent teaching and promoting Chinese to visitors during the Olympics instead of speaking English to them (*Nanfang Zhoumou* [Southern Weekly], August 16, 2007, E31).

12. To be more precise, it is inconsistent with key values of the early (original) Confucians. The neo-Confucians were deeply influenced by Daoism and Buddhism and this altered or made problematic core Confucian values (see Philip J. Ivanhoe, *Ethics in the Confucian Tradition*).

13. Confucius (in)famously argued that the care owed to elderly parents could justify covering up the crimes of one's father: "The Duke of She told Confucius, 'In my country there is a man called Upright Kung. When his father stole a sheep, he bore witness against him.' Confucius said, "In my country, the upright people are different from this. A father covers up for his son, and a son covers for his father. Uprightness lies in this" (13.18). Not surprisingly, the Legalist Han Fei Zi opposed the Confucian view that family obligations have priority over others, arguing that it is incompatible with successful warfare (he fabricated a story about Confucius rewarding a man who had run away from battle to care for his aged father, with the moral that "a man who is a filial son to his father may be a traitorous subject to his lord"). The tension between competing ties to the family and the state is a recurring theme in Chinese history. Once, at dinner time, my son reported to family members that I had wasted some food. I replied, half-jokingly, with the Confucian line that sons should cover up for their fathers. My father-in-law, an elderly revolutionary cadre (veteran of three wars), replied that Confucius's view is "wrong." Keeping in mind the value of filial piety, I resisted the urge to defend Confucius.

14. Concern for other peoples is typically motivated by familiarity and personal encounters, and globalization of various sorts has been beneficial in terms of expanding our range of concern. Consider that Adam Smith, writing in 1759, could suggest that "a man of humanity in Europe" would not lose any sleep upon hearing news that the "great empire of China, with all its myriads of inhabitants, was suddenly swallowed up by an earthquake." In comparison, the "most frivolous disaster which could befall himself would occasion a more real disturbance. If he was to lose his little finger tomorrow, he would not sleep to-night; but provided he never saw them, he will snore with the most profound security over the ruin of his brethren, and the destruction of that immense multitude seems plainly an object less interesting to him, than this paltry misfortune of his own. To prevent, therefore, this paltry misfortune to himself, would a man of humanity be willing to sacrifice the lives of a hundred millions of his brethren, provided he had never see them?" (*The Theory of Moral Sentiments*, part 3, chap. 3). Smith's general point that "we are always so much more deeply affected by whatever concerns ourselves" may be correct, but it would be difficult to imagine a contemporary Western thinker putting forward such an example, precisely because

"European" moral sensibilities have expanded due to substantial personal contact with the Chinese. Smith could write about the Chinese as though they live on another planet because few if any Europeans had developed any personal feelings for them, but obviously that's not true today (for the record, I would gladly sacrifice my little finger to save the Chinese people, if only because I'd also be swallowed up by Smith's imagined earthquake).

15. The All China Federation Trade Union is collaborating with a leading workers' union in Romania to protect the rights of Chinese workers in that country (Mirel Bran, "Pékin organise la défense des travailleurs Chinois en Roumanie," *Le Monde*, June 21, 2007).

16. It can be argued that the rhetoric of utopian cosmopolitanism might actually be more attractive to foreigners who are not expected to sympathize with the idea that China has legitimate national self-interests to pursue in the international arena. But the realities of competition in international relations would quickly show China to be hypocritical if it justifies its foreign policy with cosmopolitan rhetoric, and the result might be worse than if China occasionally appeals to national self-interest. Part of why the United States is so disliked abroad is that it appeals to supposedly universal values like democracy and freedom while not publicly admitting that its actions are often determined by national self-interest.

17. This section draws upon my book *Beyond Liberal Democracy*, chap. 2.

18. Ming Yongquan, "Youmeiyou zhengyi de zhanzheng? Yilun Rujia (wang ba zhi bian)" (Are There Just Wars? A Confucian Debate on True Kings and Hegemons), http:www.arts.cuhk.hk/~hkshp, visited October 11, 2003.

19. Mencius did say that a sage-king, who would conquer the world by means of moral power, was long overdue, but he noted that sage-kings come in five-hundred-year cycles and rarely last more than a generation or two (2B.13, 5A.5). According to Mencius's own theory, the nonideal world of competing states delimited by territorial boundaries is the reality for roughly 90 percent of the time. Note too the difference between Mencius's cyclical view of history and the linear view of progress put forward by Kang Youwei.

20. Ni Lexiong, "Zhongguo gudai junshi wenhua guannian due shijie heping de yiyi" (The Implications of Ancient Chinese Military Culture for World Peace), *Junshi lishi yanjiu* (Military History Research), vol. 2 (2001). An English translation of this article appears in *Confucian Political Ethics*, ed. Daniel A. Bell, chap. 10.

21. Gong Gang, "Shei shi quanqiu lunli de daidao shiwei" (Who is the Armed Guard of Global Ethics?), *Nanfang chuang*, September 2003, http://www.nfcmag.com/news/newsdisp.php3?NewsId=296&mod=, visited November 10, 2003.

22. As a matter of domestic policy, however, the language of human rights is much better received in China, by critics of the regime as well as official government circles.

23. Of course, the bombing (accidental, according to the U.S. government) of the Chinese embassy in Belgrade sealed the matter in the eyes of (most?) Chinese. I personally experienced the reaction in Hong Kong. The one time I was truly made to feel

like an outsider among otherwise sympathetic mainland Chinese friends and family members was when I argued that the war against Serbia was still justified, even after the bombing. I rapidly learned to keep my views to myself, in the interest of maintaining harmony with loved ones!

24. In response to such cases of apparently misguided priorities, Amnesty International has expanded its mission to include economic and social rights (see my book *Beyond Liberal Democracy*, 94).

25. Given the likely civilian casualties, however, Confucian critics would likely emphasize other means of opposition, such as remonstrance or targeted killing of the North Korean leaders responsible for the famine.

26. But would Taiwan be justified in defending itself if attacked by the mainland? For the Confucian, the judgment would depend partly on the moral character of the Taiwanese ruler, the degree of popular support in Taiwan for that leader, and the likely consequences of other options such as surrender (not so bad if the Chinese army withdraws soon after invasion and the Chinese government restores the status quo ante) or exile (Mencius holds that the humane ruler faced with certain defeat will leave his kingdom rather than expose his people to harm, and he will eventually be followed by his people [IB.15]).

27. Much of the rest of world has yet to be persuaded that China can play a responsible role in foreign affairs. According to a survey of eighteen countries carried out by the Chicago Council on Global Affairs, 52 percent of respondents said China could not be trusted to act responsibly in foreign affairs, including 76 percent of the French, 61 percent of South Koreans, and 58 percent of Americans. An NBC News/ *Wall Street Journal* poll found that Americans ranked "improving human rights" as the most important thing the government could do in the run-up to the Olympics, ahead of implementing environmental policies or practicing fair trade (*Japan Times*, September 6, 2007). Such views are reflected in my own experience. Whenever I try to humanize China to foreigners, I'm asked, "What about the Tiananmen Square massacre, Tibet, Fanlungong, etc.?" No doubt the Western press's tendency to report the bad news contributes to such views, but the Chinese government's behavior doesn't always help, to say the least.

28. In my view, it would also restore China's moral credibility in the eyes of many Chinese intellectuals. The Chinese Communist Party may fear that apologizing for June 4 may lead to pressure for it to apologize for other moral wrongs in post-1949 history, which could undermine its legitimacy. But the slaughter on June 4 was morally worse in the sense that peaceful civilians were deliberately killed by the army on the orders of the central government (far more people died in the Great Leap Forward and the Cultural Revolution, but mainly as a result of unintended consequences of central policymaking), so the government doesn't have the same moral obligation to take responsibility for other wrongs. Nor does the government have to worry that an apology would reignite the prodemocracy forces that inspired millions of Chinese in spring 1989. Several leaders of the prodemocracy movements are now active in the revival of Confucianism in China, on the assumption that political models need to be

rooted in Chinese traditions. If there is another political opening similar to spring 1989, it is highly unlikely that the galvanizing symbol would be the Statue of Liberty.

CHAPTER 3: HIERARCHICAL RITUALS FOR EGALITARIAN SOCIETIES

1. Confucian (and other) thinkers often argue for desirable social practices such as ritual with the claim that they are distinctly human and separate us from beasts. Animals do have cognitive limitations: e.g., they cannot grasp the idea that traditional rituals link them with the past or the idea that rituals can civilize our desires. But animals that live with humans can also be sensitive to the emotions that mark some rituals. At the wake for my father, my sister's two dogs showed radically different behavior. One dog, named Caesar, seemed to feel the sadness, and he hid in a corner during the wake, hardly mustering the energy to eat at mealtime. The other dog, named Bubbles, seemed uncontrollably cheerful, licking the mourners's hands and diving into her food. I still cannot forgive that dog.

2. This is not to deny that rituals may be backed up by informal sanctions, such as family or community pressure. But if people participate in rituals only because they fear sanctions (without any emotional involvement or sense of reverence for the ideals expressed by the ritual), then they do not count as rituals in Xunzi's sense.

3. Some passages seem to suggest that Xunzi also appeals to (nothing more than) the good moral sense of rulers: for example, he says that the true king should care for the "five incapacitated groups," meaning the deaf, dumb, disabled, missing an arm or leg, or dwarfed (9.1). But in the next passage (9.2) Xunzi appeals to the self-interest of the ruler, noting that such policies will contribute to the ruler's fame increasing day by day, the world longing for him, and his orders being carried out and prohibitions heeded (see also 9.4, where Xunzi notes that such polices as assistance to those in poverty and need will lead people to feel secure with the government, which eventually leads to glory and fame for the ruler). Moreover, Xunzi's suggestions for dealing with those who hold unorthodox doctrines—the first task of the sage-king should be to execute them and only then deal with thieves and robbers, "because although one can succeed in getting robbers and thieves to transform themselves, one cannot get these men to change" (5.18)—suggests that Xunzi thinks there are real limits to the possibility of moral transformation.

4. Xunzi goes on to say that "the many would inflict violence on the few and wrest their possessions from them" (23.9), presumably to persuade the rich minority that it's also in their interest to live in civilized society.

5. Xunzi himself did not conceive of the possibility of a socially egalitarian society because he thought that hierarchical society was essential for collective economic efforts. As Henry Rosemont, Jr. puts it, "no hierarchical society, no collective efforts; no collective efforts, no society whatsoever; no society, no justice whatsoever" ("State and Society in the Xunzi," in *Virtue, Nature, and Moral Agency in the Xunzi*, ed. T. C.

Kline III and Philip J. Ivanhoe, 9). Collective economic efforts may no longer require hierarchical arrangements in particular areas (like computer software design), but Xunzi's views about the need for hierarchy to secure collective economic efforts will continue to hold true so long as the mass of humanity continues to toil in fields and factories.

6. As Patricia Buckley Ebrey puts it, "Confucian texts and the rituals based on them did not simply convey social distinctions. At another level, they overcame them by fostering commonalities in the ways people performed rituals" (*Confucianism and Family Rituals in Contemporary China*, 228). In contrast to early modern Europe, Ebrey argues, "Over time class differences in the performance of family rituals seem to have narrowed rather than widened" (228).

7. The funerals of castrated criminals should be sparse and low-key compared to other funerals so as to reflect the disgraceful life of the criminal (19.10). But if such funerals are contrasted with the recommendations of Xunzi's supposed Legalist followers—cruel death by torture of the criminal himself if not his whole family—then Xunzi's humane recommendations become more apparent.

8. The dead do have interests: for example, I do not want my body to be laid out in public to be devoured by dogs and insects after I die. It could be argued that the dead can protect their own interests because they have the power to intervene in the world of the living (by means of ghosts and such), though Xunzi would likely reject such supernatural explanations for changes in the world of the living.

9. To be more precise, rituals only *seem* to be in the interests of rulers at the start, when rulers think in narrowly self-interested ways. But if rituals do what they're supposed to do, they would transform the rulers' sense of what is in their interests. That is, the rulers would begin to care more about those who participate in the rituals, including the weak and the poor, and then the rituals actually do begin to serve the (new), morally improved interests of rulers.

10. As P. J. Ivanhoe notes, another difference is the "obsession with 'fame' in the West. Fame is something that 'anyone' can win, since it has little to do with content. One can became famous for just about anything. Rituals tend to dampen the importance of fame by taking focus of the individual per se and putting it more on the relationships she or he enjoys. Those who have *renown* in ritual society gain it on the basis of their character, which tends to function to promote the common good" (email on file with author).

11. I do not mean to imply that only hierarchical rituals help to explain the relatively egalitarian distribution of wealth in East Asian societies such as Japan and South Korea. No doubt also factors, such as economic policies, international relations, and other values such as a strong work ethic and the propensity to save are crucial. My point is that rituals play an important (but difficult to quantify) role in motivating the rich and powerful to accept measures that contribute to economic equality such as high tax rates. Hierarchical rituals may also help to explain the "ethnic homogeneity" said to characterize (and underpin) relatively egalitarian East Asian societies: "ethnic homogeneity" is not a natural category; it is a subjective feeling that must be created

through a historical process, and participation in hierarchical rituals that generate a sense of commonality may also help to explain why Japanese and Koreans feel part of an "ethnic" community.

12. Needless to say, egalitarian rituals such as handshaking also take place between members of different classes. In such cases, however, they often take hierarchical characteristics: the more powerful will offer his or her hand first and the grip will be firmer. And in East Asian societies the weaker member will often lower his or her head slightly in recognition of the higher status of the powerful person.

13. In contrast, the Western host typically does not wait until the guest has physically disappeared from view. Once the taxi door closes, the Western host turns away and resumes his or her other activities. My own French Canadian mother follows such habits, and while I'm hurt at the time, I cannot blame her for following the Western ways she has yet to question. It would not be effective to raise the possibility of alternatives because she is not always as flexible as she might be (during her visit to China, she insisted on kissing my Chinese friends on the cheeks because "that's the French way"). In such cases, I've learned not to criticize my mother in order to maintain harmonious ties and adhere to the value of filial piety.

14. Music, as we will see in the following chapter, also increases the feelings of reverence and thus the likelihood that feelings of commonality develop during the course of the ritual. One may add that drinking alcohol also contributes to a sense of commonality, thus helping to explain why the ritual of toasting seems to be so common in otherwise different societies. At relatively formal Chinese meals, the host or person with highest status often goes from table to table to toast all the banquet participants.

15. Interestingly, the social status of teachers seems to be independent of their class status. In China, the average salary of teachers is quite low compared to other professions. In fact, I'd argue that the relatively low income of teachers enhances the social standing of teachers; they may be seen as relatively intelligent people who choose their profession at least partly for other-regarding reasons. In Hong Kong, university professors have very high salaries, but their social standing is lower than in China (I taught in both Hong Kong and Beijing, and the different reaction by taxi drivers suffices to demonstrate this point: in Hong Kong, the typical reaction is that I'm lucky to have found the kind of job that provides good material benefits; in Beijing, there seems to more genuine respect for my job, and the respect only increases when I respond half-jokingly that I teach students "useless" philosophy).

16. I have visited homes of migrant workers in the Beijing suburbs as well as homes of my father-in-law's relatives in impoverished rural China, and I was struck by the presence of certificates of educational prizes of children posted on the otherwise bare walls.

17. My first job was at Singapore's National University. I was only a few years older than most of my students, and I encouraged them to address me as "Daniel," but it almost never worked. Exasperated, I once scolded a student who repeatedly called me "Dr. Bell" and told him he shouldn't be so formal and should address me

as "Daniel." He immediately responded "Yes, sir!" I learned to live with "Dr. Bell" after that.

18. In Oxford, where I did my graduate studies, there is a division of labor between the academic tutor and the moral tutor. In theory, the academic tutor should deal with academic matters and the moral tutor should deal with moral and emotional matters (in practice, the academic tutor often deals with other matters, and the institution of the moral tutor is widely regarded as not very useful). It is inconceivable that such a division of labor could be implemented in East Asian universities.

19. The teacher's responsibility for the student's moral development was made explicit in Qing dynasty legal regulations: Charlotte Ikels notes that in the extreme case of the murder of a parent, the offender's principal teacher would suffer capital punishment (*Filial Piety*, 5).

20. In China, part of the responsibility or pressure is political. When the anti-Japan protests in Beijing in April 2005 threatened to get out of hand, the Tsinghua professors were told to speak to their students (on a private basis, qua supervisor) to ask them to refrain from participating in further protests.

21. The importance of establishing an emotional connection between teacher and student also shapes educational practices in primary school. It is common for the same teacher to teach the same set of students for several years (in the case of my own son, he had the same teacher for three years at the primary school attached to Tsinghua, up to the point that the students scattered to different junior high schools. Parents were invited on the last day and the farewell scenes were deeply moving).

22. The practice of communal eating in China dates from the Northern Song dynasty (*Nanfang Zhoumou* [Southern Weekly], March 9, 2006); previously, separate "Western-style" servings were served to individuals. Whatever the explanation for the change, it contributed to more harmony at mealtime and, arguably, society at in large.

23. In the context of an argument that morality counteracts our bad natures and stems from conscious commitment to ritual and moral duty, Xunzi notes that "when a person is hungry, upon seeing an elder, he or she will not eat before the elder; rather, the elder will be deferred to" (23.6). On the assumption that Xunzi is describing a common practice of his own day, we can infer that *rang* at mealtime predates communal eating practices. Perhaps the development of communal eating practices further facilitated *rang* practices.

24. In the past, it was common for children of rich families to eat separately from the adults. Such practices should be criticized if they do not effectively teach the young to defer to their elders. The rituals are only effective at generating concern for the vulnerable if they involve interaction between the different groups of society.

25. For example, the 1,800 employees at Broad Air Conditioning, in Changsha, live, work and eat together in a company town. The entire workforce participates in group singing, with many employees playing musical instruments (James Fallows, "Mr. Zhang Builds His Dream Town," *Atlantic Monthly*, March 2007).

26. At the Purple Haze restaurant in Beijing, for example, the boss-manager designs clothes for the young migrant worker waitresses at the restaurant (I am in-

volved as a minority shareholder in this restaurant, but I do not manage the restaurant and can observe such practices qua researcher).

27. The Qing dynasty established a Ministry of Rituals, but its specific function was to manage relations between tributary states rather than help the weak more generally. Still, it may have had positive effects for the weak. One might speculate that Chinese imperialism did not typically involve European-style brutality and contempt for the "natives" partly because the tributary states paid symbolic homage to the Chinese, thus establishing some sort of sense of community among the groups, and making the Chinese power-holders less likely to abuse the vulnerable people of the tributary states. I do not mean to deny that others factors, such as technological limitations, may also have played a role in limiting oppression by the Chinese overlords.

28. I still have bad memories from my childhood, when team captains would pick players in turn according to perceived ability (I was usually picked toward the end). Among Chinese children, teams are usually chosen by means of a random procedure.

29. It might take actual experience with East Asians for Westerners to really appreciate the social utility of *rang*. Several years ago, I recall arguing with my wife about which restaurant we should choose for dinner. My Korean graduate student whispered *rang* in my ear. I understood, I let her choose, and the rest of the evening went smoothly.

Chapter 4: Sex, Singing, and Civility

1. Even more surprising, perhaps, the minimum age for prostitution in Singapore is sixteen, though there has been debate about whether the age should be raised to eighteen.

2. The risk is not just HIV infection: according to a study published in the January 13, 2007, issue of the *Lancet*, syphilis has returned to China with a vengeance, and the reemergence of prostitution in the postreform era is an important cause.

3. Singapore-style government-regulated prostitution may owe more to the country's British colonial heritage. The history of legalized prostitution in Singapore goes back to the early twentieth century, when the British colonial rulers forced liberal legislation on the colony (mainly so that British soldiers could have access to prostitutes) against the advice of local authorities and Chinese community rulers.

4. Similar institutions have a long history in China. According to Charles Benn, the high-class courtesans in Tang dynasty (ca. 618–907) bordellos were trained in "the skills of their trade: singing and the rules of drinking in particular . . . [They were] prized more, or at least as much as, for their talents as entertainers at feasts than for their sexual services" (*China's Golden Age*, 65, 64). One of the hostesses I interviewed took pride in revealing the long historical heritage of her trade.

5. It could be that many Westerners do not enjoy singing because it wasn't part of their childhood education and they did not have an opportunity to develop that talent (I place myself in this category). In East Asian societies, children are often made to

learn group singing in schools and elsewhere. This may help to explain why East Asian societies are typically regarded as group-oriented societies (relative to most Western societies). Or it could be that group-oriented societies are more likely to teach group singing to young children. Of course, there are also occasions for group singing in Western societies that forge (and express) social solidarity: I attended a Premier League (English) football game at Tottenham, and the fans movingly, and spontaneously, joined in several songs that depended on the flow of the game. But such occasions are relatively few and far between (compared to East Asian societies). More common these days, perhaps, is the isolation of those plugged in to their iPod.

6. Yeeshan Yang, *Whispers and Moans: Interviews with the Men and Women of Hong Kong's Sex Industry*, 152. Not surprisingly, Yang finds that "very few of the Hong Kong local prostitutes I know like western customers, claiming that their attitude toward prostitutes is not as respectful as Chinese men" (151). The large majority of prostitutes interviewed by Yang also objected to the Westernized term "sex workers," because it implies that the women are only selling sex (153–55)

7. It is often difficult to identify the precise causal factors. I do not know of any experiment that tests whether customers would prefer karaoke-style social prostitution over Western-style individualistic market exchanges for sex, other things being equal. But I can point to one example that shows a preference for group activity over what most Westerners would consider to be private. In the male locker room for the Tsinghua University swimming pool, bathers are given the choice between group and individual showers (naked showering in both cases). To my surprise, most bathers seem to choose group showering (which often involves talking and joking) even when private showers are available (both types of showers are free).

8. For a vivid account of a "streetwalker" in Shenzhen, see Sang Ye's interview in *China Candid*, chap. 15. During a visit to Korea, I was taken on an informal tour of sites for prostitution in a remote town. There were three forms ranked in order of prestige and expense. The "lowest" form consists of brief sex for money exchanges between johns and sex workers that advertise their wares in difficult-to-find red-light districts. The next, slightly more expensive form takes place in "coffee" shops: customers sit at booths and order "ten thousand cups" of coffee, money is paid for the "coffee," and then the customer retreats to the back room for sexual liaisons. The most expensive form consists of karaoke-style prostitution.

9. Japanese-style porn films can be partly explained by laws that curb the explicit portrayal of sex organs. Porno comics in Japan—with fewer restrictions—are extremely violent and graphic.

10. One scene from the movie *Taxi Driver* expresses the nature of such exchanges. The character played by Robert de Niro is alone for the first time with the character played by Jodie Foster. The Foster character starts stripping off his clothes, asks what he wants, and puts her lit cigarette on a table as an "hourglass" to mark the time he has left. I do not mean to deny that Western-style prostitution can occasionally involve emotions of care and solidarity, particularly in cases of repeat customers. Graham Green has written with a certain amount of tenderness about his interactions

with prostitutes (for a fictitious account of a ninety-year-old who falls in love with a young prostitute, see Gabriel Garcia Marquez's *Memoirs of My Melancholy Whores*). My argument (as we will see) is that karaoke-style prostitution—because it includes the element of group singing that often leads to emotional bonding—increases the likelihood that such emotions will develop.

11. Note that conceptions of beauty often differ in East Asian societies (compared to Western societies). There is less attention paid to bodily shape and more to facial features (in Chinese, a rich vocabulary describes different eye shapes, eyelids, and eyebrows) as well as *qi* 气 (the kind of atmosphere with which one carries oneself).

12. It could be argued that there are similar scenarios in Western countries, when groups of businessmen go to strip clubs to forge social ties. But there are also significant differences. For one thing, male bonding in karaoke bars is a far more common (and commonly accepted) part of doing business in East Asia. Second, there is less emphasis in strip bars on showing self-control and deference to others (partly because there are fewer opportunities for physical interaction between customer and stripper). Third, male customers in strip clubs rarely join in the performances (unlike the joint singing in karaoke bars). Last but not least, there is no emotional component—no expectation of companionship and bonding—between customer and stripper in strip clubs.

13. In fact, he may have been critical of karaoke-style music. He praises the type of music that makes soldiers strong and united, and he criticizes songs that "causes the hearts of men to be dissipated" and warns that the exemplary person "will not let his ear hear lewd sounds or his eye gaze on the female body" (20.8). Still, it's worth noting that the most popular songs in karaoke bars should not be regarded as "lewd sounds." They are typically sweet and melodious, like the beautiful songs of the late Taiwanese songstress Deng Lijun.

14. In a fascinating paper titled "Rising to the Occasion: The Implication of Confucian Musical Virtue for Global Community" (on file with the author), Kathleen Marie Higgins argues that learning to listen is the most Confucian and most musical way to nurture cooperation. Higgins points to the insight into the nature of performing music gained by jazz saxophonist Steve Lacy when playing with Thelonious Monk. Up to that point, he had been trying to show off with his playing. Lacy reports: "I learned . . . to play with the other musicians and not get all wrapped up in my own thing and not just play interesting notes just to be interesting. . . . He got me out of the thing of trying to be too hip. . . . And Monk told me, 'Now make the drummer sound good.' And that was an enormous help to me, really. It stopped me cold, really, and changed my focus."

15. In the mid-1990s, the hostesses (*xiaojie*) were also known as *genu* 歌女 (singing women), but that term has since fallen into disuse.

16. The filtering of "creeps" can also take place at an earlier stage. One hostess told me that she doesn't smile and hides behind the others if she doesn't want to be picked by a particular customer, and that usually seems to work.

17. There are some exceptions that are explained partly by different cultural particularities. In one Beijing club, the top floor is reserved for Japanese clients who value hostesses who can speak Japanese even if they are not as physically attractive as the

ones that don't. The bottom floor is reserved for Korean customers who seem to have the opposite set of priorities (i.e., beauty over common language). In a Beijing five-star hotel, the hostesses charge more for conversation and singing (five hundred yuan per hour) because they are educated and speak English.

18. In Singapore, the sex workers are foreigners, which might reinforce negative attitudes toward women from poor countries. In Hong Kong, however, most of the sex workers have been locals, though increasingly they are coming from mainland China. The Hong Kong–born workers often feel threatened by the influx of mainland workers that offer similar services for cheaper prices, leading to conflict between the two groups (see Yeeshan Yang's *Whispers and Moans*).

19. One study found that only 1.3 percent of mainland Chinese sex workers were forced into prostitution (*Whispers and Moans*, 97–98). But for some evidence that traffickers force some Chinese women (and children) into prostitution, see http://www.uri.edu/artsci/wms/hughes/china.htm and http://www.uri.edu/artsci/wms/hughes/china.htm (sites visited September 11, 2007). According to the later site, the Ministry of Public Security estimates that nine thousand women and a thousand children are kidnapped and sold illegally each year. Though the number may be on the low side, it is still a tiny proportion of the sex workers in China.

20. In the mid-1990s, it was more common for government officials to visit karaoke clubs and pay for themselves. They were big spenders, as they paid with public money without any worries about being penalized. One male manager of a karaoke club in Beijing told me that 80 percent of his customers were government officials. Due to closer monitoring of public funds, that number has substantially decreased.

21. The anonymous author of an extensive Chinese-language report on the karaoke trade in Taiyuan reports that the term *xiansheng* ("mister" or "husband") was first used to describe karaoke-style male prostitutes (perhaps because it's the complementary term for *xiaojie*, lady). But the term didn't take hold and was soon replaced by the term *yazi* (duck) in popular usage. I would speculate that the term *yazi* won out because it sounds more humorous.

22. Surprisingly, perhaps, there are not many karaoke parlors for the gay community (in Western countries, much of the trade in male prostitution serves the gay community). Perhaps there is less demand for male prostitution in East Asian societies because of the widespread presence of gay saunas and bathhouses where men can go for free sex. Even the predominantly Muslim city of Kuala Lumpur in Malaysia has a gay sauna. One particularity of gay saunas in East Asia is that sexual intercourse tends to be carried out in private cubicles. One contact who has frequented many gay bars in Asian cities tells me that there he has yet to see one like the gay bathhouses in San Francisco or Sydney that are characterized by public displays of gay sex involving many individuals.

23. The influence of Christianity (along with Western medical ideas) in Hong Kong, according to the University of Hong Kong's Mark King, may also help to explain why seemingly more liberal Hong Kongers tend to be less supportive of transgenderism and transsexuality compared to mainland Chinese (*Time Out Beijing*, September 2007, 78). In Shenzhen, across the border from Hong Kong, the Sunshine

hospital is paying for the sex change operation of Shen Xiaoyong, who had used the media to highlight her plight, in return for media attention. It is unlikely that a sex reassignment story would be regarded as good PR for a hospital in Hong Kong.

24. In Southeast Asia, traditional conceptions of what's taboo may also influence the form and extent of prostitution. Female prostitution is far more common in pre-dominantly Buddhist Thailand than in predominantly Muslim Malaysia, notwith-standing similar levels of economic development. According to Chandran Muzaffar, this phenomenon may be related to the different religions: Whereas Islam celebrates sex within marriage and condemns it outside marriage, Buddhism tends to denigrate the sexual act no matter what the context. The implication is that for Buddhists, pros-titutes may not be all that much worse morally than those engaged in marital sex. One of the commonly remarked features of sex workers in Thailand (such as those who perform in clubs doing sexual acts of various sorts) is that they tend to "turn off," as though their minds are elsewhere. But Buddhism may also pose some problems. The Chinese newspaper *Nanfang Zhoumou* (Southern Weekly), February 23, 2006, reports on the case of a prostitute who worried about her Buddhist commitments because she feared that her profession would cause her to be reincarnated in subhuman form. A Buddhist friend subsequently told her that since she engaged in prostitution to raise money for needy family members, then it was good (善) and she will not suffer adverse consequences in her next life. That eased her conscience, and she decided to stop do-ing sex work without worrying about what would happen to her in future lives.

25. Without explaining the source of the revenue, needless to say. One hostess I spoke to said she gave a ten-thousand-yuan gift to her brother as a wedding present. She had only recently begun to work as a hostess, and I asked her how her brother could believe that such a large sum had been earned in such a short time. She said she told him that she got the money from a rich boyfriend.

26. Filial piety can be extended to elderly parents besides one's own. One hostess told me that she broke up with her boyfriend of five years after he physically abused her and refused to apologize afterward. But she continues to visit her former boy-friend's parents and does not tell the parents that she has separated with their son. As she explained to me: "His parents are old and sick now. I do not want to upset them before they die."

27. Several weeks after the interview, this hostess quit her job after she met a re-cently divorced Taiwanese businessman in a karaoke bar who supports her.

28. After the Korean government's crackdown on the domestic sex industry in 2004, an association of sex workers publicly (but with sunglasses that hid their iden-tity) urged the government to abolish the antiprostitution law, explaining at a press conference that it "chases sex laborers away to the streets, making our lives more miserable. Brothels are our precious workplace through which we can make our futures better." Moreover, the crackdown also lead to an exodus of Korean sex work-ers to other countries (*Korea Times*, March 21, 2007).

29. The Chinese word for "comrade"—*tongzhi* 同志—has become the commonly used term for "gay" in the streets of mainland China (and Hong Kong and Taiwan).

30. Mao, of course, was the glorious exception to the rule.

31. One difference between the Chinese mafia and the Italian mafia is that the former are mainly motivated by money rather than territory, and prostitution is an important element of their trade. The Italian mafia has been traditionally resistant to dealing with prostitution because it is seen as "dishonorable" to make money from women.

32. One possibility short of outright legalization that would make sex work into a normal form of work is decriminalization, like the policy regarding euthanasia in Holland. But if the government is not involved in regulating the trade, the health and security situation for sex workers would only be marginally better than the status quo.

33. Another possible disadvantage is that the hostesses might not want to be officially recognized, for fear that the nature of their work might be made known to families and friends back home. But it should be possible to recognize the trade in particular locales with guarantees that the identities of the hostesses would not be made public.

34. Hong Kong, perhaps due to its British liberal heritage, has the opposite set of legal arrangements. Private prostitution, meaning one-on-one exchanges between sex workers and customers, is legal, but karaoke-style prostitution is not. Individual prostitutes can advertise their trade, and they may be "reviewed" by "Fatty Dragon" in the Chinese-language tabloid *Apple Daily* (next to the horse-racing coverage). In reality, there is also some illegal karaoke-style prostitution (including one club in a five-star hotel) that is controlled by the triads (Hong Kong mafia).

35. The point about de facto polygamy may seem inconsistent with the earlier point that there are fewer affairs in East Asian societies (compared to Western societies). But even if we want to define "de facto polygamy" under the category of "extramarital affairs" (meaning consensual, unpaid sex outside of the monogamous relationship between legally married husband and wife), there are relatively few such relationships (only a small minority of wealthy people can typically afford de facto polygamy) so the total number of extramarital affairs may still be lower in East Asian societies with karaoke bars.

36. In practice, according the Pueng Vongs, the "new concubinage" has been less oppressive than old-style concubinage: "Now the woman has the upper hand, as far as the material perks of the arrangement go. The tradition of keeping concubines was once a measurement of a man's success. Today it is often the woman who calls the shots, as she chooses from an array of newly flush suitors. . . . She now has her own, fully funded pad, with an allowance for clothes, jewelry and leisure activities often spent with her own lover" (*Pacific News Service*, January 22, 2004).

37. This essay draws on interviews with contacts that frequent karaoke clubs, three "mamas" ("Public Relations Manageress," according to the English translation on one name card), one male manager, as well as several hostesses in Beijing. The hostesses were told about my research, and they were asked the following questions: (1) How did you find this job? (2) Are you happy with this job? What are the main advan-

tages? The main disadvantages? (3) Why did you take this job? (4) What kind of customers do you like? Dislike? (5) What kind of bosses do you like? Dislike? (6) Is karaoke an important element of your job? (7) How can the karaoke scene be improved? Do you have any suggestions for change? How to improve relations between bosses and workers? Workers and customers? Should the trade be legalized?

There are legitimate questions to be asked about methodology that relies on anonymous contacts and informal conversation with the people involved. But it is difficult otherwise to get at the truth when most participants are rarely willing to openly discuss what really happens.

CHAPTER 5: HOW SHOULD EMPLOYERS TREAT DOMESTIC WORKERS?

1. The same friend came to visit me in Beijing a couple of years ago. My wife, a lawyer at an international firm, hired a driver because she never learned to drive herself. The driver came to pick up my friend at the airport, but we told him that she (the driver) is our friend. I didn't mean to lie (actually, it wasn't really a lie, because we do have friendly ties with our driver), but I worried that my academic friend would raise objections (or make fun of the alleged gap between my leftist commitments and my "bourgeois" lifestyle) if I admitted that we now have a helper and a driver.

2. Marx didn't write about the politics of domestic work, however. Perhaps the least illustrious episode of his life is the affair he carried out with his domestic helper, leading to the birth of an illegitimate child (and Engels taking it away from him, thus avoiding a family scandal), which may help to explain Marx's reluctance to confront the topic.

3. This chapter draws on my book *Beyond Liberal Democracy*, chap. 11.

4. The extension of family-like labels can also be manifested in highly unusual circumstances. On Chinese television, an experienced police detective who specializes in rescuing kidnap victims described his "velvet glove" methods: he talks to the kidnapper, softens him up by calling him "younger brother," and more often than not the kidnapper eventually relents and gives up. In an American context, the extension of family-like labels takes place, strangely enough, in women's prisons. Instead of forming gangs (as in male prisons), female prisoners form "families," with elder women acting as "grandparents," middle-aged women as "parents," and younger ones as "children."

5. I use the feminine pronoun to refer to domestic workers, because they are usually female. In mainland Chinese cities, however, there are some male domestic workers, especially to help care for disabled and elderly people. The assumption seems to be that such care can require heavy physical labor (e.g., to lift the patient into a bath) that men are typically better able to provide.

6. She still refused to take the money. I did ask her son for help again, and I gave him the money (for help on both occasions), which he accepted, after some initial protestation.

7. I do not mean to imply that liberals actually live according to their theory. For example, my dear liberal friend mentioned above is warm and compassionate in everyday life.

8. Such strict defense of moral principles may be particularly common among liberal political theorists. Left-leaning economists and political activists are often more willing to bend principles and recognize trade-offs among competing values. For example, the Bush administration's proposal for a guest-worker program—to my mind, one of the few sensible proposals to emerge from that administration—was defended by left-leaning politicians such as Ted Kennedy (the proposal was opposed and ultimately defeated by conservative forces who worried about granting "amnesty" to illegal immigrants).

9. For an interesting account of the Western tradition, see Samuel Fleischacker, *A Short History of Distributive Justice*. Fleischacker argues that Adam Smith (!) first took seriously the idea of the state's responsibility for alleviating poverty (other theorists, such as Aristotle and Machiavelli, objected to large gaps between rich and poor because they valued political stability, not because they objected to poverty per se; and Christians generally favored private charity as a way of dealing with poverty).

10. The economic benefits of remittances by migrant foreign workers are substantial. As UN secretary-general Ban Ki-moon puts it, "Last year migrants sent home 131 billion [English pounds], three times all international aid. In some countries, a third of families rely on these remittances to keep them out of poverty. Across the developing world, remittances underwrite healthcare, education and grassroots entrepreneurship" (*The Guardian*, July 10, 2007).

11. The economist Lant Pritchett has argued that giant guest-worker programs—workers would stay three to five years, with no path to citizenship—that put millions of the world's poorest people to work in its richest economies is best able to combat global poverty. Pritchett assumes that most receiving countries would not allow them to bring families, but he argues that the benefits for global development outweigh the cost. In reply, Jeffrey Sachs says, "Let them come as a family? Having tens of millions of men separated from their families in temporary living conditions is hardly going to be conducive to the kind of world we're aiming to build" (quoted in Jason DeParle, "Should We Globalize Labor Too?" *New York Times Magazine*, June 10, 2007). But what if such choices must be made to alleviate global poverty?

12. Interestingly, this moral outlook still seems to inform the practices of Asian immigrants to other societies. According to the *New York Times* (August 11, 2001), fewer than one in five whites in the United States helps care for or provide financial support for their parents, in-laws, or other relatives, compared with 28% of African Americans, 34% of Hispanic Americans, and 42% of Asian Americans. Those who provide the most care also feel the most guilt that they are not doing enough. Almost three-quarters of Asian Americans say they should do more for their parents, compared with two-thirds of Hispanics, slightly more than half the African Americans and fewer than half the whites.

13. Greater involvement by adult sons in the caregiving process will be essential in the future because the one child per family policy in China will make it even more challenging to provide at-home care for elderly parents.

Chapter 6: The Politics of Sports

1. One might predict that there will be a rise in interest in national affairs if the media opens up and the political system democratizes, with controversial national issues being publicly aired and discussed. There may also be a corresponding *decrease* in interest in international affairs. In Taiwan, arguably, democratization has focused debates on national affairs, and there is, consequently, less interest in international affairs, including international sports. The recent political opening may help to explain why the World Cup did not generate the same level of enthusiasm in Taiwan as in mainland China (there are other factors, such as Taiwanese enthusiasm for baseball).

2. Paik Wooyeal has noted that the tendency to cheer against neighboring country teams may be more universal. For example, the Swiss Germans cheer against the German team, the English against the French, and so on. Could it be that the history of warfare between neighbors still forms preferences in sports? Or perhaps there is a natural tendency to be jealous of a neighbor's success?

3. Ghana eliminated the United States from the 2006 World Cup with a thrilling 2 to 1 victory (with the aid, admittedly, of a dubious penalty), but I could not make my joy too explicit during the game itself. I watched the game with my son, who holds an American passport, and since he was cheering for the United States. I did not want to upset him. It is difficult to persuade children that their team allegiances should be determined at least partly by principles of international economic justice.

4. In my view, it is impossible to translate the word "underdog" in Chinese with the right nuances (the weaker party who wins our hearts).

5. Huang eventually lost his job as soccer announcer with CCTV, but he found another one with the privately run Phoenix TV station. He also appeared in a humorous television commercial for a job-seeking agency that was run several times a day (on CCTV!).

6. In China, children are often asked which parent they feel closest to. This question is considered to be highly inappropriate in Western societies.

7. The Clinton administration claimed that the bombing was unintentional and apologized for the bombing and the loss of life, but there is widespread skepticism in China regarding the official U.S. explanation.

8. I do not mean to imply that the quest for gold medals should be entirely subordinated to the concern for Confucian civility. I've yet to recover form the disappointment that Canada did not win any gold medals during the 1976 Olympics in Montreal (nor am I proud of the fact that Canada remains the only country ever to host the summer Olympics without winning a gold medal). My point is that Confucian civility

should be an important concern and that national glory should not simply be focused on the quest for victory. Nations engaged in international sporting competitions can also take pride in their civility, decency, and sense of justice.

9. In the same vein, the Korean soccer team's civility after its loss to Turkey in the semifinals of the 2002 World Cup may be explained partly by the fact that it did so well before, surpassing even the most optimistic projections.

10. On the other hand, there are informal constraints on the expulsion of mucus that Westerners may find puzzling. For example, it is considered rude, in a Chinese context, to expel nose mucus (blow one's nose) at mealtime. More than once, I've seen Westerners do this in the presence of Chinese hosts, who are invariably too polite to issue disapproving glances (in contrast, Westerners are only too ready to show disapproval to Chinese who spit on public streets).

11. Zhao Zonglai, "Beijing Aoyunhui de fushi liyi changyishu" (The Proposals for Attire and Rites at the Beijing Olympics), http://www.xici.net/b723831/d50774546.htm, April 5, 2007, site visited August 28, 2007.

12. After the violent crackdown on peaceful protesters on June 4, 1989 in Beijing, Wang Meng lost his job as minister of culture because he refused the order (by claiming ill health) to demonstrate loyalty to the Party by visiting the few hospitalized soldiers ("heroes in suppressing the counterrevolutionary riot").

13. To continue the Olympic tradition in which one school in the host country supports another country to foster grassroots cultural understanding, the Huajiadi Elementary School in northeast Beijing has been chosen by the Olympic authorities to cheer and support athletes from Japan. Japan's national flag is on display in classrooms, and students have learned to speak a few words of Japanese as well as aspects of Japanese culture (*Asahi Shimbun*, March 28, 2007).

14. Wang Meng, "Aoyun ying zhuzhong biaoda dui bisai duishou de zunzhong he youyi" (The Olympics Should Emphasize the Expression of Respect and Friendship toward Opponents in Competitions), http://news.sohu.com/20070312/n248674721.shtml, visited September 11, 2007.

15. On August 22, 2007, the *New York Times* published an op-ed by Ross Terrill titled "In Beijing, Orwell Goes to the Olympics". The op-ed portrays the attempt to clean up bad English as an expression of an "Orwellian impulse to remake the truth." One might argue that it's the opposite of an "Orwellian impulse" to turn the meaning of language on its head (to the extent the campaign to correct bad English reflects anything deeper, it could be seen as an extension of the Confucian injunction to "rectify names," to make language accord with the truth of things). And what's wrong with correcting bad English if there's no punishment attached to it? For example, one "Ethnic Peoples' Park" (民族园) was infamously (mis)translated as "Racist Park." Should the state take a hands-off approach to such matters? The comment goes on to conclude that "sport should just be sport" and politics should be left out of it. But that also seems wrong. For example, if the Berlin Olympics had been held in 1944 (rather than 1936), when Nazi Germany was clearly responsible for killing millions of innocent people, should other countries have sent athletes there? To me, the answer is

clearly no. Of course the dispute now is whether China's responsibility for the slaughter in Sudan should justify boycott of the 2008 Beijing Olympics. To my mind, the answer is also no: the extent of China's responsibility for the killings is not so direct, and the Chinese government seems to be more active in collaborating with the international community's efforts at dealing with the problem (it can be argued that the change in the Chinese government's stance was brought about by the threat to boycott the Olympics, but even if that's true there is no longer any reason to maintain the threat of boycott). In any case, there are other, equally, if not more controversial international developments that might be used to justify boycotts now. The Carter administration pulled the U.S. team out of the Moscow Olympics over the Soviet invasion of Afghanistan. Should the U.S. be barred from competition at the Beijing Olympics because of its invasion of Iraq, carried out in defiance of international opinion?

16. Again, it's tempting to think that only authoritarian political systems officially promote civility, but state-sponsored civility also characterizes democratic countries with a Confucian heritage: in the Spain-Korea quarter-final 2002 World Cup game hosted by democratic South Korea, there was a cheering section for Spain composed of South Koreans.

17. I hope to be proven wrong (again), but I'm not optimistic that the Western world will pay much attention to the "civil" aspects of the 2008 Olympic Games. So far, the reporting from the Western press has been almost entirely negative: the pollution in Beijing, how Chinese athletes are forced by vain parents to sacrifice their physical and personal well-being for the sake of Olympic glory, how the state is forcing poor people out of their dwellings to make room for Olympic-related developments, how ordinary citizens take pride in "showing up the foreigners," and how bad news is being covered up by an authoritarian government that seeks to preserve a façade of national glory. I do not mean to criticize such coverage (though sometimes it seems to glorify attention-seekers and play into the hands of forces that seek to demonize China). It's perfectly natural—indeed, desirable—for journalists to report on the dark side of the global event, to remind people that the Olympics will be accompanied by suffering and misery on the part of disadvantaged sectors of the population. But it's not the whole story.

Chapter 7: A Critique of Critical Thinking

1. The Confucian tradition is rich and varied, and my account is necessarily highly selective. What drives my account is an attempt to identify Confucian perspectives on education that differ from liberal views and may still be defensible in the contemporary world. I rely mainly on quotes from *The Analects of Confucius*—among the most famous quotes in the text, well known to most educated Chinese—so my interpretation of Confucianism should not be viewed as too eccentric. Of course, I do not mean to speak "for" Confucius or to imply that he would endorse the details of the views I'm putting forth. But perhaps he would endorse the effort to "review the old as a means of realizing the new" (*The Analects*, 2.11).

2. Confucius, from another perspective, lives on via his teachings and his ancestors. About ten years ago, I gave a talk at Beijing University, and one of Confucius's descendants surnamed Kong gave me my first Chinese copy of *The Analects of Confucius*. We subsequently became friends, and he hosted my family during a visit to his (and Confucius's) hometown, Qufu, in Shandong province.

3. To the extent there is any similarity with an actual person, it would be Hu Shi, not Hu Jintao. Hu Shi was an early twentieth century Chinese liberal influenced by John Dewey who criticized Confucianism as unsuitable for modern life and promoted vernacular language to replace what he regarded as the "dead" classical writing style.

4. I was reminded of such limits when my wife was giving birth to our child. I had taken the prenatal courses with my wife, and I learned about breathing techniques intended to reduce the pain associated with contractions. The natural drug-free birth process was protracted and difficult due to the unexpectedly large size of our son (ten pounds, two ounces). In between one of the contractions, I told my wife not to worry: "I'm with you, I'm breathing with you, and I understand what you're going through." She screamed back at me: "No you don't, you don't understand!" Of course she was right.

5. See, e.g., the neat experiment by Shali Wu and Boaz Keysar demonstrating "that cultural differences induce different patterns of perspective taking: Chinese culture, which emphasizes interdependence, focuses attention on other people, whereas American culture, which emphasizes independence, focuses attention on the self. Consequently, compared with Americans, Chinese are better at solving perspective-taking problems, make fewer errors in assessing the intentions of another person, and are less distracted by their own private perspective" (Shali Wu and Boaz Keysar, "The Effect of Culture on Perspective Taking," *Psychological Science*, vol. 18, no. 7 [2007], 605). For a general survey of experimental findings that reveal cognitive differences between East Asians and Westerners, see Richard Nisbett, *The Geography of Thought: How Asians and Westerners Think Differently . . . and Why* (New York: Free Press, 2003).

6. I've borrowed and slightly modified the famous example from Mencius. It's worth noting that wells were holes in the ground in ancient China, hence increasing the likelihood that young children might fall into them.

7. The liberal theorist Martha Nussbaum has also written about the importance of educating people's emotions. She argues for the importance of reading novels because readers come to be sensitive to the plight of the marginalized. But the mechanism is different. The Confucian perspective is that the motivation for caring comes largely from informal interaction with needy intimates, empathetic feelings that are then extended to others. And the end is different. Nussbaum's view may be closer to the Christian idea of the Good Samaritan, with Jesus praising the one who helps a total stranger. The Confucian perspective is that feelings are extended to others, but with diminishing intensity. In cases of distress, help would be provided first and foremost to intimates, not strangers.

8. Of course, the actual Confucius did not say that women should be given equal opportunities. But neither did he say that women could not be exemplary persons or that women are biologically inferior (à la Aristotle). Arguably, the commitments of early Confucians can find common ground with a range of contemporary feminist values and needn't hinder gender equality (see the contributions by Sin Yee Chan and Chenyang Li in *Confucian Political Ethics*, ed. Daniel A. Bell).

9. Note that the Chinese word for "elite"—*jingying* 精英—is not pejorative; quite the opposite, it has a positive connotation. Also, the idea that the political purpose of higher education is to train an elite with better-than-average political decision-making abilities is not so controversial in East Asian societies with a Confucian heritage. For example, Underwood International College—an English-language liberal arts college associated with Yonsei University in Seoul, Korea—advertises itself as educating "Asian Leadership." Though the reality in Western countries may not be all that different, the typical liberal arts college might downplay, at least publicly, the elitist aspect of its educational mission. In the United States, interestingly, military academies and colleges for historically marginalized groups, such as women and African Americans, tend to make explicit the focus on training leaders.

10. We do not know Confucius's own views regarding imperial examinations because they were implemented long after his death. The influential twelfth-century scholar Zhu Xi, who believed that the key to understanding the moral principles of the classics lies in scrubbing the mind clean, followed by careful reading, recitation, memorization, and reflection upon the meaning of the texts, condemned the "pernicious influence of the examination essay" on the grounds that "men make up their minds to seek the unusual in the texts even before they read them—and pay no attention whatsoever to the original meaning. Having got the unusual from them, they imitate it in their examination essays; in the end, they're accomplished only at using the unusual in texts" (*Learning to be a Sage*, trans. Daniel K. Gardner, 142). Zhu Xi did say that the texts should be read so that they were personally meaningful, but he seemed to think that careful reading of the texts would reveal "the" correct moral principles, and he objected to "unusual" interpretations that seemed to be rewarded by the examination authorities. On the other hand, the seventeenth-century Confucian scholar Huang Zongxi condemned the examinations of his day for rewarding superficiality and plagiarism. Huang didn't oppose testing for knowledge of the classics and subsequent commentaries, but he emphasized that candidates must also offer their own interpretations of the classics, so that examinations test for independent thought (see "The Selection of Scholar Officials, Part I," in *Waiting for the Dawn: A Plan for the Prince*, trans. Wm. Theodore de Bary).

11. Chinese schools emphasize memorization at the primary and secondary level. Many Chinese intellectuals think it's a sound educational practice, and I agree with them. Students are made to memorize poems and classics when they are young and their minds find it relatively easy to absorb knowledge, and when they are older they can (and should) make the effort to understand what they have learned as well as consider the implications for the way they lead their lives. If the latter stage is done

well, then the earlier knowledge can be creatively applied in new situations: for example, it's common for Chinese intellectuals to invoke variations of memorized idioms (*chengyu* 成语) in new situations, for both serious and humorous purposes. There are also aesthetic pleasures associated with early memorization: when Chinese intellectuals visit historical sites in China, they derive pleasure from invoking the poems about those sites they had memorized as children.

12. Avner de-Shalit defends such an approach to the teaching of political theory. See his book *Power to the People: Democratizing Political Theory*.

13. When I look back on my own educational experience as an undergraduate student, I regret my tendency to make quick judgments without having made the effort to properly understand complex texts. In my defense, it was a common tendency of my contemporaries. I find that my Chinese students are less inclined to early judgment; they are often humble and hardworking in the way I wish I had been. Interestingly, local practices also seem to influence visiting American students. One teacher-administrator of a Tsinghua-based program that hosts visiting American students tells me that the students make progress in the sense that they become more cautious and less willing to voice uninformed opinions as the year progresses. They learn to speak less and listen more.

14. Note that Professor Kong doesn't say anything about the content and authorship of Great Works, perhaps because his own case is quite complicated (there are endless debates about whether the *Analects* is the work of a single author, whether it's one book or several, when the various passages were written, and what order they should be presented in; moreover, the *Analects* was only made a "classic" in the Song dynasty, and the historian Qin Hui remarks that Confucius would be upset if he had known that contemporary people regarded the *Analects* as one of the "six classics" (*Nanfang Zhoumou*, July 12, 2007). My own view is that study of the "classics" refers to works that have "stood the test of time" and that are widely regarded as the product of deep and innovative thinking. In the contemporary world, I also think that we should take a multicultural approach to the study of Great Works (see chapter 8 of my book *Beyond Liberal Democracy*). Of course I do not mean to deny that what people regard as "classics" can (and perhaps should) change over time.

15. Regrettably, we have lost the score of the *shao* music that Confucius refers to.

16. A former professor at Stanford told me that Rice, qua provost at Stanford, eliminated the "Cultures, Ideas, and Values" track from the Stanford undergraduate curriculum. My source comments: "I found her to be wholly *unmusical* to any sense of humanity, claiming to be a 'scientist' herself."

17. In East Asian countries with a Confucian heritage, music is part of the educational curriculum in primary schools and sometimes secondary schools, thus helping to explain why Koreans, Chinese, and Japanese often develop a taste for karaoke (in contrast, musical education is typically regarded as less central in North American schools, and it is often the first thing to be cut in cases of budget or time constraints). But music is rarely part of the curriculum in East Asian universities, and if Confucius

were around today, I surmise that he would be arguing for musical education in higher education too.

18. Mencius told King Xuan of Qi that if he has "great fondness for music, then there is great hope for the state of Qi" (IB.1). The king admits that he is fond of popular music rather than the classical music favored by Confucians, but Mencius replies that it doesn't matter so long as the king shares his fondness in the company of the common people. Mencius does not appeal simply to the altruism of the king, he suggests that the king will enjoy the music more fully if he shares it with others. In other words, music that unites us has a more positive impact on human well-being than music enjoyed alone.

19. For an extended defense of this view, see Steve Angle's essay "Challenging Harmony: Consistency, Conflicts, and the Status Quo" (on file with author).

20. Such views may lead to conflict in work settings as well. One Chinese lawyer friend trained in both Western and Chinese universities said it took her a while to "unlearn" the view that she shouldn't speak up without proper understanding of the legal issues. In her American law firm, she observed American colleagues being rewarded for speaking up with confidence about complex and ambiguous legal issues (the partners were too busy to know the details of the legal issues at stake). Eventually, my Chinese friend learned to speak with authority about issues that she knew were more complex and ambiguous than she was letting on, and her career took off.

21. On Teacher's Day in September 2006, I appeared on a national television show along with two Chinese professors to discuss what it means to be a teacher in contemporary China. One relatively elderly distinguished professor emphasized that teachers should be moral authorities to their students. As part of living up to this standard, he refuses the gifts that are offered to him on Teacher's Day and emphasizes that his greatest reward is that students learn well and improve their lives (thus challenging my earlier view that it's rude not to accept gifts). He presented his views in an informal, charming way, without any trace of arrogance or self-righteousness, and clearly embodied the kind of teaching ideal that would inspire his students.

22. I'm drawing all these examples from current practices at Tsinghua University, though I do not mean to imply that they are explicitly justified in Confucian terms. Regarding admittance, the university awards extra points to students with musical ability: students who pass the benchmark on the national examinations (*gaokao*) have a better chance of being admitted (but I suspect that such ability is viewed as a talent, rather than as an important part of moral development). Regarding musical activities, all graduate students are Tsinghua are strongly encouraged to participate in the singing competition intended to commemorate the December 9, 1935, anti-Japanese (invaders) movement led by Tsinghua students. The activity is not compulsory, but participants get extra points relevant for scholarships equivalent to writing one scholarly article. Regarding letters of recommendation, Tsinghua referees are asked to comment on the student's moral character (though it might seem strange if the referee were to comment on musical ability in this section).

23. An important reason for memorizing historical events and persons is that they can provide a ready-to-hand store of model examples when teachers (or other moral authorities, such as parents) discuss appropriate ways of life in different contexts.

CHAPTER 8: TEACHING POLITICAL THEORY IN BEIJING

1. The preuniversity compulsory military training at Beijing University has since been reduced to one month, in line with other Chinese universities. It is worth noting that mainland China does not have an extended period of compulsory military service (unlike Taiwan, Korea, and Singapore), but periods of military training are widespread in schools: my own son underwent a military training period of one week prior to the start of each school year at his primary school (the primary school attached to Tsinghua University).

2. To be more precise, huge numbers (tens if not hundreds of thousands) would have to be killed (or under imminent threat of being killed) before the moral case for foreign military intervention would begin to seem plausible (that's another reason nobody called for foreign military intervention after June 4; the number of people killed was small in comparison to Rwanda or the former Yugoslavia). State sovereignty does serve, on the whole, to secure people's vital interests in life and security, and the barriers to foreign military intervention should be high. But I don't see any moral difference if, say, huge numbers are being killed because they belong to a certain class (as in Stalin's liquidation of Kulaks) rather than an ethnic group.

3. There is no such risk in written communication. The students sometimes write papers and send emails in Chinese (I usually comment and respond in English), and if I'm missing something I can consult the dictionary.

4. It's worth noting that the idea of a "syllabus," with the particular week's reading and discussion decided long before term time, is less common in Chinese universities. Most teachers assign a general reading list of a few topics and related books and articles, without trying to fit X amount of material in a particular week. This poses a problem for American universities that seek to establish links with Chinese universities. Administrators and teachers at American universities often seem disappointed by the syllabi of Chinese professors, with the consequence that many American import their own professors for their "study abroad" programs in China. In my view, visiting students are thus deprived of different and potentially enriching learning experiences.

5. This expectation may be partly due to the fact that my first book on (Western) communitarianism has been translated into Chinese, and some students know me as a (Western) communitarian. But after my interest in Chinese philosophy becomes more apparent, there is more willingness to discuss Chinese material. And there is no such prejudice among Chinese academics when I discuss Chinese and comparative philosophy.

6. With the exception of Kymlicka's chapter on Marxism: the normally curious and critical students did not object to (or even mention) this discrepancy.

7. There is a literal translation for "professor," but I once introduced myself as "Professor Bell," and my (Chinese) wife said it sounded arrogant—I should say that I'm "Teacher Bell." I've since learned that most professors refer to each other as "teacher," the same term that is used to refer to teachers of all levels. The term is also used to refer to departmental administrators (for example, students would call our departmental administrator "Teacher Bai"). Such linguistic practices may stem from a mixture of Confucian humility and Maoist egalitarianism.

8. There is also an order to the seating arrangement. The senior professor should sit at the part of the round table that gives him (or, more rarely, her), a view of the whole dining room.

9. A few weeks after I gave my talk, U.S. defense secretary Donald H. Rumsfeld gave a talk to midcareer Communist Party officials preparing for senior leadership positions at the Central Party School (the school has two parts—one for graduate students and one for midlevel cadres—but both groups meet on Friday mornings for a joint lecture). The Pentagon specifically requested this setting for Rumfeld's talk. Rumsfeld criticized China's military expansion, saying that it prompted "questions whether China will make the right choices—choices that will serve the world's real interests in regional peace and stability"—one wonders if he was so self-deluded as to think members of the crowd would look to his administration for guidance regarding "the world's interests in regional peace and stability." The only defense of the invasion of Iraq I've heard in China came from a party official who was pleased that the U.S. forces were stretched in Iraq, thus reducing the likelihood that the United States would lend military support to proindependence forces in Taiwan.

10. The main reason for the relative freedom at speech at the Central Party School may be that students and professors can be trusted as committed nationalists and Communists; they are not likely to rock the boat no matter what kind of critical information they are exposed to.

11. The lake at nearby Beijing University is called Unnamed Lake (未名湖), but this lake really doesn't seem to have a name.

12. Middlebury College in Vermont is famous for its intensive summer language programs: students live on campus and must sign a language pledge that bars them from speaking English the whole summer.

13. In contrast, articles that "demonize" China are often given full play in major Western newspapers. To my mind, the one-sided coverage reflects Western fears about the rise of China rather than anything about the "essence" of China itself.

14. I now work with the translator and we ask the websites that no changes be made without our consent.

15. Many Internet sites are blocked and there is an Internet police force, thousands strong, that monitors the content of the Internet. But much of that is meant to block pornography (not a bad idea, I say, as the father of a thirteen-year-old), and there are so many sites that not everything can be monitored efficiently. In the case of "political"

websites, once one picks up a potentially sensitive article, others usually follow. And those with technical savvy can usually get around the restrictions (or so I'm told; in my case, I ask friends and former students from abroad to send restricted information via email).

16. It may also be worth noting that academic "censorship" takes different forms in Western countries. Of course the state rarely if ever directly interferes with academic publications. But the tenure system, designed to protect free academic speech, often seems to have the opposite effect: more than once, I've heard it said that young scholars should be cautious before getting tenure, they should concentrate their efforts on writing things that senior people in their discipline want to hear rather than writing about what they really find interesting (if it were up to me, I'd abolish tenure, and replace the system with renewable ten-year contracts without any monitoring in between). And there are certain issues that seem off-limits in "politically correct" circles: an earlier version of chapter 4 was turned down by an American periodical that had previously published my China-related essays because it was too "controversial."

17. I've probably run into more problems lecturing—and, especially, answering questions—in English. I recently gave a talk in Germany, and my wife (sitting in the audience) told me afterward that her heart sank every time I began to answer: either what I said was not to the point or too frank for my own good. She took notes during the lecture and told me what I should have said afterward.

18. It takes a while for the Westerner to get used to doing things on very short notice, which is how things tend to work in Beijing. I once made an appointment with a Chinese acquaintance a couple of weeks in advance, and I became upset when he failed to show up (now I know I should have phoned him a few hours beforehand to make sure we were still on). The idea of making appointments long in advance seems too formal, perhaps, in the relatively spontaneous, easygoing northern Chinese culture (as Confucius says, a friend visiting from afar is one of life's greatest pleasures, with the implication that one shouldn't be bound by prior appointments if a friend really does visit from afar). It may also explain why many Chinese academics prefer to use the phone rather than communicate by relatively impersonal emails.

19. The northern campus, however, is still off-limits to those without special invitations. I did go once—for a conference on democracy in December 2007—and I can report that it is even more beautiful than the open southern campus.

20. We were in England at the time, but almost the entire Chinese overseas student community was involved in supporting the student demonstrators in Beijing. One day, after a particularly exhilarating march in central London, I told my to-be wife "You know, it's a cool time to be Chinese." She replied: "It's a cool time to be with a Chinese."

CHAPTER 9: ON BEING CONFUCIAN

1. I live in the northwest part of Beijing, where few foreigners live, and thus kids are sometimes surprised to see me there. When they say "waiguoren" (foreigner), I turn around and say "zai nar?" (where?), but that only seems to generate a laugh by the kids' parents. No doubt the parents will go on to explain "the truth" to their confused children.

2. In this sense, I've learned more from Confucianism than from my earlier engagement with Western communitarianism. I was attracted to communitarianism mainly because the arguments of modern-day "communitarian" thinkers seemed to make sense of my preexisting moral commitments, but my engagement with communitarianism didn't substantially change my "value system" or "way of life" (it could be argued that communitarianism is meant to articulate moral commitments rather than challenge them, but once articulated, such commitments, e.g., the commitment to active political participation, should also have to power to improve one's way of life).

3. Liberalism as a political philosophy inspired by such thinkers as Locke, Mill, and Rawls should not be confused with the common usage of the term in the U.S. (left-wing supporters of the Democratic Party) or France (right-wing defenders of the free market).

4. Nor do they have to worry about the extent to which their own personal experience shapes their political views. Let me tell a story about John Rawls, perhaps the greatest liberal philosopher of the twentieth century. He was commissioned to write an article on the topic of whether or not the United States should have used atomic bombs in Japan. He argued that it should not have done so, but he left out one (crucial?) fact: that he himself fought in the war and his troop train went through the recently devastated city of Hiroshima.

5. I've lived with my Chinese mother- and father-in-law for several years, and my Western friends occasionally praise me for this fact while noting that they couldn't do it themselves. Of course, there are conflicts, but I try to remind myself of the value of filial piety and defer to the wishes of my parents-in-law to the extent possible. And when I fail to do so, my wife reminds me of the gap between my theoretical commitment to filial piety and my way of life, and I try to change my ways. Admittedly, however, there remains a substantial gap. For example, I objected when my mother-in-law started to play the *erhu* (the "Chinese violin") at home because the less-than-harmonious sounds interfered with my studies. Upon reflection, I realized a better (more filial) way of dealing with the situation would be to get my mother-in-law a teacher so that she would improve. She agreed, notwithstanding worries about the cost (which I lied about). That seems to have worked somewhat, though occasionally I still need to struggle not to grimace (and to be fair to my mother-in-law, she now plays in her room behind closed doors).

6. Why is it important, from a moral point of view, to be liked by others? Because ties of affection underpin the trust that allows for mutual criticism and hence self-improvement (see section on humor). People who evoke the dislike of others cannot evoke the trust of others and hence find it more difficult to improve themselves.

7. There is an interesting contrast with Aristotle's views. In the *Politics*, Aristotle says that "deliberation needs the maturity of wisdom," and he argues for a division of labor, with the young sticking to military affairs and the mature deliberating about matters of public interest and justice (book 7, chap. 9, 1329a). However, he also suggests—unlike Confucius—that moral judgment begins to decline after a certain age (book 2, chap. 9, 1270a) and that the aged should stick to the service of public worship. In the *Rhetoric*, the aged are described as cynical, distrustful, small-minded, selfish, cowardly, overly fond of themselves, concerned with what's useful rather than what's noble, shameless, slaves to the love of gain, and querulous (book 2, part 13). It could be argued that Aristotle's purpose is just to warn against character defects, similar to Confucius's claim that those aspiring to be exemplary persons should guard against the tendency to be acquisitive when elderly (16.7). But Aristotle clearly presents his account as a descriptive claim (at the end of the passage he says "such are the characters" of elderly men), and he goes on to say that the middle age is the best because the middle-aged possess the merits of both youth and old age and they reduce the defects of both (book 2, part 14). Moreover, there is a political purpose to Aristotle's account: he aims to give an extra share of power to the middle-aged. Interestingly, Singapore senior statesmen Lee Kuan Yew has put forward an "Aristotelian view" regarding age and citizenship, arguing for a voting procedure that would give extra votes to persons between the ages of thirty-five and sixty (married and with families) because the middle-aged are the most responsible, whereas the young are too capricious and the elderly more likely to vote in selfish ways that penalize productive people and future generations (*Straits Times*, July 30, 1994). The elderly Lee might seem to be undermining his own authority when he puts forward such arguments (as would the elderly Aristotle qua teacher to Alexander), but he would probably reply that there are great individuals such as himself who can rise above these general tendencies. For an outsider, however, the fact that Lee's son is prime minister and other family members control key levers of the Singaporean economy leads one to wonder if Lee's account of the "selfishness" of elderly people may be informed by his own experience.

8. In nonmoral disciplines such as mathematics, it is often said that the best work is done by the young, when the mind may be more creative and less bound by traditional ways. But the task for exemplary persons is not so much to create as to learn what others have said about morality. Even the tiny minority of philosophers that develop new ideas about morality usually need to first learn what others have said about the subject. As Rosalind Hursthouse puts it, "There are youthful mathematical geniuses but rarely, if ever, youthful moral geniuses" ("Virtue Theory and Abortion," in *Virtue Ethics*, ed. Roger Crisp and Michael Slote, 224).

9. There is an obvious evolutionary reason for "enslaving" young people with the sexual drive: it increases the likelihood that the species will be propagated. But once

people pass their sexual peak, then such traits as empathy and compassion may be better from an evolutionary point of view. In a similar vein, Laura Carstensen and Corrinna E. Lockenhoff of Stanford University have posited an evolutionary reason to explain recent experimental findings that people get wiser (in the sense of being able to exercise control over their emotions and relying on more complex and nuanced emotions) as they get older: "Emphasizing emotional connection and kinship at an older age may increase the survival ability of one's children and grandchildren (and their genes) in the future" (see Stephen S. Hall, "The Older-and-Wiser Hypothesis," *New York Times Magazine*, May 6, 2007).

10. The same may be true of other desires that can cause harm, such as the desire for thrills by driving fast. Car insurance companies penalize young people not because of any prejudice against the young but because numbers show that they are more prone to accidents due to reckless driving. In Quebec, my home province, one can obtain a driving license at sixteen years old, and when I look at my past driving behavior I consider myself lucky to be alive today. Now I'd favor a minimum driving age of at least eighteen.

11. In Western societies, it seems that sexuality is often viewed as an important part of the good life, and there may be less of an imperative to reduce, if not extinguish, the sexual urge. Quite the opposite, in fact: those who manage to counteract what seems like the natural decline of the sexual urge are praised in the popular media (one often hears reports of elderly people who carry on "healthy" and "normal" sex lives, as though that's a good thing). Why should we encourage elderly people to have sex, and make them feel bad if they're not? Isn't it better to try to lead a moral life without having to worry about fulfilling our hedonistic desires?

12. A sage (*shengren*) is morally superior to an exemplary person, because the sage can change the ways of the universe, not just the human world (see the end of the *Zhongyong*).

13. Confucius notes that exemplary persons need to guard against lust in their youth, bellicosity in middle age, and acquisitiveness when old (16.7). This passage can be read to imply that that young (and middle-aged) people can also be exemplary persons, but perhaps what Confucius is really saying is that the process of trying to become an exemplary person starts at a young age, and there are different natural tendencies to guard against at different stages of life.

14. See Christopher Harbsmeier's highly entertaining article, "Confucius Ridens: Humor in The Analects," *Harvard Journal of Asiatic Studies* (June 1990), 131-61. Harbsmeier is generally persuasive, but goes a bit overboard when he suggests that Confucius is not a "merchant of morality." In my view, Confucius cares about promoting morality, but he thinks that creating an informal, joking atmosphere among a group of diverse and intelligent students is the best means for self-improvement (because gentle teasing among intimates allows for criticisms without anybody taking offense). I do not mean to imply that such concerns actually motivated Confucius's behavior in everyday life; the tendency to humor may not be so instrumental. Perhaps it's more a matter of unchosen character traits, and Confucius is naturally inclined to

joking and informality, with self-improvement as the by-product rather than the purpose. Put differently, it may be difficult for relatively serious, missionary types to practice informality and humor if they aren't already inclined to that way of being.

15. Cohen's "gay" character is used to expose the moral vacuity of the fashion industry.

16. I watch Cohen videos with my thirteen-year-old child, and I sometimes need to make the political message explicit in order to avert misunderstandings. The videos can also be used as educational tools: for example, my son didn't get the joke about euthanasia (a term that Cohen, playing Ali G., intentionally misunderstood as "youth in Asia") because he wasn't familiar with the concept of assisted dying, and it was a good occasion to explain the controversy.

17. Aristotle says more explicitly that one of the benefits of music is its power of "gladdening" hearts; therefore, "We may conclude that the pleasure it gives is one of the reasons why children ought to be educated in music" (*Politics*, book 8, chap. 5, 1339b). Like Confucius, he also praises music for its contribution to moral training, with the difference that Aristotle is mainly concerned with music's contribution to improving the individual soul rather than its contribution to group harmony. As a result, Aristotle writes more about the individual's relation to particular instruments than about group musical performances.

18. Even the normally stern Mencius says that the content of music is the happiness that arises from it (the same character—乐—refers to both happiness and music, in classical Chinese as well as today). And when the joy cannot be stopped, the listener begins to "unselfconsciously dance with one's feet and wave one's arms" (IVA.27). As he's scolding King Zhuang Bao for not sharing the joy of music with his people, Mencius adds that the joy of music can be even greater when it is experienced in the company of others (IB.1) (I'd add some qualifications: see note 5). Here too, an analogy can be drawn with humor: we enjoy humor more when it is shared with others, especially people we care about (one might put it even stronger than that: humor is essentially communal. There is something deeply wrong with somebody who enjoys telling jokes to himself and has no desire to share them with others; in that sense, humor is even more social than music, because individual enjoyment of music is not so strange).

19. I've added "in the immediate aftermath" because an Israeli friend tells me that some Israelis do tell "black jokes" about suicide bombers, perhaps as a way of coping with the anxiety of living with the threat of such bombers. But it's far worse, morally speaking, to tell a joke right after such bombings. Such jokes are conceivable (e.g., you don't look so well today) and could make their appearance in, say, Quentin Tarentino movies, but anybody who makes such jokes in reality must have a moral compass that's seriously out of whack.

20. Huang Zongxi, *Waiting for the Dawn: A Plan for the Prince*, trans. Wm. Theodore de Bary, 92 (modified).

21. See Philip J. Ivanhoe, "Lessons from the Past: Zhang Xuecheng and the Ethical Dimensions of History," unpublished manuscript on file with the author.

22. One seemingly puzzling passage in the *Analects* (11.26) where Confucius seems to be arguing in favor of a life of leisure over social commitment should instead be taken to mean that informal social interaction is foundational to social harmony and rule by moral power rather than coercion (see appendix 1).

23. This passage may not be as controversial as it sounds. It may just mean that family members should not be forced to incriminate each other, which is not very different from the "Western-style" immunity that protects spouses from testifying against each other (though Confucians would want to extend that immunity to the relationship between adult children and their elderly parents).

24. There may be controversy regarding the degree of "badness" of rulers. In the Yuan dynasty (ruled by Mongols), two famous Confucians chose different paths: Xu Heng chose to collaborate with the authorities in the hope that he could help bring about the Confucian way, whereas Liu Yin withdrew from politics on the grounds that the Confucian way could not prevail if scholars accept Mongol masters. Today, there are similar debates. Some Confucian scholars, such as Yu Ying-shih, seem to think that the Chinese Communist Party is irredeemably tainted with evil, to the point that they would refuse to have anything to do with it (such as refusing to visit mainland China). Others, such as Jiang Qing, advise political rulers if they are called upon to do so. I personally side with the latter. My view is that withdrawal may have been reasonable during the Cultural Revolution, but things have changed for the better since then. If my students chose to work for the Party with the hope of reforming it from the inside, I would not object.

25. And perhaps I'm ripping the quotes from the *Analects* of Confucius from their context and my interpretations are completely wrong. But I lack the detailed historical knowledge that would allow me to evaluate such claims.

APPENDIX 1: DEPOLITICIZING THE *ANALECTS*

1. This view is qualified somewhat later in the text, when Yu Dan notes that talented people in modern societies may face obstacles in their careers if they refrain from expressing good things about themselves (72).

2. She was criticized for mistranslating passages for the purpose of softening the misogynist parts of the *Analects*, but such mistakes have been fixed in the published version of her lectures (in the more popular version of her book, she doesn't mention anything about Confucian views on women). In the longer version of her book, including a complete translation and interpretation of the *Analects*, here's how she explains the infamous passage where women are compared to petty people (17.25): "In this passage, Confucius belittles women's thought. Such views were consistently advocated by Confucian thinkers, and subsequently led to such patriarchal expressions as "respecting the male and belittling the female" and "relationships with females are the least important." In this case, clearly, there is no attempt to beautify the text.

3. One brief passage earlier in the book (48-49) does mention that elites have special responsibilities for the well-being of the world (but with the qualification that focus on self-cultivation and individual well-being come first).

4. Yu Dan, of course, wouldn't be the first interpreter to do so. The view she attributes to Confucius about sagehood was widely accepted by neo-Confucians. Followers of Wang Yangming not only claimed that everyone could be a sage; they insisted that everyone already was a sage, but that most people had not understood and realized their true nature. Zhu Xi also believed that our original natures were perfectly pure and everyone had the potential for sagehood.

5. Without any textual support, Yu Dan refers to Confucius as a sage (6), an even higher status than exemplary person. To be fair, she won't be the first interpretator to do so. For a different view—i.e., that Confucius is not a sage, see 李零(Li Ling)'s more scholarly interpretation of the *Analects*, 丧家狗 (Homeless Dog).

6. It can be argued that one way of practicing filial piety is to make elderly parents feel useful, so allowing them to care for grandchildren can be seen as an expression of filial piety. But Yu Dan seems to shy away from arguments that calls for taking seriously our moral duties to others.

7. Mencius explicitly said that common people would fall astray and into excesses without dependable means of support (1A.7).

8. Surely there are some limits to creative interpretations. It makes no more sense to make Confucius into a proponent of an apolitical, individualist, and carefree lifestyle than it does to interpret the Bible as a text that denies the existence of God.

9. Strangely enough, Yu Dan deploys concepts from the Western liberal tradition to make such points, as when she says that women who talk or complain too much are exploiting other people's right to choose their topics (78). I must confess I've never heard anybody defend such a right!

10. For example, if I lack work opportunities I should reflect on my own failures (80) rather than social and economic structures and patterns of ownership.

APPENDIX 2: JIANG QING'S *POLITICAL CONFUCIANISM*

1. The "P" refers to 蒋庆, 政治儒学: 当代儒学的转向, 特质与发展 (北京: 三联书店, 2003) (Jiang Qing, *Political Confucianism: The Transformation, Special Characteristics, and Development of Contemporary Confucianism* (Beijing: Sanlian shudian, 2003). This book, unfortunately, has yet to be translated in English.

2. Jiang offers several other reasons to favor the Gongyang tradition in *Political Confucianism*, pages 28-39.

3. References to this book will be noted by the letter "L," followed by the page number.

4. See Gan Yang's (Chinese language) article, available on the following website: http://www.wyzxwyzx.com/Article/Class17/200704/17083.html, visited September 11, 2007.

5. One might add that there is also a need for exemplary decision-makers to take into account of the interests of those who are often unjustifiably neglected by democratically selected governments, such as minority groups with legitimate interests in protecting their language.

6. I translate the names of the houses freely, according to my interpretation of the meaning.

7. The United States has three branches of government, but the judiciary, at least in theory, is meant to interpret the law, not engage in political decision-making. Jiang doesn't mention the judiciary, but it is hard to imagine that any modern society could effectively function without a judiciary. So if we include the judiciary, it would mean four branches of government under his scheme.

8. In Western countries, democracy (by logic) wasn't deeply rooted when it was first adopted, but it eventually became so, and one can imagine that China would undergo the same historical process.

9. The translation "civil service examinations" is somewhat misleading, because the people selected were meant to exercise political power, not simply implement the decisions of others.

10. See Stephen C. Angle, "Confucianism Is Not Islam: Epistemological Dimensions of Traditions' Engagement with Human Rights," unpublished manuscript on file with author.

11. Such questions are addressed in the context of a similar proposal for a meritocratic house inspired by the ideas of Huang Zongxi in my books *Beyond Liberal Democracy*, chap. 6 and *East Meets West*, chap. 5.

12. See 蒋庆, 关于重建中国儒教的沟想 (Jiang Qing, "Reflections on the Establishment of Confucianism as the State Religion of China"), article sent to me by email.

13. See 秦晖: 儒家的命运 (Qin Hui, "The Fate of Confucianism"), http://www.southcn.com/nflr/llzhuanti/lndjt/wqhg/200704020641.htm, visited September 11, 2007.

14. Note the contrast with Marx's relatively individualistic account of the "communist" way of life in the *German Ideology*: "hunt in the morning, fish in the afternoon, rear cattle in the evening, criticize after dinner."

15. I've met more than one person—including highly educated types—who consider Jiang Qing to be a modern-day sage who appears once every few hundred years.

16. My own studies have been tremendously enriched by conversations with our driver. She reads in her spare time and has an impressively detailed grasp of Chinese culture and history.

Index

Abu Ghraib, 35
Afghanistan, 34
age: Confucianism and, 151–54; moral
    judgment and, 224–25n.9, 224n.7; sex
    drive in the elderly, Western view of,
    225n.11
All China Federation Trade Union,
    199n.15
Ames, Roger T., 161
Amnesty International, 34, 200n.24
Analects of Confucius, The: on
    education, 215n.1; on harmony, 14; on
    moral power, 52–53; self-description
    of life of Confucius, 151; on sex,
    153; Yu Dan's book on (*see* Yu Dan)
Anderson, Bridget, 81
Angle, Stephen C., 47
Aristotle, 99, 212n.9, 217n.8, 224n.7,
    226n.17

Ban Ki-moon, 212n.10
Bass, Gary, 196n.23
Beijing University, 130–31, 220n.1
Bell, Daniel, 194n.6
Benn, Charles, 205n.4
Bingdian (Freezing Point), 143
British Broadcasting Channel,
    141
Buddhism, 188, 198n.12, 209n.24
buildings, Confucian ethics and the
    design of, 11
Burma, 22
businessmen, bonding in karaoke
    bars by, 63, 67, 207n.12. *See also*
    prostitution

Cai Dingjian, 16
Cankao Xiaoxi, 92
Caplan, Bryan, 196n.23
Carens, Joseph, 89
Carstensen, Laura, 225n.9
CCP. *See* Chinese Communist Party
censorship, 129–30, 144, 222n.16
Central (Chinese Communist) Party
    School, 131, 140–42, 145–47,
    194–95n.15, 221nn.9–10
Chan, Joseph, 27
Chan Sin Yee, 217n.8
Chen Lai, 12
China, imperial, the tributary system,
    34–35, 205n.27
China, People's Republic of: foreign
    policy/international politics (*see*
    foreign policy; international politics);
    government of (*see* government of
    China); political future of (*see*
    political future of China); territorial
    boundaries within, 197n.7
Chinese Communist Party (CCP):
    Confucianism and, 10, 12; hair dye
    used by senior leaders of, 10; June 4,
    1989 (*see* June 4, 1989); Marxism and,
    4–6; meritocracy within, 195n.16;
    "primary stage of socialism," the current
    political system as, 3, 177; social welfare
    measures, call for, 5–6; Translation
    Bureau of the Central Committee, 7.
    See also government of China
Chinese Cultural College, 195n.15
Chineseness, 148, 161–62
citizenship: economic benefits of
    differentiated, 85–89; unequal for

citizenship (*continued*)
  migrant workers and the *hukou*
    system, 85–87
Clausewitz, Carl von, 35
Clinton, Bill, 132, 150
Cohen, Sacha Baron, 155
communism, 4–8
communitarianism, 223n.2
competition, ritual as civilizing
  influence on, 54
Confucianism: adaptation of to meet
  contemporary challenges, xxvii;
  civility, revival of for the Olympics,
  101–3; critical thinking without
  empathy, dangers of, 112; cultural and
  linguistic particularity of, 161–62; on
  families, 76–78, 89, 109–10; family
  insiders and nonfamily outsiders,
  distinction between, 79; foreign policy
  and, 22–27, 37; gender equality and,
  149, 164, 217n.8, 227n.2; the Gongyang tradition, 175–79; Great
  Harmony, ideal of, 27, 110, 112;
  humor and, 154–57, 225–26n.14; Jiang
  Qing on (*see* Jiang Qing); liberal
  democracy and, compatibility of,
  13–18; on marital arrangements,
  68–69, 74; on meritocracy and
  differences in abilities, 13–14, 113–15,
  166–67; moral growth with age,
  151–54; music, moral benefits of,
  63–64, 119–21, 126, 155–56; personal
  life and theoretical commitments,
  convergence of, 150–51; politics of,
  157–61, 170–74 (*see also* Jiang Qing);
  prisons, use in, 194n.12; the revival of,
  8–13; on rituals, 39–45, 52–53, 111; on
  rulers, 227n.24; socialism, Confucian,
  178; soft power and, 20 (*see also* soft
  power); on sporting competitions,
  99–100; as state religion, Jiang's
  proposal to enshrine, 187–88;
  stereotype of Confucian philosophers,

151; strands of, xxix–xxx, 175–78 (*see
  also* left Confucianism; Legalism);
  Tian Xia, ideal of, 23–26, 28; unequal
  rights, reasons to accept, 87–88; war,
  on just and unjust, 28–36; way of life,
  as, 151–52; the Xinxing tradition,
  176–77; Yu Dan's popularization of
  (*see* Yu Dan)
Confucius: age and the process of
  becoming an exemplary person, 153,
  225n.13; the archer, account of, 100;
  education in the humanities, aims of,
  108–16; education in the humanities,
  content of, 116–21; education in the
  humanities, methods of, 121–27; on
  filial piety, 77, 168, 198n.13 (*see also*
  filial piety); on friends visiting from
  afar, importance of, 222n.18; Golden
  Rule, Chinese equivalent of, 102;
  humor/seriousness of, 154–57,
  225–26n.14; leaders, moral power of,
  35; "original Confucianism" of, xxx;
  people's subsistence, government's
  obligation regarding, 87; on physical
  beauty, 68; political stance of, 157–60,
  170–74; ritual as means of civilizing
  competition, 54; self-description of
  the life of, 151, 168; singing, appreciation of, 63, 120, 155–56; trust of the
  people, government's need to secure,
  190; on women, 227n.2
Confucius Institutes, 9, 26
cosmopolitan ideal, the (Tian Xia),
  23–26, 28, 197n.7
Cui Zhiyuan, 6, 193n.5
Cultural Revolution, 108, 158, 195n.21

Daoism, 169, 172–73, 188, 198n.12
Da Tong (Great Harmony), 23–24, 26–27
de Bary, William Theodore, 157
democracy: Confucians in South Korea
  and, 195n.17; elected leaders in

Taiwan and South Korea, problems regarding, 196n.24; legitimacy of, 179–80; meritocracy and, 14–18, 196n.25; Western-style liberal (*see* liberals, liberalism, and liberal democracy). *See also* elections

Deng Lijun, 207n.13

Deng Xiaoping, 4

de Niro, Robert, 206n.10

de-Shalit, Avner, 218n.12

Dewey, John, 216n.3

Dissent, 142, 144

domestic workers: Chinese and Western employers, differential treatment by, 78–79; employer's family, implications of being treated as, 77–85; foreign, relationship between employers and, 75–76; foreign, unequal rights system faced by, 85–90; trade-offs between affective ties and rights, 81–85. *See also* migrant workers

Dong Zhongshu, 176

East Asia: Confucian values regarding family responsibilities in contemporary, 77–78; family values and prostitution in, 68–70; gay saunas and bathhouses in, 208n.22; hierarchy and egalitarianism in, 38–39; rituals in contemporary, 45–51. *See also* names of countries

Ebrey, Patricia Buckley, 202n.6

economic equality/inequality: hierarchical rituals and, 46–51; income gap in China, 9, 52; social equality/inequality and, 38–39, 45

education: Central Party School, talks given at the, 140–42, 145–47; Confucianism, teaching of, 11–12; critical thinking in, 107–8; cultural challenges for a teacher of political theory, 135–39, 144–47; elites,

training of, 217n.9; examinations, 196n.22, 217n.10; Great Thinkers/ Works, role of studying, 116–21; in the humanities, aims of, 108–16; in the humanities, content of, 116–21; in the humanities, methods of, 121–27; memorization in, 217–18n.11, 220n.23; music as part of, 218–19n.17, 219n.22; political challenges for a teacher of political theory, 128–35, 143–44; Socratic method in, 122, 124; syllabus, use of in China and America, 220n.4; the teacher, conceptions of the role of, 125; teacher's social status and salary levels in China and Hong Kong, 203n.15; teacher-student relationship, rituals in, 48

elections: competence of voters in, 196n.23; potential for and doubts regarding, 14–16. *See also* democracy

employment: of domestic workers (*see* domestic workers); the economic benefits of differentiated citizenship, 85–89; migrant workers (*see* migrant workers); misuse of family rhetoric to argue against workers' rights, 81–82; prostitution (*see* prostitution); ritual in relationships between bosses and workers, 49–50

Engels, Friedrich, 76, 211n.2

environment, the, 21–22, 196n.25

equality: economic (*see* economic equality/inequality); egalitarian rituals, 45–46; social (*see* social equality/inequality). *See also* meritocracy

ethnic homogeneity, 202–3n.11

families: Confucian conception of, 89; Confucian values and, 10–11, 76–78, 198n.13; domestic workers and, 77–85; filial piety, 10–11, 49, 77, 152,

families (*continued*)
    168, 198n.13, 209n.26, 223n.5;
    financial support for others in,
    cross-cultural data regarding,
    212n.12; marital arrangements, 68,
    73–74, 74; mealtime rituals in,
    49, 51; of migrants, impact of
    unequal rights system on, 88;
    obligations that bind together,
    intensity of, 27; one child per family
    rule, 194n.8, 213n.13; prostitution's
    impact on, 61, 68–70, 72–73 (*see also*
    prostitution)
feminist theorists and Confucianism,
    149
filial piety, 10–11, 49, 77, 152, 168,
    198n.13, 209n.26, 223n.5
Fleischacker, Samuel, 212n.9
foreign policy: Confucianism as guide
    for, 22–27, 37; the cosmopolitan ideal
    and, 23–26; the Great Harmony ideal
    and, 27; humanitarian interventions
    (*see* humanitarian interventions); just
    and unjust war, 27–36, 132–34;
    Legalism in, 20–22; soft power,
    political values underlying, 19–20;
    state sovereignty to global harmony as
    changing emphasis of, 20–23; Sudan,
    change in stance regarding, 215n.15;
    teaching a course addressing, 131–34;
    the United States, responding to
    actions of, 37. *See also* international
    politics
Foster, Jodie, 206n.10
Foucault, Michel, 46
Friedman, Thomas L., 33, 197n.9
future of China, political. *See* political
    future of China

Gan Yang, xxx, 178
gay community, male prostitution for,
    208n.22

gender equality: Confucianism and,
    149, 164, 217n.8, 227n.2. *See also*
    women
Ghana, 93, 213n.3
Gong Gang, 31–32
Gongyang tradition, 175–79
Gore, Al, 196n.25
government of China: civil service
    examinations, 195n.16; Confucianism
    and, 8–10, 12–13; disciplining of
    sports announcer, 96; rituals,
    proposed agency for promoting,
    51–53; the world's concerns regarding,
    200n.27. *See also* Chinese Commu-
    nist Party (CCP)
Great Harmony (Da Tong), age and
    ideal of, 23–24, 26–27
Great Learning, The, 26–27
Greece, sporting competitions in
    ancient, 99
Green, Graham, 206–7n.10
Gries, Peter Hays, 194n.7
Grosso, Fabio, 94
Gu Yanwu, xxx, 172
Gulf Wars: first, 31–32; second (*see* Iraq
    War)

hair color, 10
Han Fei Zi, 20, 198n.13
Harbsmeier, Christopher, 225n.14
He Baogang, 86
He Weifang, 144
Hegel, Georg Wilhelm Friedrich, 182
hierarchy: in rituals, 42–44; in rituals,
    egalitarian consequences of, 46–51; in
    rituals, reviving in contemporary
    China, 51–53; social (*see* social
    equality/inequality)
Higgins, Kathleen Marie, 207n.14
Hong Kong: boundaries of within
    China, 197n.7; foreign domestic
    workers in, 75, 77–80, 83–85, 88–90;

Legislative Council of, 182–83; prostitution in, 61, 66–67, 208n.18, 210n.34; teacher's social status and salary levels in, 203n.15; transgenderism and transsexuality in, 208–9n.23

household registration system (hukou), 50, 85–87, 129, 197n.7

Hu Jintao, 7, 9, 194n.9

Huang Jianxiang, 94–97

Hu Shi, 216n.3

Huang Zongxi, xxx, 157–58, 170, 217n.10, 229n.11

Huanqiu Shibao (Global Times), 92

hukou system (household registration system), 50, 85–87, 129, 197n.7

humanitarian interventions: barriers to foreign military intervention, 220n.2; liberal vs. Confucian judgments regarding, 33–34; Mencius's conditions for, 30–31; teaching of a course addressing, 132–34

human rights: American concerns regarding, 200n.27; Chinese response to Western criticism regarding, 21; justifying military actions by referring to, 32–33; rule of law, excessive focus on by Western promoters of, 55; sovereignty vs., 132; wartime morality and, 32–34

humor, Confucianism and, 154–57, 225–26n.14

Hursthouse, Rosalind, 224n.8

Ignatieff, Michael, 33

Ikels, Charlotte, 204n.19

Indonesia, 22

inequality: economic (see economic equality/inequality); social (see social equality/inequality)

international politics: athletic competitions as political struggle, 98–99;

Chinese support for countries with long and rich histories, 93–94, 100–1; just and unjust war, 28–36, 132–34; realist paradigm, teaching alternatives to, 131–34; self-regarding nationalism, dangers of, 97–100; the world's view of the Chinese government, 200n.27. See also foreign policy

Internet, monitoring of content on, 221–22n.15

Iraq War: Chinese view of, 221n.9; humanitarian intervention as justification for, 33, 132–33; just and unjust war theory applied to, 28, 32; torture of prisoners at Abu Ghraib, 35

Ivanhoe, P. J., 103, 202n.10

Japan: the boss-worker relationship and workplace rituals, 49; environmental impact of Chinese economic growth experienced by, 21; hierarchy and egalitarianism in, 38; karaoke in, 61–62; Legalist ideas in, 20–21; needy family members, caring for in, 77; Olympic athletes of, Chinese school supporting, 214n.13; soccer team from, lack of Chinese support for, 93

Jiang Qing: advising of political rulers, 227n.24; Gongyang tradition, revival of, 175–78; legitimacy, political implications of types of, 178–80; personal impressions of, 188–89; political Confucianism of, 12–14, 175; responses to criticisms of his proposals, 189–91; socialist ideals in the Confucianism of, xxx; tricameral legislature, proposal for, 180–88

Jing Jun, 70

Jin Guantao, 10

Jin Yong, 10–11, 194n.10

June 4, 1989: crackdown on protesters, loss of moral credibility from, 36–37; government apology for the slaughter on, considerations regarding, 200–1 n.28; question in classroom discussion regarding, 133; student elites as leaders among demonstrators, 195n.21

just and unjust war, 28–36, 132–34

Kang Xiaoguang, 20
Kang Youwei, 13, 23–24, 26–27, 74, 176, 199n.19
Kant, Immanuel, 68
karaoke clubs/parlors: prevalence and operation of, 60–61; Western strip clubs and, comparison between, 207n.12. *See also* prostitution
Kennedy, Ted, 212n.8
Keysar, Boaz, 216n.5
Korea, Democratic People's Republic of (North), 34
Korea, Republic of (South): Confucians and democracy in, 195n.17; elected leaders, problem regarding, 196n.24; environmental impact of Chinese economic development experienced in, 21; hierarchy and egalitarianism in, 38; needy family members, caring for, 77; prostitution in, 206n.8, 209n.28; soccer team from, 92–93, 100
Kosovo intervention by NATO, 32, 132, 199–200n.23
Kymlicka, Will, 85, 136, 221n.6

labor. *See* employment
Lacy, Steve, 207n.14
language: as a challenge for foreigner teaching in China, 135–36; Chinese as a global, 198n.11; Confucianism and, 161–62

law and legal mechanisms, rituals and, 54–55
Lee Kuan Yew, 16, 115, 184, 195nn.19–20, 224n.7
left Confucianism, xxix–xxx, 178. *See also* "new left" intellectuals
Legalism: Confucianism and, combination of, xxix; family obligations, opposition to Confucian view of, 198n.13; in Singapore, 195n.19; state sovereignty/power and, 20–21; Xunzi and, 39
Liang Qichao, 13, 24
Liang Shuming, 177
liberals, liberalism, and liberal democracy: American common usage of "liberal," not to be confused with, 223n.3; Confucianism and, compatibility of, 13–18; domestic workers, perspective on, 75–76, 81–85; elderly parents, caring for, 90; hierarchical rituals, denunciation of, 43; migrant workers, providing rights vs. economic benefits for, 86–90; "political" and "personal," distinction between, 150; unequal citizenship, rejection of, 85–88
Li Chenyang, 217n.8
Li Jinxi, 24
Li Zehou, 10
Little Red Book (Mao), xxix, 163
Liu Junning, 144
Liu Xiang, 102
Liu Yin, 227n.24
Lockenhoff, Corrinna E., 225n.9
Lu Xun, 194n.10

Macau, 197n.7
Machiavelli, Niccolo, 212n.9
MacIntyre, Alasdair, 139
Mao Zedong: Confucianism in the beliefs of, 10; and Cultural Revolution,

108, 158; "Da Tong" as goal of the
youthful, 24; and Legalism, 21; *Little
Red Book*, xxix, 163
Marx, Karl, xxx, 4–8, 76, 193n.2, 211n.2,
229n.14
Marxism/Marxists: Chinese-style,
explanations of, 10; end of in China,
4–8, 177; hierarchical rituals,
denunciation of, 43; teaching of, 131
McGreevey, James, 194n.9
Mencius: the archer, account of, 99;
censorship of comments about,
129–30; criticism of imperialism and,
xxvii; cyclical view of history of,
199n.19; ethical instincts, four basic,
197n.8; on family relations, 79, 89;
human relations, government's
obligation regarding, xxx; on just and
unjust wars, 28–33, 35–36; and
monogamy, 69; moral earnestness of,
156; on music, 219n.18, 226n.18;
"original Confucianism" of, xxx;
people's subsistence, moral necessity
of providing means for, 87, 228n.7;
political stance of, 157; on rulers faced
with certain defeat by an invader,
200n.26; on well-field system, 177
meritocracy: Confucian belief in
differences in ability and, 13–14,
113–15, 166–67; democracy and,
14–18; in government and the Chinese
Communist Party, 195n.16; in Jiang's
proposal for a tricameral legislature,
186–87; in Singapore, 16–17
Mexico, 21
Middlebury College, 221n.12
migrant workers: family life, impact of
migration on, 88; foreign domestic
workers, employers and, 75–78, 90 (*see
also* domestic workers); guest-worker
proposals, 212n.8, 212n.11; making
prostitution available to, 71–72;
remittances by, value of, 212n.10;

rituals and, 50–51; unequal citizenship and the *hukou* system, 85–87
military training, compulsory, 220n.1
Ming Yongqian, 28
Monk, Thelonious, 207n.14
Mou Zongsan, 197n.8
mourning rituals, 41, 44
Mozi, 36, 63, 90, 136
mucus expulsion, spitting vs.
nose-blowing, 214n.10
music: Aristotle on, 226n.17; Confucians' belief in the moral benefits of,
119–21, 126, 155–56; education and,
218–19n.17, 219n.22; humor, impact
of compared to, 155–56; Mencius on,
219n.18, 226n.18; moral benefits of
and karaoke, 63–64. *See also* singing
Muzaffar, Chandran, 209n.24

Nanfang Zhoumou (Southern Weekend),
14, 209n.24
nationalism, dangers of self-regarding,
97–100
National University of Singapore,
128–29
"new left" intellectuals, 6–7, 178
Ni Lexiong, 31
Niu Gensheng, 12
Nussbaum, Martha, 216n.7

Olympic Games: Chinese nationalism,
pursuit of gold medals as expression
of, 98–99; civility, governmental
promotion of, 101–3; politics and,
214–15n.15; Western press coverage in
Beijing prior to 2008, 215n.17. *See also*
sports

Paik Wooyeal, 213n.2
Peerenboom, Randall, 196n.24

Philippines, domestic workers from, 77–78

political future of China, 3–4; Confucianism, revival of, 8–13; liberal democracy and Confucianism, compatibility of, 13–18; Marxist ideology, end of, 4–8

polygamy, 73–74

power, soft. See soft power

Pritchett, Lant, 212n.11

prostitution: affairs and polygamy as alternatives to, 73–74; decriminalization, 210n.32; economic benefits of, 59–61, 66–67; for the gay community, 208n.22; health concerns associated with, 61, 205n.2; in Hong Kong, 61, 66–67, 208n.18, 210n.34; karaoke-style, impact on families of, 68–70, 72–73; karaoke-style, impact on women of, 64–68, 72; karaoke-style for well-to-do women, 67–68; karaoke-style in northeast Asia, 61–62; in Korea, 206n.8, 209n.28; legalization of, 59–61, 70–73; the mafia and, 210n.31; methodology for studying, 210–11n.37; morality of karaoke-style, 62–64; in Singapore, 59, 65–66, 205n.1, 205n.3, 208n.18; in Southeast Asia, Buddhism and, 209n.24; Western and East Asian contrasted, 62

Przeworski, Adam, 18

Qin Hui, 188, 218n.14

Rawls, John, 223n.4

Record of Rites, 23, 26–27

Rice, Condoleeza, 120

Rise of Great Powers, The (China Central Television), 19

rituals: animals and, 201n.1; in boss-worker relationships, 49–50; in contemporary East Asian societies, 45–51; egalitarian, 45–46; fame and, 202n.10; hierarchical, egalitarian consequences of, 46–51; legalistic, rights-based cultures, difficulty of promoting in, 54–55; mealtime, 48–49, 51, 204nn.22–24; mourning, 41, 44; political rulers and, 43; reviving hierarchical in contemporary China, 51–53; in teacher-student relationships, 48; toasting along with drinking alcohol, 203n.14; universal value of, 53–55; village wine ceremony, 44; Xunzi's philosophy of, 39–45

Romania, 199n.15

Rosemont, Henry, Jr., 201n.5

Rumsfeld, Donald, 221n.9

Rwanda genocide, 132

Sachs, Jeffrey, 212n.11

Saddam Hussein, 33

Sang Ye, 99, 206n.8

Satz, Debra, 66

sex drive: of the elderly, Western view of, 225n.11; moral judgment and the diminishment of, 153, 224–25n.9

sex trade and workers. See prostitution

sexual affairs, karaoke-style prostitution vs., 73

shareholding-cooperative system, 193n.5

Shen Xiaoyong, 209n.23

Sheng Bin, 93

showering, group vs. individual, 206n.7

Singapore: democracy in, 16–17; Legalism in the political system of, 195n.19; legalized prostitution in, 59, 65–66, 205n.1, 205n.3, 208n.18; likely experience of censorship in, 130

singing: author's lack of ability regarding, 145; boss-worker relationships and, 49–50; joint of employers and domestic workers, 81; karaoke and prostitution, 62–64, 73 (see also prostitution); in Western vs. East Asian societies, 205–6n.5. See also music

Sisci, Francesco, 92–93

Smith, Adam, 198–99n.14, 212n.9

social contract tradition, 55

social equality/inequality: economic equality/inequality and, 38–39, 45. See also hierarchy

socialism: the current political system as the "primary stage" of, 3, 177; left Confucianism and, xxx

social justice: government's actions regarding, 5–6; "new left" intellectuals' call for, 6–7

Socrates, 122

soft power: Confucianism and, 22–27; just and unjust war, 28–36; political values underlying, issue of, 19–20; the world's actions and the prospects for, 37

Southeast Asia, prostitution in, 209n.24

sports: announcers, bias vs. neutrality of, 94–97; athletic competitions as political struggle, 98–99; "civility" for the Olympics, 101–3 (see also Olympic Games); Confucian vs. Greek athletic ideals, 99–100; nationalism among a team's supporters, dangers of, 97–100; rituals in, 54; traditional soccer powers, Chinese support for, 92–94, 100–1; World Cup games played in Beijing, enthusiasm for, 91

state sovereignty, 21, 132, 220n.2. See also foreign policy

Straits Times, 130

Sudan, 21–22, 215n.15

Sun Yat-sen, 13, 24

Sunzi, 142

Taiwan: elected leaders in, problem regarding, 196n.24; justification of self-defense if attacked by the mainland, question of, 200n.26; karaoke-style prostitution in, 61; self-censorship of paper touching upon relations with, 130; sports vs. national affairs, interest in, 213n.1

Tan, Sor-Hoon, 13

Taxi Driver, 206n.10

technology, in the Marxist framework, 4–5

Terrill, Ross, 214n.15

Thailand, 209n.24

Tian Xia (the cosmopolitan ideal), 23–26, 28, 197n.7

Tibet, 86

Totti, Francesco, 95

Translation Bureau of the Central Committee of the Chinese Communist Party, 7

Travel, Taylor, 22

Underwood International College, 217n.9

United Nations peacekeeping missions, Chinese participation in, 22

United States: anxiety over "Made in China" label, 21; Chinese foreign policy as responsive to actions of, 37; guest-worker proposal by the Bush administration, 212n.8; Hurricane Katrina, Chinese offer of aid following, 22; messianic impulse in, 197n.9; political values associated with, 19–20; social equality and economic inequality in, 38, 45, 52

village wine ceremony, 44

Voice of America, 141

Vongs, Pueng, 210n.36

Waley, Arthur, 156
Wall Street Journal, 61
Wal-Mart, 5
Walzer, Michael, 32, 132–33
Wang Hui, 6
Wang Juntao, 13
Wang Meng, 102, 214n.12
Wang Yangming, 228n.4
war: humanitarian interventions (*see* humanitarian interventions); just and unjust, classroom discussion regarding, 132–34; just and unjust, Confucianism and thinking regarding, 27–36; moral evaluation of, teaching of theories that allow, 131–34; moral quality of political and military leaders in, 35
welfare states: comparisons with China, 193n.3; praise of in the Chinese media, 6; rights-based, reliance on legal mechanisms in, 55
Wen Jiabao, 9, 193n.1
women: and caring for elderly parents, 77, 90; Confucianism and gender equality, 149, 164, 217n.8, 227n.2; family-like labels in prisons for, 211n.4; and karaoke clubs, 67–68; karaoke-style prostitution's impact on, 64–68, 72 (*see also* prostitution); kidnapping and illegal sale of, 208n.19; polygamy, impact of revival of, 74
Wong, Eva, 12
Woodruff, Paul, 47
World Cup: announcer's enthusiasm during Italy-Australia match in 2006, 94–97; Chinese support for traditional soccer powers, 92–94; enthusiasm for 2006 games played in Beijing, 91; nationalism among fans, 97–100
Wu Ming, 86–87
Wu Shali, 216n.5
Wu Zhongmin, 6

Xinxing tradition, 176–77
Xu Heng, 227n.24
Xunzi: on caring for dead bodies, 44, 152; collective economic efforts, hierarchy as essential for, 201–2n.5; on just conduct in war, 36; on the limits of moral transformation, 201n.3; on mealtime practices, 204n.23; moral earnestness of, 156; on music, 63–64; and "original Confucianism," xxx; political stance of, 157–58; on rituals, 39–48, 51, 53

Yang Fan, 60
Yang Mingchang, 194n.12
Yang Yeeshan, 62, 67, 206n.6, 208n.18
Yan Hui, 114, 122–23, 125, 169, 171
Yao Ming, 102
Yu Dan: criticisms of her book, 166–70; depoliticizing of the *Analects* by, xxix, 170–74; misogyny in the *Analects*, softening of, 227n.2; popularity of her book, 11, 163–65
Yu Keping, 15–16
Yu Maochun, 92
Yu Ying-shih, 227n.24

Zambia, 21
Zhang Xuecheng, 159, 170
Zhao Tingyang, 24–26
Zheng Tiantian, 63
Zhou Enlai, 193n.1
Zhu Xi, 26, 173, 177, 217n.10, 228n.4
Zhuangzi, 169, 173
Zidane, Zinedine, 98
Zimbabwe, 22
Zuo Zhuan, 172